Politics of preferential development

Trans-global study of affirmative action and ethnic
conflict in Fiji, Malaysia and South Africa

Politics of preferential development

Trans-global study of affirmative action and ethnic conflict in Fiji, Malaysia and South Africa

Steven Ratuva

Australian
National
University

E PRESS

ANU
E PRESS

Published by ANU E Press
The Australian National University
Canberra ACT 0200, Australia
Email: anuepress@anu.edu.au
This title is also available online at http://epress.anu.edu.au

---

National Library of Australia Cataloguing-in-Publication entry

Author: Ratuva, Steven, author.

Title: Politics of preferential development : trans-global study of affirmative action and
           ethnic conflict in Fiji, Malaysia and South Africa / Steven Ratuva.

ISBN: 9781925021028 (paperback) 9781925021035 (ebook)

Subjects: Minorities--Political aspects--Fiji.
          Minorities--Political aspects--Malaysia
          Minorities--Political aspects--South Africa.
          Fiji--Ethnic relations--Political aspects.
          Fiji--Race relations--Political aspects.
          Malaysia--Ethnic relations--Political aspects.
          Malaysia--Race relations--Political aspects.
          South Africa--Ethnic relations--Political aspects.
          South Africa--Race relations--Political aspects.

Dewey Number: 305.8

Cover design and layout by ANU E Press

Cover image: The multi-coloured design on the cover is a mural at the back of the stage of the
Lambert Hall at Marist Brothers High School, Suva, Fiji. It was painted by the author when
he was a 16 year old student and depicts multidimensional forms of political and cultural
relationships such as conflict, domination, accommodation and respect in a multi-ethnic society
like Fiji.

Contents

Acknowledgements

I take this opportunity to thank a number of people for making this book possible. My gracious thanks to the Faculty of Arts at the University of Auckland for providing me with the Faculty Research Fund which enabled me to carry out research on some parts of the Fiji chapters. My hearty thanks go to the four reviewers, three anonymous and Prof Bob Norton. Dr Norton's meticulous review and incisive comments were invaluable indeed. Similar sentiments can be expressed for Prof Stewart Firth for his scholarly insights during the review process. My gratitude also goes to John Moriarty for his professionalism in copyediting the manuscript as well as Duncan Beard of the ANU E Press for his technical advice and Nausica Pinar for her technical skills in designing the cover.

I express my deep appreciation for my wife Adi Mere as well as my children Natasha and Joji for their prayers and moral support. I reserve my warmest gratitude for my mother Olita and late father Joeli, to whom this book is dedicated, for their inspiration.

Cover design

The multi-coloured design on the cover depicts the mural on the stage of the Lambert Hall at Marist Brothers High School, Suva, Fiji. It was painted by the author himself when he was a 16 year old student and depicts multidimensional and complex forms of moral, social and political relationships and principles relating to conflict, domination, inter-cultural accommodation, respect, social justice and equity in multi-ethnic societies such as Fiji. It uses a deconstructed and one-dimensionalized derivative of Pablo Picasso's multi-dimensional cubism with shades of Fijian cultural symbolism to construct a multi-patterned jigsaw representing the vibrancy of ethnic diversity as well as the myriad of challenges in creating a multicultural world. The mural is one of the largest works of contemporary art in the Pacific.

1. Affirmative action and trans-global study

Exploring affirmative action

Affirmative action refers to programs designed and implemented to address the socio-economic and political situations of those considered historically 'disadvantaged'. However, the questions, 'Who constitutes the disadvantaged?' and, 'What type of preferential programs are appropriate?' can be contentious because the term 'disadvantaged' can be defined in different ways in different situations by different people; and often, certain definitions may favour certain groups ahead of others.

Affirmative action policies range from 'strong' approaches based on highly institutionalized quota-based and sanction-driven policies imposed by the state to 'soft' approaches based on very informal and voluntary systems. The most common preferential policies relate to special political representation, improved educational opportunities, provision for employment and access to means of economic advancement for social groups which may be identified as disadvantaged on the basis of gender, class, caste, ethnicity or physical disability (Kellough 2006; Lipson 2006; Sterba 2009). The role of the government is important in the identification, categorization and prioritization of designated groups as well as in the conceptualization, planning and implementation of affirmative action programs (Sowell 2005). However, it should be noted that in some cases affirmative action can also be a result of voluntary decisions by corporations, civil society organizations, educational institutions and other relevant groups to provide assistance to those considered to be in need of preferential treatment given their marginalized position.

The discourse on affirmative action spans a number of disciplinary boundaries, with scholars emphasizing different aspects of preferential programs. Those taking the legalistic approach often focus on preferential legislation and disputes over the legality of quotas in education and the labour market, as well as the deeper issues of equity and justice (Girardeau 2000). Economic arguments are concerned with the issue of the re-distribution of public resources and often raise questions about the relationship between affirmative action and economic growth and the potential of affirmative action to undermine growth or to feed on it (Chand 2007). In recent years the psychological aspect has been considered a significant area of study because of the way in which preferential treatment defines in-group and intergroup perceptions and behavioural dispositions and how this shapes relationships within or between communities (Bobo 1998; Skitka and Crosby 2003). Political scientists tend to focus on the power dynamics of preferential policies relating to political governance and the policy-making process and how affirmative action is used to serve political interests (Neblo 2008; 2009). The sociological perspective tends to provide a broad approach and tends to focus on the relationship between affirmative action and the labour market, ethnic relations, conflict, culture, power and equality (Choo and Feree 2010; Jain, Sloane, and Horwitz 2003). Increasingly the study of affirmative action transcends disciplinary boundaries because of its multidimensional nature. Similarly, this book takes an interdisciplinary approach.

The justifications used to support affirmative action are specific to local contexts and might include correcting historical wrongs and providing compensation, as in the US (Pincus 2003), South Africa (Horwitz 2009), Canada (Agocs 2009) and Namibia (Usiku 2009); addressing inequality, as in Malaysia (Gomez 2009; Gomez and Jomo 1999), Brazil (Bernardino-Costa 2010), Northern Ireland (Harvey 2010) and India (Parikh 2010); or resolving ethnic conflict, as in Fiji (Ratuva 2010). Some countries use either one or a combination of two or three justifications, depending on context. Often, affirmative action is associated with the moral virtues of equity and justice as well as a pragmatic need to contain tension and maintain stability. The assumption is that addressing historical wrongs and injustices helps to redress grievances and resolve long-standing ethnic conflict and this may lead to social transformation and progress (Kende 2009).

The affirmative action debate

The preferential treatment of one group over another has raised a number of moral and philosophical questions, which continue to be contentious. While there is a consensus that affirmative action should, fundamentally, be based on the principles of justice and equality, controversy begins when the rights of a group are seen to be undermined while the disadvantaged situation of another group is being addressed.

From another perspective, affirmative action is considered by some as a form of "reverse discrimination" on the grounds that "if arbitrary discrimination has occurred because morally irrelevant characteristics of persons – such as sex, religion or race – have been taken into account to treat them differently, it would not be permissible to take into account the same characteristics in order to compensate them for the initial act of discrimination" (Faundez 1994: 4). In other words, reverse discrimination occurs when ethnicity (for instance) is used as the basis for affirmative action just because previous acts of discrimination that are being compensated for were based on ethnicity. Under this logic, one may argue that even if affirmative action is compensatory it is still unjustified because it embodies hallmarks of reverse discrimination. The counter-argument is that since affirmative action involves redressing past wrongs and compensation for them as a way of contributing to good relations and future stability, it should not be seen as a form of discrimination at all (Pincus 2003).

Another contentious issue relates to the question of whether affirmative action should be associated with group or individual rights. An argument against group rights is that affirmative action is justified only as a remedy for individuals who have suffered discrimination. On the other hand, it can also be argued that the need of individuals for redress is because they are part of a group that suffered discrimination and, hence, the best solution is for the entire group to be compensated. This idea is linked to the notion of distributive justice, premised on the utilitarian notion of the provision of the greatest good for the greatest number of people. Thus, providing opportunity for the disadvantaged, in particular the poorer sections of a community, is considered a morally justified way of serving the entire community. In this context, affirmative action is seen as essential in fostering greater equality, reducing tension and enhancing social and national integration.

Affirmative action based on ethnicity is often subject to emotional reaction because of the complex, and often nebulous, way ethnicity is linked to political and ideological interests. Because of its links with culture and identity, ethnicity is deeply embedded within a group's collective consciousness. People tend to mobilize and politicize ethnic group consciousness readily, even to the extent of invoking extreme violence if they feel protective of their identity or feel insecure as a group. Ethnicity as a mode of stratification is more pronounced in some countries than others and, because of ethnicity's sensitive and potentially flammable nature, some states are sensitive to reaction when designing affirmative action policies around ethnicity (Stanley 2009). To avoid such reactions, it has been suggested policy should move away from affirmative action towards alternative approaches such as labour market "diversity", which involves the deliberate creation of a multi-cultural and multi-skilled workforce without the use of targeted quotas (Thomas 1990).

Quotas in education and employment are intended to ensure access to higher education and employment opportunities for groups which, historically, have been disadvantaged and which have thus lacked social mobility. Critics of quotas often argue that quotas victimise deserving people in the non-designated groups on the basis of their ethnic category and not on the basis of merit and there have been legal challenges to educational quotas in the US and in India. Nevertheless, as international studies have shown, there is still a recognition in some parts of the world that preferential policies in education and employment play a vital role as mechanisms of social levelling in order to create equal opportunities. (Zhou and Maxwell 2009).

Affirmative action can also be used as a political and ideological tool by the state to appease ethnic minority groups or assimilate them into a dominant culture (Katznelson 2005). The mere practice of affirmative action can be a powerful ideologically symbolic exercise to project the image of proactive policy for social justice and national integration. However, this can be misleading because, as Wise (2005) points out, in the case of the US, behind the veneer of justice and equality at the rhetorical level, there are still layers of denial that hide institutionalized racism in everyday life. There is a perception that, despite affirmative action in the US, black and white middle classes, although inextricably linked, still exist entirely on different economic planes and that the achievement of equality is an immense challenge.

Sometimes, minorities which feel oppressed take the initiative to engage in direct ethnic bargaining and political negotiations for special programs, and even autonomy and secession, rather than wait for the state to take the initiative. Some prominent past cases included Sudeten Germans in interwar Czechoslovakia; Slovaks and Moravians in post-communist Czechoslovakia; Hungarians in Romania, Slovakia, and Vojvodina; and Albanians in Kosovo (Jenne 2006).

Affirmative action based on ethnicity is fraught with multiple challenges especially in relation to social issues of inequality, human rights, inclusiveness, citizenship and group recognition. Such challenges are even more pronounced in developing countries, where the policy development capacity of state institutions may not be as well developed as it is in developed countries, and where structural inequality is stark and firmly embedded. The governance process and the role of political elites are determining factors in the policy making and implementation process because even if affirmative action programs are ethically and philosophically sound they can still be subject to political manipulation to serve the interests of a selected few.

Because of its multidimensional nature, debates on affirmative action can contribute to national discussions on broader issues of ethics, merit, redistribution of resources and power in society. Attempts to undermine the legitimacy of affirmative action through court challenges and political action take place at the same time as attempts to justify and promote it. For instance, Kende (2009) observes that resistance to affirmative action in the US has shaped ethnic relations and perceptions of the state as well as inter-group perception in significant ways. This is indeed the case in Fiji, Malaysia and South Africa, as this book demonstrates. The continuing debate on affirmative action in many countries is indicative of their complex history, which has given rise to a range of antagonistic groups and discourses clamouring for political advantage and policy influence (Bowser 2007).

Contextualising the trans-global approach

This book is a trans-global study of affirmative action in post-colonial multi-ethnic states and focuses on the interplay between ethnic politics and preferential programs in Fiji, Malaysia and South Africa. These countries have been chosen because they provide the most prominent examples of affirmative action based on ethnicity in post-colonial Africa, South East Asia and Oceania.

The term 'trans-global' is used in the book instead of 'comparative' because the latter is often associated with the use of 'ideal' variables to determine the similarities and differences between two or more countries. As such, it tends to be quite mechanical, through an over emphasis on the primacy of comparative methodology over in-depth analysis of unique experiences of the case studies (Lijphart 1971). This book is not aimed at comparing and contrasting the three case studies but is an attempt to highlight their unique characteristics and experiences, including the lessons they have learnt from each other. These unique experiences, often lost in comparative studies, need to be understood and appreciated in their own specific historical and cultural contexts. In providing an alternative approach to comparative study, this trans-global approach highlights the specific realities of individual case studies across the globe and examines their links rather than simply focusing on appearances of generalized similarities and differences. In short, the unique experiences of countries and the global links between these individual experiences are central to the trans-global approach. This approach is important in the light of the cross-border transfer of ideas, experiences and models associated with affirmative action and development generally. Affirmative action has become trans-global in nature, with countries 'borrowing' policies and models they deem to be appropriate to their own situation from other countries. Fascinated with Malaysia's affirmative action programs, both Fiji and South Africa borrowed, modified and implemented aspects of Malaysian affirmative action they believed to be appropriate to their local requirements, with sometimes similar and sometimes different consequences.

It is not often that a trans-global study between small Pacific island states (SPIS) and bigger states in Asia and Africa is carried out. This is probably because of the assumption that SPIS are too insignificant in size and influence to be appropriate for trans-global study with bigger and more prominent countries. Reinforcing this line of thinking is the tendency to depict SPIS as marginal and vulnerable entities whose future as sustainable and viable states is questionable (Santos-Paulino, McGillivray and Naude 2010).

This study negates that view and emphasises that no matter how small or how big countries are, they all have unique histories and experiences, which deserve attention. Many post-colonial societies have unique features, as well as shared experiences that were shaped by their own colonial and post-colonial histories and which must be given serious consideration in their own right. The SPIS's borrowing and localization of global ideas and institutions, as well as their contribution to shaping global cultures, make trans-global study of SPIS important (Lamour 2005).

The book critically examines the three case studies in terms of their unique historical, cultural, political and economic dynamics and draws together a number of common threads to enable us to understand affirmative action in other countries in a more informed manner. The countries in the case studies have all experienced ethnic inequality and tension although there are significant differences in how that inequality and tension has been manifested.

Fiji's colonial history was characterized by ethnic demarcation, which continued to some degree after independence. Ethnic tension led to political instability, which contributed to coups on six occasions. Similarly, Malaysia's colonial history created the conditions for ethnic demarcation and tension, which culminated in ethnic violence in 1969. In both Fiji and Malaysia, post-colonial politics revolved around negotiating political balance and concessions through affirmative action. In contrast, South Africa had a highly repressive apartheid state and an extremely unequal economic structure controlled by a white minority. Political power shifted to the black majority following the 1994 election and ever since there has been a concerted effort to provide greater economic and educational opportunities for blacks through affirmative action. While there was ethnic segregation in Fiji and Malaysia, it was not as rigid and coercive as South Africa's apartheid system. Besides, there was still space for inter-ethnic political cooperation in the two countries, unlike in South Africa, where the majority blacks were denied basic rights for a long time. The three countries have had their share of ethno-political violence in the form of coups in Fiji, ethnic riots in Malaysia and various forms of community-based and state-sponsored violence in South Africa.

Another shared characteristic of the three countries is that affirmative action is considered a major social engineering undertaking, rather than just a policy prescription, to restructure society as a way of addressing what Stewart, Brown and Langer (2007) refer to as "horizontal inequality", or the differences between ethno-cultural groups. This entails engineering a new middle class and new patterns of ownership and power relations, with the hope of creating a more equitable, just and stable society. One of the latent effects of the economic advancement and empowerment of the indigenous middle class, as we will see in the three case studies, is an increase in inequality within the designated community.

Another feature common to all three societies studied here is the role of elites who use their strategic position both as ethnic leaders, as well as state elites, in accessing state resources in the name of affirmative action for their communities. Associated with this is the formation of networks of patronage, consisting of political elites, state bureaucrats and businessmen who stand to gain from affirmative action. It is common practice in the three case studies to use affirmative action as a payoff for political loyalty. The distribution of affirmative action resources through the patronage system and the focus on creating an indigenous middle class contributes directly to intra-communal inequality.

Affirmative action in the three countries is justified by ideological notions such as "paramountcy of Fijian interest" in Fiji, Malay "special privilege" in Malaysia and "black empowerment" in South Africa. These ideological constructs not only identify the designated ethnic categories, they also give affirmative action a sense of possessing a political imperative and primordial destiny, often associated with the notion of divine right. Public articulation and wide acceptance of these ideological notions and implementation of affirmative action programs are relatively easily achieved in the three countries because the designated groups are demographically and politically dominant.

The case studies also show the constant tension and accommodation between neoliberal development policies and preferential programs. While affirmative action is seen by neoliberal policy thinkers as a distortion of economic development, there is also a belief that it should be targeted at poverty eradication across ethnic groups. The compromise between neoliberal policies and preferential programs is best represented in the effort to create an indigenous middle class. Privatized state assets often end up in the hands of state-aligned elites and the middle class.

While affirmative action has helped lessen inequality, it has not removed ethnic tension as initially envisaged. The ultimate question is whether affirmative action has led to a fairer, more just and peaceful society or whether it has simply worsened the existing situation. The book takes the view that the answer is a mixed one and reflects the complexity of the situation, rather than one which is simply positive or negative.

The book centres on Fiji, while Malaysia and South Africa provide the trans-global cases. The Fiji section consists of six chapters (Chapters 2 to 7). Chapter 2 examines the pro-indigenous affirmative action programs during the British colonial period. Most were rural focused and were meant to introduce indigenous Fijians into the cash economy but within the ambit of communal life under the native regulations. Indigenous Fijians were locked into a communal social order under rigid colonial laws that prevented them from full participation in the mainstream economy and education. This later bred ethno-nationalist grievances when indigenous Fijians realised that they were lagging behind other ethnic groups in commerce, education and professional employment.

Chapter 3 contains a discussion of the pro-indigenous policies of Ratu Sir Kamisese Mara's Alliance Party after independence in 1970. These were no different from the colonial rural development strategy, except for the differences in scale and diversity. Some of the development projects worked and some did not. Many major agricultural projects failed, but the most successful project was the special educational scholarships for indigenous Fijians.

Chapter 4 looks at the political dynamics associated with the 1987 coup, including political and constitutional transformations. It argues that the 1987 coup was in fact a form of "political" affirmative action. It looks at how affirmative action was constitutionalized (both by the 1990 and 1997 Constitutions) and at the use of decrees to drive affirmative action policies which led to the Fijianization of the civil service and other areas of Fiji society. It also discusses some of the policies meant to enhance indigenous Fijian participation in the corporate sector as a way of consolidating an indigenous middle class.

Chapter 5 examines in detail the mandates and activities of institutions tasked with carrying out the state's affirmative action programs. This includes the Fiji Development Board, National Bank of Fiji, Fijian Holdings Ltd, Native Land Trust Board and others. It discusses the failure of these institutions to deliver as a result of lack of capacity, corruption and political incompetence and patronage.

Chapter 6 deals with the affirmative action programs from 1999 after Mahendra Chaudhry became the first Indo-Fijian prime minister to 2006, when a further coup took place. It examines the differences between Chaudhry's appeasement strategy and Laisenia Qarase's social engineering approach after the 2000 coup, and how both approaches turned out to be disastrous for the two men's political career and for the country's political future.

Chapter 7 discusses the capture of state power by Commodore Bainimarama in 2006 and some of the contradictory tendencies of his indigenous development strategies. On the one hand he demonized affirmative action but on the other hand he reinvented it under the rubric of rural development in order to mobilize support and gain legitimacy amongst indigenous Fijians for the purpose of electoral gain.

Chapter 8 is a discussion of affirmative action in Malaysia, its origin, justification, implementation and results. Where possible, parallels with Fiji are made. Chapter 9 examines affirmative action in South Africa in the context of creating a new social order after the collapse of apartheid. Chapter 10 draws together some of the commonalities between the three case studies and provides a discussion of some of the trans-global lessons learnt.

2. Proto-affirmative action: Indigenous Fijian development from cession to independence

Although the term 'affirmative action' was not used until after the 1987 military coup, various policies aimed at improving the socio-economic conditions of indigenous Fijians were adopted from the early days of colonialism. However, there were contradictory perceptions and policies as to how the question of indigenous Fijian 'progress' was to be dealt with. The first view, advocated by Governor im Thurn in the early 1900s as well as many white farmers, was that there should be a total liberalization of the indigenous Fijian system including the commercialization and individualization of the landownership system. On the opposite side of the continuum were those like Sir Arthur Gordon, the first Governor, and later Ratu Sir Lala Sukuna, an indigenous statesman, who wanted a tight communal system which would facilitate the gradual evolution of indigenous Fijians in a social Darwinian way. In between was the perception that, while locked in communal organization, indigenous Fijians could be integrated slowly into the cash economy through participation in the copra and banana industries as famers and salesmen. It appeared that the third view prevailed because, as we shall see later, a number of projects to introduce indigenous Fijians to the cash economy were introduced, but within the ambit of communal hegemony.

The interaction with the market economy was not based on sharing the control of the production process but on the provision of labour for village-based cash crops. Village-based semi-subsistence production was a low-cost production system that greatly subsidized the production cost, which enabled middlemen and exporters to make sizeable profits. Nevertheless, despite these economic engagements, the impact of such interaction with the market economy on the indigenous Fijian community in terms of socio-economic development was minimal. One of the restraining factors was that full entrepreneurship was considered destructive to the fabric of Fijian social life.

From 1874, when Fiji became a British colony, to independence in 1970, two separate but related modes of development were in place in Fiji. On the one hand was the entrenchment of communalism under the colonial native policy put in place in 1876, and on the other was the consolidation of the capitalist economy. The communal mode of production sustained a semi-subsistence way of life under the hegemony of chiefs, at the same time as capitalist economic development was creating fundamental socio-economic changes such as the growth of an embryonic indigenous Fijian working class whose new mode of consciousness which came into conflict with the communal ethos of the native policy. After the 1940s serious attempts were made to reform the native administration with a view to strengthen communal hegemony rather than liberalize it. The liberalization process did not take place until the 1960s, as independence approached.

This chapter looks at some early attempts to assimilate indigenous Fijians into the mainstream market economy and some of the consequent challenges. The first part looks briefly at the period from 1874, when Fiji became a British colony, to 1970, when Fiji gained independence.

Indigenous Fijians in the embryonic market economy

A quick glance at the growing capitalist economy in Fiji in the 19th century should give us an idea of the broader socio-economic space within which the indigenous communal system existed. The growth of a capitalist economy had direct bearing on the use of indigenous Fijian land, labour and a lukewarm involvement of indigenous Fijians in the market economy. The colonial economy from 1874 was dominated by sugar production, which was under the monopoly of the Colonial Sugar Refining Company (CSR). The colonial state played a direct role in facilitating the accumulation process, such as the importation of indentured labourers from India (Gillion 1962; Lal 1989). The use of indigenous Fijian labour was restricted by the native policy and there were reservations concerning the use of indigenous labour because of a fear of the breakdown of the indigenous social system, already threatened by western influence. By the beginning of the twentieth century, CSR-produced sugar accounted for about 80% of total export value (Narsey 1979). Like sugar, copra production was also an activity dominated by Europeans, using indigenous Fijian and Indo-Fijian labour. But use of indigenous Fijian labour in this case was piecemeal and officially controlled under the Native Labour Ordinance. An Australian Company, Burns Philp (BP), one of the biggest companies operating in the Pacific, was responsible for the purchase and shipping of copra. In 1903, copra exports were worth 91,051 pounds sterling, compared to sugar exports worth 403,301 pounds sterling. Heavy subsidies by the colonial state for sugar and copra production accounted for the high rates of return. For instance, there was a dramatic increase in copra production to 98,382 tonnes in 1970 from a mere 29,969 tonnes in 1900. While this boosted the involvement of indigenous Fijians in the copra industry, they participated only as small-scale semi-subsistence farmers and labourers.

By the beginning of the twentieth century expatriate capital had substantially increased and virtually controlled all merchandising, insurance, banking and overseas shipping. Competition between European-run companies such as BP and Morris Hedstrom (MH) provided dynamism in the economy. Local companies, which consisted mostly of retailers, were too small to compete. The growth of European capital on the one hand and the rigid communal existence of indigenous Fijians on the other raised some concern. Governor Im Thurn saw authoritarian chiefly rule as a stumbling block to the progress of the indigenous Fijian people. This view was reflected in a speech to the Great Council of Chiefs in 1905, in which he accused chiefs of unfairly becoming prosperous through the imposition of exactions which prevented "…(ordinary Fijians) from gaining anything for themselves – any property to make life interesting to them". He advocated "individuality" as "the habit of thought which we (government) and you (chiefs) should encourage in the Fijians" (Fiji Government 1905: 2-3). The means of social reform suggested by Im Thurn included teaching English in village schools to enable indigenous Fijians more cultural liberalization and social mobility, and the "freeing up" of some of the communal land for individual ownership and settlement by indigenous Fijians under the Native Land Ordinance No.14 of 1905. The idea of liberalization was resisted by chiefs, who preferred to continue ruling over an obedient community (Grattan 1963). Nevertheless, some of the land was "freed up" and sold and, as Scarr (1984: 112) noted, between 1905 and 1908, about 105,000 acres of land were sold as freehold and an additional 170,000 acres were put on long-term lease. Land liberalisation was later stopped after a fierce campaign in London by Lord Stanmore (Sir Arthur Gordon), who saw it as a threat to his native policy. Lord Stanmore vigorously defended his policies in Britain's House of Lords in reaction to im Thurn's reforms (Routledge 1985). It was also realised that speculation, rather than settlement, was taking place and the policy was stopped in 1911.

This dramatic sequence of events showed that indirect rule through the chiefs continued to provide institutional resistance towards indigenous Fijian enterprise. Later, in 1915, a motion in the Legislative Council by council member Sir Henry Scott, which required that government was to take all the land that was not required for use by indigenous Fijians for European settlement, was defeated. According to Spate, "this date at latest may be taken as marking official endorsement of the view that Fijian interests were completely paramount" (Spate 1959: 16). The notion of the paramountcy of Fijian interest was initially conceived as a protective mechanism to shield indigenous Fijians from contesting forces; but later, especially as a result of the rise of ethno-nationalism from the 1970s onwards, it became a rallying cry for indigenous Fijian political dominance.

Although largely 'marginalised' from the mainstream colonial economy by a paternalistic native policy, indigenous Fijians were still subject to the demands of a modern economy through seasonal labour recruitment and taxation.[1] The taxation burden compelled many indigenous Fijians to 'commute' between subsistence life and cash employment.[2] They had to pay tax in kind and a significant number left their villages to work on European plantations and cane farms in order to be able to pay tax and avoid the penalty (Burns 1963). In fact by the 1880s 35% of indigenous Fijians paid their taxes in cane. This piecemeal 'proletarianisation' was strictly controlled by the Native Labour Ordinance, which restricted the use of native labour (Narayan 1984). After the indentured system stopped in 1916, there was a growing demand for indigenous Fijian labour to work in the plantations, docks and other areas of commercial growth. Slow liberalisation of indigenous Fijian labour was still subject to the hegemonic control of the colonial state-chiefly system historical bloc.

Indigenous labourers were, however, continuously constrained by increasing demands, by chiefs for provision of communal labour and by the colonial state with its attempts, against the current of its own introduced capitalist economy, to contain Fijians in villages as subsistence producers. These constraints limited the involvement and active participation of indigenous Fijians in the developing colonial capitalist economy. The dilemma for indigenous Fijians was the minimal opportunities they had to earn an income in the face of increasing capitalist penetration of the economy and villages (Plange 1996: 215).

By the 1930s, the real growth was in mining, which was largely controlled by Emperor Gold Mines of Australia. Many indigenous Fijians were recruited from villages, with the help of the chiefs, to provide labour.[3] Emberson-Bain (1994) observed that the recruitment of indigenous Fijian labour into the mines was done within the context of communal labour and under the supervision of

---

1   From 1874, when Fiji became a colony, indigenous Fijian labourers were recruited piecemeal from villages to work on plantations, and within eight years indigenous plantation workers totalled more than 4,000, about 25% of the total able-bodied men. The trend continued into the 1920s and 30s with the setting up of mines. In the mines, ethnic-Fijian workers were "subjected to class and racial exploitation" under a hierarchy of European, part-European, Rotuman and Indian bosses (ranked in that order). See Emberson-Bain (1994). The growth of the ethnic-Fijian working class did not lead directly to the development of a fully-fledged and independent proletarian class, as they were in many ways still subject to the patronising hegemony of the chiefly system. The development of class consciousness was subsumed under ethnic hegemony and provincial division and conflict within the indigenous Fijian labour force. At the time of the recruitment of Indian indentured workers, ethnic hegemony and the uneven development of capitalism laid the foundation for the separate production and reproduction of ethnic identities.
2   This practice is still very common today. While many indigenous Fijians who live in villages commute to work every morning, a large number who live far away from urban centres 'commute' between villages and towns once a month or so to look for casual employment.
3   The extent of the deplorable working conditions in the mines has been well documented (Emberson-Bain 1994). The conditions in the mines led directly to the formation of the first indigenous Fijian labour union. Strikes in the mines were suppressed through the intervention of chiefs, acting on behalf of the colonial state and mining companies to remind indigenous Fijian miners that striking is "un-Fijian" and a sign of disrespect for Fijian chiefs.

chiefs. At the mines, indigenous Fijian miners maintained their province-based communal identity. But in the context of the wider class structure, indigenous Fijians were at the bottom of the socio-economic strata, *vis-a-vis* Indo-Fijians, Rotumans, part-Europeans and Europeans (in that upward order of hierarchy). Chiefs were used effectively to break strikes and neutralise working class consciousness through ethnic and communal appeal (Howard 1989).

The inter-war years were characterised by increased politicisation and mobilisation of class-consciousness. Colonial hegemony and the degrading working conditions it created were being challenged by the increasingly confident mobilisation of Indo-Fijian workers. In 1920[4] and 1921 two major strikes were organised to demand better wages and working conditions.[5] Both strikes were repressed by force, using the largely indigenous Fijian militia. The use of indigenous Fijian military and police by the state against the Indo-Fijians helped to buttress the ethnic wedge of "divide and rule" entrenched by the Native Policy in support of capital. This became a common trend throughout the history of Fiji, where the alliance between chiefs and the state consolidated a power bloc to protect capital accumulation as well as "Fijian interest."

On the political front, although Indo-Fijians were granted elected representation to the Legislative Council in 1929, indigenous Fijians were still "represented" through nominations. The indigenous Fijian representatives were mostly chiefs who, in effect, were the link between the 'separate' Native Administration mentioned earlier and the central government. The structure of the Legislative Council from the 1930s to the 1960s was an institutionalised form of ethnic segregation, reflecting the ethnic division in society generally.[6] Through the nomination system, indigenous Fijians continued to be subservient to the chiefly authority and were deprived of direct experience in formal democracy. This was to contribute to the ambivalent attitude of indigenous Fijians towards democratic politics in later years.

---

4   The strikes were organised by an Indian barrister sent by Gandhi to organise Indo-Fijian workers.
5   In fact the very first strikes in Fiji occurred in February 1886 and March of the same year. The grievances concerned low wages.
6   For instance, under the amended 1937 Constitution, the Legislative Council consisted of: the Governor as President; 3 ex officio members; 13 official members; 5 European members; of whom 3 were elected and 2 nominated; 5 Fijian nominated members; and 5 Indian members, of whom 3 were elected and 2 nominated. Voters were male only (voting was later extended to women in 1961), there was a minimum voting age of 21 years and voters had to pass certain property and income qualifications (Fiji Government, 1938). Voting was strictly on the basis of the communal franchise system.

Reforms and transition to independence, 1940 to 1970

By the end of the Second World War a number of major changes had been made to the Fijian administration by Ratu Sir Lala Sukuna[7] and Governor Mitchell. Amongst these were the setting up of the Native Land Trust Board (NLTB) or *Vale ni Volavola ni Qele Maroroi* under the 1940 Native Land Trust Ordinance to administer Fijian land. The setting up of the NLTB ensured that administration of all native land was to come under a central authority. The NLTB was to oversee the leasing of land, codification of the ownership system and was to ensure that native land was put into productive use (NLTB 1990). As part of the reform, the post of Secretary for Fijian Affairs was created, with Sukuna as office holder, under the Fijian Affairs Ordinance of 1945. His title was *Ai Talai ni Kovana* or governor's representative. This new structure was a shift towards a more indirect rule, and, culturally, became the prism through which indigenous Fijians continued to define their collective identity in later years. It was "...a system empowered by law to organise some of the activities of the Fijian people for their own social, economic and political development as well as for the preservation of their traditional way of life" (Nayacakalou 1975: 85). These changes further consolidated chiefly hegemony within the indigenous Fijian political sphere, at the same time acting as leverage for communal segregation. But these changes were deemed to be justified because of the perceived political 'threat' from Indo-Fijians, who, as shown in Table 1.1, out-numbered the indigenous Fijians by the mid-1940s.

Table 1.1 Population changes 1921-1946

Year	Fijian (%)	Indian (%)	European (%)	Others (%)	Total (000)
1921	54	39	4	4	127
1936	50	43	4	3	198
1946	45	46	4	4	260

Source: Fiji Government 1974.

The reforms of the1940s effectively reversed some of the earlier attempts at liberalising the Fijian Administration, attempts which in the 1930s had been in abeyance. Some of the early 'liberal' reforms included Im Thurn's revision of the Native Regulation in 1912, by which the Governor attempted

---

7 Ratu Sir Lala Sukuna is regarded by many as the most prominent indigenous Fijian to date. He was the first indigenous Fijian graduate as well as the first to be knighted. He became speaker of the Legislative Council and is considered to be the founder of the Native Land Trust Board (NLTB), Fijian Affairs Board (FAB) and a number of policies and institutions that govern indigenous Fijian political and land rights. See Scarr (1980), for a detailed biography of Sukuna.

to reduce the hegemonic power of chiefs; the modification of the Native Administration in 1914 by Governor Bickham Sweet Escott, to ensure more European administration at the district levels; and the increase in the number of Europeans in the Native Administration in 1915, followed by the abolition of the Native Affairs Department in 1916. The Native Affairs Department was revamped as the Fijian Affairs Board (FAB). However, Sukuna tried to complement consolidation of chiefly hegemony with neutralisation of worker consciousness and solidarity by deliberately fostering exclusively ethnic labour unions to ensure that indigenous Fijian workers were directly under chiefly control to maintain communal cohesion. In 1946, as part of the consolidation of indigenous communal solidarity, the racially exclusive Seaman's Union was formed (Europeans were not allowed membership) and the wholly indigenous Fijian Fiji Mine Workers Union was formed in 1948. This, as Howard (1985: 115) puts it, "not only served to divide further organised labour, but it also obviously was intended to create unions that were less likely to be militant since it was felt that the chiefs would exercise a restraining influence on the members of such unions."

Part of the reform was to incorporate indigenous Fijians into mainstream institutions slowly through gradual evolution within the Fijian Administration structure (NLTB 1996). Sukuna suggested in the Legislative Council on 25 February 1944, that it was necessary to train chiefs and people in orderly, sound and progressive local government the better to fit them eventually for the give-and-take of democratic institutions. Hence a number of initiatives were made within the framework of the Fijian Administration in the decade after the war to facilitate indigenous Fijian development. Apart from the restructuring of the Fijian Administration, these included: the setting up of the co-operative movement (*Soqosoqo Cokovata ni Veivoli*) under the Co-operative Ordinance of 1947; the setting up of the Fijian Banana Venture in 1950; the setting up of the Fijian Development Fund (*Lavo Musuki in Veivakatorocaketaki*) by Ordinance No.14 of 1951; the creation of Economic Development Officer positions in 1954 (following the incorporation of an economic development agenda into the Fijian Administration); and more rigid control of the *galala* (independent farming) system. These changes were part of attempts to gradually introduce indigenous Fijians into the market economy but within the context of communal hegemony under the rigid regulations of the Fijian Administration. However, one could argue that these initiatives were perhaps amongst the very first forms of affirmative action consciously carried out specifically for the purpose of enhancing the socio-economic position of indigenous Fijians.

The Co-operative Society, set up under the 1947 Co-operative Ordinance, was seen as a viable alternative for indigenous Fijians instead of fully-fledged individualism. Although the Society was intended to be independent, over time it was progressively influenced by the dictates of the Fijian Administration. It was initially assumed that because of their "communal" orientation, "Fijians were naturally inclined to co-operative effort" (Fiji Co-operative Dept. 1948: 49). Within ten years of formation, the ethnic distribution of co-operative societies in Fiji were as follows: 51 for indigenous Fijians, 5 for Indo-Fijians, and 22 for other ethnic groups and mixed membership (Fiji Co-operative Dept. 1958). Nevertheless, the co-operative movement encouraged self-help, self-management and self-discipline and this came into conflict with the authoritarian communal requirements of the Native Administration. There was conflict at the level of leadership between elected co-operative officials and hereditary chiefs and in many cases local chiefs used their power to control local co-operative movements, and as a result many collapsed. There were constant attempts by hostile Fijian Administration officials to intervene and direct policies in keeping with the Fijian Administration agenda, away from what they saw as a movement which would threaten communal cohesion. There were other problems such as reckless extension of credit to kinsmen and inter-village jealousies (Spate 1959). The main focus of conflict was between the communalistic structure favoured by chiefs and Fijian Administration officials on one hand, and the collectivist co-operative system based on mutual co-operation, democratic leadership and expectations of financial bonus (depending on performance) favoured by many ordinary villagers, on the other.

Thus over the years one of the biggest barriers to the efficiency of the co-operative movement was the way the authoritarian chiefly rule and communal obligations interfered with the operation of many co-operative societies (Young 1984). In a major review in 1959, Spate concluded that "the movement's history of difficulties illustrates perhaps better than anything else the inherent obstacles to economic advance imposed by the traditional system" (Spate 1959: 55). I take issue with Spate's modernizationist generalization here. The problem was not so much the "traditional system," but rather how certain individuals in the system used their status to siphon off benefits to themselves. Belshaw (1964), who was doing fieldwork almost around the same time, found cases of village-based enterprises which were running well.

The Fijian Banana Venture (FBV), sponsored by the Fijian Administration in 1950 as a way of developing banana cultivation and marketing amongst indigenous Fijians, had mixed results due to a number of factors including the difficult logistics involved. Production was principally at the village level on a communal basis, although some producers were independent farmers. Banana cultivation went through difficulties and did not perform as expected, and in many parts of the banana growing area such as Nadroga production was in a "sorry state" (Belshaw 1964: 45).

In his seminal study of rural socio-economic life in the 1950s, Belshaw observed a number of "specialized or expansionist enterprises" in various Fijian villages in Vitilevu, including village store keepers; cash-oriented farmers, some of whom engaged also in auxiliary business; cattle raisers; and marketing middle men. These were relatively small in number but at the same time they provided the engine for socio-economic development in villages. A problem was that these enterprises were tied up with a complex array of institutional forces such as the Fijian Affairs Board, cooperatives, community associations, provincial government and national government; and faced community obligations.

The setting up of the Fijian Development Fund (FDF) in 1951 was one of the first of a series of attempts to encourage saving amongst indigenous Fijians. It was set up primarily for copra farmers, to ensure that part of their earnings was directed to communal development. The initial success of the FDF was due to the high post-war copra prices. The FDF dealt with items in three main categories: first, relatively small items, say up to F£1,000 in value, which were widely distributed (ploughs, bullocks, tractors, cocoa machines, copra driers and surveying); second, 'intermediate' projects, about F£5,000 in value (fisheries, small mining, cattle); and third, projects requiring high capitalisation and skilled management (land development, purchase and development of estates, timber projects).

Rather than mobilising resources for generating income on a long-term basis, the FDF was concerned mostly with improvement of communal life through the development of village amenities (Fijian Affairs Board 1990). A compulsory deduction of F£10 per ton of copra produced by copra farmers was collected by the Fijian Affairs Board and credited to accounts of individuals or co-operative producers and sometimes to village accounts, bearing a 2% interest rate, and requiring a flat rate ledger fee of 10 shillings per account. Copra was sold only to Fijian Affairs Board (FAB) agents or licensed buyers. The FDF was controlled by a board of which the Secretary of Fijian Affairs was the Chair. Other members consisted of FAB members; legal and financial advisors to the board; and a number of European and indigenous Fijian nominated members. The FDF was highly bureaucratic and paternalistic and discouraged individual economic enterprise outside the ambit of the Fijian Administration.

Aside from the development institutions, agents responsible for the day-to-day operation of Fijian development were the Economic Development Officers (EDOs), who were appointed in 1954 for the purpose of bridging the divide between the development policies of the government's Agricultural Department (which encouraged individual farming) and the Fijian Administration (which encouraged communal farming). By employing EDOs, it was hoped that there would be "less danger of conflicting policies being pursued and that agricultural assistance for Fijians would be developed within the framework of the well-established communal system rather than as in the past concentrated on a comparatively few individuals" (Fiji Government 1954). The EDOs' development program was laid down in a 1954 resolution of the Great Council of Chiefs: cultivation of economic crops should be organised as a communal service on family lands; building and repairing of houses to be done outside the development program; and EDOs were to see that programs of work were drawn up in consultation with those concerned and that those programs were in fact carried out. The EDOs were mostly high chiefs with diverse communal responsibilities and charged with the task of consolidating communal cohesion through economic development along the old *tikina* and *koro* program of work (Fiji Government 1957). Two of the EDOs, Ratu Sir George Cakobau and Ratu Penaia Ganilau, later became Governor General and President of Fiji respectively. Other EDOs included the paramount chiefs of Rewa and Nadroga. These were men of power with no expertise on 'development' who used their traditional status to act as comprador for the colonial state to keep the state system operational and to control indigenous Fijian labour. Most of them had influence at various levels of the state system from the top to the bottom, as shown in the case of the EDO for the Northern provinces (in Vanua Levu). Ganilau was the Roko Tui Cakaudrove (a state-designated civil servant/chief of Cakaudrove Province) and was a member of the following: Legislative Council; Legislative Council Standing Committee; Fijian Affairs Board; Fijian Development Fund Board; Central Road Board; Macuata Road Board; Taveuni Rural Authority; Taveuni Hospital Board of Visitors; Taveuni Native Land Trust Board Local Committee; and Taveuni Liquor Permit Committee. This example provides an indication of the extent of political authority and influence EDOs had.

Thus, paradoxically, under the EDO Fijian development was far from being a liberating process to catapult indigenous Fijians into the entrepreneurial world. Rather, it was part of a bigger design to help indigenous Fijians engage in the cash economy – but within the ambit of the state, province and chiefly control.

Another significant change was the increased regulation of the *galala* system (individual farming) in 1955. Under Governor Gordon's Land Ordinance XXI of 1880, it was envisaged that indigenous Fijians would eventually be granted individual holding when the time was ripe. In the early twentieth century, Governor Im Thurn, as we saw earlier, also favoured liberalisation of land holdings. In the 1930s, with the encouragement of the Department of Agriculture, there were cases of independent farmers settling outside the communal system, although special exemption had to be granted by the District Administration. The number of exemptions increased during the war in the 1940s as part of the effort to produce supplies for the forces. Sukuna, alarmed by the increasing number of exemptions, declared in 1944 in a memorandum to the Administrative Officers Conference that, while a number of indigenous Fijians desired to "live as peasant farmers, independently of the system, either on their own lands or elsewhere", government and the Fijian Regulations were prepared to "encourage" it -but "within the limits laid down in the Native Regulations" (Sukuna 1944: 1). In 1955 changes to the *galala* conditions under Native Regulations No.6 made commutation between the village and independent settlement more rigid. It also specified a number of conditions related to production which the *galala* should strictly follow.[8] These conditions ensured that while independent farming was encouraged, it was to be carried out under the terms of the Native Regulations.

If anything, the 'reforms' mentioned above merely further crystallised communal hegemony by reinforcing chiefly control and did little to advance the economic situation of indigenous Fijians, at a time when the colonial economy had progressively shown a clear link between ethnicity and socio-economic position. The class structure in the 1940s and 1950s had a distinctive ethnic dimension. The economy was dominated by expatriate and local European capital; below was a growing class of Indo-Fijian and Chinese petite-bourgeoisie and at the bottom was a large mass of impoverished Indo-Fijian cane farmers and indigenous Fijians in the semi-subsistence sector (Narayan 1984; Plange 1996). However, it needs to be mentioned that amongst the indigenous Fijians was a class of comprador chiefs who were co-opted into the civil service or who, through the native regulations, wielded substantial power over the indigenous community.

In addition, ethnic relations worsened during the war because of the refusal of the Indo-Fijians to join the army to fight the invading Japanese, and their demand for equal rights with Europeans as a condition for signing up. Instead, in 1943 the Indo-Fijian sugar workers went on strike to demand better prices for cane. Unlike the 1920 and 1921 strikes, the 1943 strike was led by union leaders. The organising unions were the Kisan Sangh (formed in the late 1930s) and the Akhil Fiji Krisnak Maha Sangh (All-Fiji Farmers' Great Association), formed in 1941. The 1943 strike, like the previous ones, reinforced the indigenous Fijian nationalist stereotype (encouraged by the 'ethnic wedging' technique of the colonial state) that Indo-Fijians were 'scheming' and were not to be trusted when it came to situations of national and security interest.

During the post-war period there was a concerted effort to increase exports (Knapman 1987). Europeans still dominated agricultural production, despite the increase in the number of Indo-Fijian and indigenous Fijian farmers. In the late 1950s, for instance, 557 Europeans were able to produce and export produce to the value of £2,159 each; 22,000 Indo-Fijians produced exports worth about £337; and indigenous Fijians produced exports to the value of £72.10s.

---

8   The 1956 Census estimated that there were about 1,300 *galala*. This represented a little over 3.5% of all ratepayers and a little over 5.5% of all indigenous Fijians engaged in agriculture.

Europeans had much larger and more productive commercial estates, while at the other extreme, indigenous Fijians were mostly subsistence village farmers with occasional semi-commercial farming operations.

By the 1950s little had changed in relation to indigenous Fijian participation in commerce. The Fijian administration still played a hegemonic role and largely controlled the political and economic direction of indigenous Fijian 'development', in a way that promoted communalism and undermined independent enterprise. In terms of the latter, communal ownership of land was a major obstacle. For instance, by 1956, a mere 0.2% of freehold land, which constituted the most productive commercially used land, was owned by indigenous Fijians. Within the commercial farming sector (excluding cattle farming), ethnic distribution of average per capita acres (land under commercial farming) in 1958 showed that there were 131.0 acres for Europeans, 7.0 acres for Indo-Fijians, 6.4 acres for Chinese and other Islanders and 4.8 acres for indigenous Fijians. If we include 36,000 acres of improved pastureland for cattle farming and 600 acres of fodder crops under European ownership, then the average per capita area in use by Europeans was over 192 acres or 27.7% of the total farm land in Fiji (Narayan 1984: 67). In sugar production (the largest industry in the colony) in terms of tons harvested, indigenous Fijians produced only 4.3% in 1953; 4.84% in 1954; 3.49% in 1955; 4.43% in 1956; and 3.25% in 1957 (Colonial Sugar Refinery 1959). Despite efforts to increase indigenous Fijian productivity in sugar farming – including the setting up of a CSR school in Drasa, to train young indigenous Fijians in a three-year practical course on sugarcane farming – indigenous Fijian production never exceeded 5% of total production. Most of the indigenous Fijian cane famers leased their own communal land and a few leased land from the Fiji Sugar Corporation (Belshaw 1964).

One of the drawbacks of agricultural development for indigenous Fijian farmers was the difficulty in getting a commercial loan. For instance in the 1950s and 1960s, ethnic allocation of loans by the Agricultural and Industrial Loans Board (later to become the Fiji Development Bank), which was set up to provide capital for agricultural development, disadvantaged indigenous Fijians. European borrowers, who accounted for only 15% of the total number of loans, received 53% of the total loan value; Indo-Fijian borrowers accounted for 53% of the total number of loans and received 34% of the total loan value; and indigenous Fijians received 25% of the total number of loans but only 7% of the total value (Sutherland 1998). The figures for the financial year for 1960/61 showed that the average size of a loan to an indigenous Fijian was half that of loans to Indo-Fijians and one tenth that of loans to Europeans. The bank was generally blamed for "favouring" Indo-Fijians. But the real situation was that indigenous Fijian land was communally owned and could not be used as collateral for loans (Burns

1963). In law, the bank could not make a claim on communally owned land. Even houses could not be used as collateral since they were built on communal land. Because of their distrust of banks, many indigenous Fijians joined credit unions. The credit union movement was introduced by Father Ganey in 1954. At the end of 1957 there were 231 unions with a total membership of 24,148. Members were, predominantly, indigenous Fijians. Many of the loans went to meet communal obligations (Schultze 1982).

While communal land ownership was meant to 'protect' indigenous Fijian land, it also became a major barrier to economic development. On the other hand, Indo-Fijians used sugar cane crops on their leased farms as collateral for loans. A few indigenous Fijians who ventured into commercial farming on leased land were able to do likewise.

Sukuna's communal paradigm not only retarded progress in economic entrepreneurship, it also disadvantaged education for indigenous Fijians at large. Sukuna's idea was that cohesion within Fijian communal life could only be sustained through absolute loyalty to chiefs, who were the only ones with the right to be educated. It was feared that educated commoners would pose a threat to chiefly authority and communal cohesion. An educated commoner intelligentsia, according to Sukuna, would be potentially subversive by "undermining and confusing authority to their own ends" (quoted in Scarr 1980:146). The first secondary schools were set up primarily for children of chiefs (Whitehead 1981).

The overall impact of the protective and paternalistic communalism under the native policy no doubt led to the relatively low achievement of indigenous Fijians in various areas of the economy and professional service. For instance in 1953, as Table 1.2 shows, the per capita cash income of Europeans and part-Europeans (F$468) was highest, followed by Chinese (F$279), who were mostly shopkeepers, and then Indo-Fijians (F$113), while the indigenous Fijians had the lowest per capita of only F$60. However, differences in per capita income for both cash and subsistence between indigenous Fijians (F$121) and Indo-Fijians (F$128) was not very significant, due to the substantial involvement of indigenous Fijians in the subsistence economy (Fiji 1956). The figures show a low level of indigenous Fijian participation in the capitalist sector of the economy compared to other ethnic groups.

Table 1.2 Estimated per capita income by ethnicity, 1953 (F$)

Ethnic Group	Income per head (Cash and Subsistence)	Income per head (Cash only)
Indigenous Fijians	121	60
Indo-Fijians	128	113
Europeans/Part-Europeans	468	468
Chinese	302	279
Other Categories	147	113

Source: Fiji Legislative Council Paper No.44 of 1956.

Also, in 1958, as Table 1.3 shows, in the various professions including lawyers, doctors and dentists, there were 2 indigenous Fijians, 58 Indo-Fijians, 1 Chinese, 2 part-Europeans and 74 Europeans (Fiji 1960). Despite their under-representation in the areas of commerce and professional services, indigenous Fijians seemed, by virtue of their preponderance in small scale, semi-subsistence agriculture, to have performed well in crop cultivation for local consumption. For instance, they cultivated about 45% of the 80,000 acres of crops for local consumption. But they farmed only a little under 32% of the acreage used for export crops. Indigenous Fijians dominated banana cultivation; but a relatively low number of indigenous Fijians participated in rice and sugar farming.

Table 1.3 Numbers qualified in selected professions, by ethnic group 1958

Ethnic Group	Lawyers	Doctors	Dentists	Total
Ethnic-Fijians	-	1	1	2
Indo-Fijians	38	12	8	58
Chinese	-	1	-	1
Part-Europeans	1	1	-	2
Europeans	17	51	6	74
Total	**56**	**66**	**15**	**137**

Source: Fiji Legislative Council Papers No.1 of 1960: 12.

This trend continued into the 1960s. Table 1.4 provides a general picture of the distribution of gross income in 1967, three years before independence. It shows that the proportion of indigenous Fijians receiving cash income above F$5,000 was only 4%, compared to 16% for Indo-Fijians, 38% for Europeans and 24% for Chinese. In other words, indigenous Fijians were the least represented in the higher socio-economic strata. Indigenous Fijians predominated in the low-income bracket (F$0-1,000), while there was an almost equal proportion of indigenous Fijians and Indo-Fijians within the F$1,001-2,000 range.

Table 1.4 Distribution of gross cash income of individuals, by ethnic groups, 1967, in percentages

Income Range (F$)	Fijians (%)	Indo-Fijians (%)	Europeans (%)	Chinese (%)
0-1,000	30	22	5	9
1,001-2,000	35	34	14	22
2,001-5,000	31	28	43	44
over 5,000	4	16	38	24
Total	100	100	100	100

Source: Fiji Inland Revenue Department, National Accounts Report 1967: 5.

Around the same period (1966), the ratios of indigenous Fijian lawyers, doctors and dentists to Indo-Fijians in those occupations were; 0 indigenous Fijian to 38 Indo-Fijians; 1 indigenous Fijian to 12 Indo-Fijians; and 1 indigenous Fijian to 8 Indo-Fijians, respectively (Fiji 1966).

The continuing disparity in indicators and the lack of indigenous Fijian progress in socio-economic terms were the subject of two major investigations by Spate and Burns. In his report, *The Fijian People: Economic Problems and Prospects*, Professor Spate argued that the lack of progress of indigenous Fijians in commerce could be attributed to the rigid communal system under the native policy (Spate 1959). Later, the Burns Report concurred with Spate's findings and emphasised the fact that communal ownership of land undermined the economic progress of indigenous Fijians (Burns 1963).

By the late 1950s and 1960s, the establishment of the forestry and tourism industries provided some hope for the future development of indigenous Fijians. Both these industries became important to indigenous Fijians because of the use of native forests (and native labour) for logging and the use of indigenous Fijian land (and labour in tourism development). But in both cases, the investors were foreign companies, sometimes with local shareholders. The Forestry Department was largely Fijian staffed. This created some difficulties with local chiefs, who saw it as their right to direct department officials as to which forest to log. One of the first sawmills to be set up under the Fijian Development Fund was the Kadavu sawmill in 1957. Complicated negotiations had to take place with the 31 *mataqalis* who owned the land.

The 1956 Census showed that about 600 out of the 1,000 workers in lumbering and sawmilling were indigenous Fijians. Indigenous Fijians accounted for two-thirds of the supervisory and clerical workers and all 192 skilled workers. But over half the proprietary and managerial grades were occupied by Indo-Fijians and Europeans. Tourism, in particular, went through a period of unprecedented boom after the 1962 legislation to allow duty-free trading and the 1964 Hotel Aids Ordinance, which encouraged tourism investment. The growth of the service industries associated with tourism (travel services, taxis, duty-free shopping and so on) largely benefited European capitalists, the Indo-Fijian petit-bourgeoisie and indigenous Fijian chiefs whose land was leased to hotel companies. The lowest-paid jobs were reserved for indigenous Fijians recruited from villages around hotel resorts. They were (and still are) largely used as marketing exhibits for the "smiling" and "friendly" Fijian image on which Fiji's tourism has thrived. This was to be the trend until independence.

Also in the 1950s and 1960s, an emergent proletarian class, and class-consciousness, had developed across communal boundaries and strikes had become commonplace (Narayan 1984). The colonial state even suspected that some were instigated by the Communist Party of Australia (CPA), which by then was at the forefront of worker agitation in Australia. Perhaps one of the most significant strikes in this period was the 1955 Vatukoula gold miners' strike, because it manifested a growing contradiction between communalism and working-class consciousness. Although miners lived and were organised along provincial lines in the mining town, the exploitative conditions of the work made it a necessity to seek new principles of social action. Despite pleas from four high-ranking chiefs, together with the Commissioner of Labour and District Commissioner, the strike went ahead and the arbitration ruled in the strikers' favour. Perhaps the most important class-based resistance was the first ever multi-racial strike in 1959 against European employers and the colonial state, which was seen as evidence of a growing class alliance between the Indo-Fijian and indigenous Fijian proletariats (Sutherland 1993). The strike led to street riots in which European shops were targeted.

Some of the strikes in the 1960s were directly linked to the demand for independence, particularly by Indo-Fijians. To strengthen their political cause, the militant cane growers' unions formed the Federation Party (FP). In a show of defiance, the members of the FP walked out of the Legislative Council in 1967 to show their support for a "common roll" (one person one vote) as opposed to "communal roll" (voting for one's own ethnic representative). The communal roll was generally preferred by the indigenous Fijians because it complemented the Fijian Administration communal organisation in 'protecting' indigenous Fijian interests (Ali 1982).

There were dramatic changes in the 1960s as part of the transition towards independence. The franchise was extended to indigenous Fijians (although only partially) for the first time in 1961, and further constitutional changes took place in succession in 1964 and 1965 to allow for greater electoral representation. In 1966 the first full election took place with both common and communal rolls. The distribution of seats, shown in Table 1.5, shows that of the 34 elected members of the Legislative Council, there were 12 Indo-Fijians 1, 2 indigenous

Fijians and 10 Europeans. The population distribution of 42% indigenous Fijians, 51% Indo-Fijians and 4% Europeans meant that Europeans were much over-represented *vis-a-vis* other ethnic groups.

Table 1.5 Seat distribution of Legislative Council 1966

Voters	Communal Seats	Cross voting Seats	Total
Indigenous Fijian	9	3	12
Indo-Fijian	9	3	12
General Voter (European and Part-European)	7	3	10
Total Elected	25	9	34
Elected by Great Council of Chiefs	-	-	2
Nominated by Governor	-	-	4
Total			40

Source: Ali 1982.

Indigenous Fijians were granted the franchise for the first time in 1963. The 1965 Constitution incorporated Rotumans and other Pacific Islanders into the Fijian roll. Although voting was not entirely on the basis of the communal roll, the extensive use of ethnic discourse and mobilization during the election campaigns further reinforced communalism at the local level.[9] Communalism at the national level, through the communal franchise, acted as the legitimising framework for communal mobilisation at the local level. A universal franchise did not undermine communalism, rather it merely reinforced it.

The year 1966 was also important because it was then that the Fijian Association became a prominent electoral force. It later became the dominant group within the Alliance Party, the umbrella organisation that also incorporated the Indian Alliance (for Indo-Fijians) and General Electors' Association (for Europeans, part-Europeans, Chinese and Pacific Islanders). Despite its "multi-racial" rhetoric and organisation, the Alliance Party became closely identified with the Fijian Administration and communal and chiefly hegemony.

Perhaps one of the most significant changes in the 1960s was the gradual relaxation of the rigid native policy rules. That relaxation was led by Dr Rusiate

---

9   At this stage we need to distinguish between the 'communal' and the 'common' franchise. The concept of communal franchise referred to various ethnic categories voting only for representatives within their communal constituencies. The common roll franchise allowed everyone to vote for candidates from other ethnic categories. Communal franchise, a British colonial legacy, was first introduced for Europeans in 1904, and later extended to Indians in 1929 and eventually to Fijians in 1963. It assumed that stability was possible by allowing colonised people a small parliamentary political space within which they could articulate their frustrations, without having to resort to extra-legal means. It was believed that 'communal safeguards' would help to reinforce 'national safeguards'. The communal franchise system encapsulated ethnic separation and helped make ethnic hegemony, especially the paramountcy of Fijian interest, an entrenched part of the political culture.

Nayacakalou, the leading indigenous Fijian scholar at the time. The thrust of the reform was based on Nayacakalou's perception that greater liberalization was important for adaptation to modern realities (Nayacakalou 1975). There was a general feeling that Fijians needed to be emancipated from the control of the Fijian Regulations and central authority. This emancipation was part of the gradual opening up process to introduce indigenous Fijians into democratic politics and more individualistic living. At one level, social and political liberalisation was taking place, but at another, this was not so. Although the native regulations were lifted, and legally imposed and communal mobilisation was no longer the norm, communal institutions still existed in the form of the Great Council of Chiefs, Fijian Affairs Board, Native Land Trust Board, Fijian Development Fund and a number of pieces of legislation. Importantly, after almost half a century of coerced conformity, communalism had become an entrenched component of mainstream indigenous Fijian social psyche. It continued to be the social basis for mobilisation in politics and economic development.

By 1969 independence was inevitable and negotiations over parliamentary representation started between the two major political parties, the National Federation Party [NFP] (representing the Indo-Fijians) and the Alliance Party (representing the indigenous Fijians and 'Others' category). The Alliance Party insisted on protection of indigenous Fijian communal interests. To safeguard this it was important to create a fine balance between the communal franchise on the one hand and the common franchise on the other. The result was an independence constitution which provided for a delicate ethnic balance by allocating 22 seats to indigenous Fijians, 22 to Indians and 8 to the General voters. Of these, 27 were classed as communal seats (12 Fijians 12 Indo-Fijian and 3 General Electors), and 25 were reserved ethnic seats in common-roll electorates.[10] The seat allocation was intended to draw a balance between the changing demographic pattern and the need to maintain the "paramountcy of Fijian interest". Although Indo-Fijians made up 51% and indigenous Fijians only 43% of the population in 1969 and 1970, it was felt that there was a need to keep a political 'balance' through recognition of the special interests of indigenous Fijians.

The 1970 Constitution was the result of accommodation among elites, where leaders of the various communities bargained their way to an eventual consociationalist solution. Interestingly, the Malaysian consociationalist model in the form of the Malaysian Alliance, consisting of political parties representing different ethnic communities, was seen as a possible model for Fiji. In fact the Malaysian Alliance Party, which later became a national umbrella political organization, was the model for the Alliance Party in Fiji. The optimism for

---

10   Under the 1970 Constitution, the Fiji electoral system was quite complex. Voters had to vote on four separate ballot papers altogether in the communal and national seats (Fiji Government, 1970).

the Malaysian model was thwarted after the May 1969 ethnic riots in Malaysia, which revealed some of the fundamental contradictions and weaknesses of the Malaysian consociationalist approach.

Despite provision for a universal franchise, first given in 1963, the independence constitution still perpetuated communalism through various 'protective' mechanisms in order to ensure the paramountcy of Fijian interests. Amongst these were legislation to preserve the inalienability of native land, provisions for institutional prominence of the Fijian Administration and provisions for the communal franchise. Thus communalism at the political level also found expression at the grassroots in terms of development initiatives and other forms of social organisation.

Conclusion: Effects of the colonial native policy on the indigenous Fijian community

The native policy transformed the indigenous Fijian community in significant ways. At the cultural level it helped to shape a homogeneous collective ethnic identity. The Fijian Administration became the dominant institutional force around which indigenous Fijians defined their world view as a collective *Taukei* in relation to others. This homogeneous identity, crafted out of the diverse identities amongst the different tribes, later became institutionalised 'officially' in such institutions as the Fijian Affairs Board, Ministry of Fijian Affairs, Native Land Trust Board and even the 1970 and 1990 Constitutions. It also became the basis for political mobilisation and ethno-nationalism in later years (Norton, 1994).

At the socio-economic level, the native policy locked indigenous Fijians into the village subsistence economy, and marginalised them in terms of the mainstream commercial arena, except as a source of seasonal cheap labour in the newly created plantations and as workers in the mines. Individual entrepreneurship was half-heartedly encouraged, although individuals were later allowed to pursue commercial farming on their *galala*, or individually leased communally owned land, on a limited basis. The lack of commercial and educational opportunities was a direct consequence of the restrictions deliberately imposed by the rigid communal system. When the restrictions were finally lifted in the 1960s, indigenous Fijians found themselves at a disadvantage in terms of formal employment, commerce and education in relation to other ethnic groups. The indigenous elites saw greater economic and educational empowerment as an urgent priority even as Fiji was moving towards independence.

3. Politicized affirmative action: Independence in 1970 to the 1987 military coup

By the time of independence in 1970, Fiji was faced with a number of dilemmas. The first was how to create a collective national identity while maintaining distinctive cultural identities; the second was how to address indigenous Fijian development while ensuring an open market economy; and the third was how to consolidate a pluralistic parliamentary democracy while maintaining distinctive ethnic political rights through communally reserved parliamentary seats. Negotiating these sets of seemingly dichotomous variables required a political process which was ethno-politically sensitive, ideologically balanced and able to accommodate and ameliorate diverse and often antagonistic interests.

Perhaps the most pressing issue was the question of indigenous Fijian development; and, in particular, how to articulate preferential development policies for indigenous Fijians while pursuing a multi-ethnic ideological stance and free market economy at the same time. The colonial economy had locked indigenous Fijians into the subsistence sector under the native policy and, in the process, had kept them outside mainstream commercial activities and higher education. By the time the rigid system was liberalized and indigenous Fijians were freed from the confinements of the native policies, they were suddenly awakened to the fact that economic and educational opportunities were being lost and other ethnic groups had done relatively well in relation to participation in the modern market economy. This bred multiple sentiments: the desire to fast track indigenous Fijian development and education, envy of other ethnic groups' commercial success, demand for political empowerment to balance Indo-Fijian prowess in commerce and high expectation for the Alliance Party's ability to drive indigenous Fijian development. This required not only strong and decisive leadership but also flexibility to be able to accommodate tension and negotiate differences. These were the major dilemmas faced by the Alliance Party under Mara after independence. To understand the complex dilemmas facing the Alliance and the contradictions of Alliance policies, a good place to start is to examine the party's own structure and ideology.

The post-independence dominance of the Alliance Party

While on the surface independent Fiji appeared peaceful, there were underlying fissures, which the leaders of the two major ethnic groups tried very hard to keep under wraps. A way of doing this was a consociational agreement to have a constitution which provided political balance between the ethnic groups. Apart from this the British had carefully nurtured an indigenous Fijian elite within the Alliance Party to take over political power upon independence. But the transition was not a simple matter. There were socio-economic and political complexities derived from the past that had to be addressed, in particular the ethnically divisive strategy of the colonial state as well as the issue of socio-economic inequality and grievances.

Dealing with the issue of economic redistribution would be a challenge for two reasons. Firstly, a culture of ethno-political competition over control of state power had been established, encouraged by an ethnically based party system in response to the constitutional provisions for communally reserved seats. Given this ethnicized political environment, any attempt to put in place pro-indigenous preferential policies was going to be met with stiff resistance, particularly by Indo-Fijians. The Alliance Party had to convince Indo-Fijians that affirmative action was good for ethnic relations. Secondly, the powerful European and Indo-Fijian business supporters of the Alliance Party needed to be convinced that redistributive policies through affirmative action were complementary and not adversarial to the ideology of multiracialism and would not threaten their economic and political interests.

For the European, Chinese and Indo-Fijian business elites, the Alliance Party provided the political stability and security they needed. They saw the Alliance as the only political force to keep the agitating Indo-Fijian farmers and disgruntled indigenous nationalists under control. To the ordinary indigenous Fijians the Alliance Party, whose leadership was dominated by chiefs, encapsulated their socio-cultural and political identity as well as their socio-economic interests. To many ordinary Indo-Fijians, it was just another "Fijian" Party supported by only a few members of the Indian elite in the same way that the National Federation Party (NFP) was perceived by ordinary indigenous Fijians as just another "Indian" party supported by a handful of misplaced Fijians. Some more moderate Indo-Fijians saw the Alliance as the only political force which could run and sustain a multi-ethnic Fiji and protect Indo-Fijian interest in the face of competing ethno-political demands.

The Alliance Party's multiracial philosophy was the brainchild of Mara, whose propensity towards racial inclusiveness was nurtured during his student days at the Marist Brothers High School, a Catholic school and the first multi-racial school in Fiji. Most of the leading ethnic leaders of the Alliance government, consisting of indigenous Fijians, Indo-Fijians, Chinese and part-Europeans were old boys of the school. The "Marist Old Boy network" became a powerful political, social and economic force in Fiji over the years after independence.

The structure of the Alliance Party was based on the post-independence Malaysian Alliance Party, which was a consociationalist arrangement incorporating three major political groups, the United Malays National Organisation (UMNO), the Malaysian Indian Congress (MIC) and the Malaysian Chinese Association (MCA). In a similar configuration, the Alliance Party consisted of the Fijian Association, Indian Alliance and General Electors Association (representing Europeans, part-Europeans, Chinese and Pacific Islanders).[1] Ideologically, the Alliance Party advanced two seemingly contradictory principles: multi-racialism and communalism. While the notion of multi-racialism embraced pluralism, communalism emphasised ethnic compartmentalisation and the paramountcy of Fijian interests. Paradoxically, the two seemed mutually linked because multi-racialism itself implied ethnic diversity, but this diversity was conceptualised in terms of ethnic distinctiveness. It was based on the ethnic pluralist notion of co-existence but distinctiveness and separation of cultures.

The main political power base of the Alliance Party was the Fijian Association, which was intimately linked with the institutions of the Fijian Administration, such as the Fijian Affairs Board, Native Land Trust Board and Great Council of Chiefs, and also the predominantly indigenous Fijian military. In other words, the Alliance Party was not only a political party in the 'normal' sense, but more than that, it acted as the 'political arm' of the chiefly establishment and indigenous Fijian communalism in the sphere of liberal democratic power politics. Through this, Alliance Party hegemony permeated various levels of the indigenous Fijian community, from the national parliamentary structure to the village level. It was a re-adaptation of the native policy, but now, instead of the colonial state, the Alliance government itself was the centripetal political force. This schema largely defined and reproduced the boundaries of indigenous Fijian political identity and loyalty both in the 'traditional' and liberal democratic sense.

The Alliance cleverly used chiefly authority as an instrumentalist and ideological tool to legitimise and consolidate political leadership in the modern

---

1   Although the Alliance Party proper was formed in 1966, the Fijian Association, the dominant group in the Alliance, was formed in 1956 to mobilise indigenous Fijian political support for the chiefly system and indigenous Fijian privileges. Ascribed chiefly leadership was regarded as legitimate and sacrosanct and could not be opposed. The Indian Alliance was started by small groups opposed to the National Federation Party. These were the Fiji National Congress, the Muslim Political Front, and the Muslim-based Fiji Minority Party. The General Electors Association was formed in 1966 to ensure greater effective participation of other minorities.

context. The convergence of traditional and modern politics was personified by the Alliance leader himself, Mara, who was groomed by Sukuna and the colonial state to take over political leadership upon independence. Mara, like Sukuna, was an Oxford graduate and a high chief. His colourful political career was characterised by his astute ability to utilise both his manoeuvring skills in modern power politics and the mythical *mana* of chiefly authority. His aloof and authoritarian style of leadership was resented by many, but to many indigenous Fijians it was a mark of divinely ordained chiefly rule. Mara was a complex leader who operated at the level of intellectual idealism and the pragmatism of *realpolitik* simultaneously. Despite his commitment to the ideals of multi-racialism, he was also a great advocate of communalism because that was where his real political power base lay. The Alliance's political ideology was based on this contradictory dualism; on the one hand the Alliance adhered to multi-racialism to portray a universally acceptable political image and on the other hand it was pragmatically committed to the communalistic agenda, to mobilise indigenous Fijian support (Norton 1994).

The Alliance fought and won the first post-independence General Election in 1972 on the basis of this apparently contradictory philosophy by mobilising indigenous Fijian support using communal leverage and appealing to other ethnic groups through multi-racial rhetoric. The Alliance Party won a total of 33 seats. This included all the indigenous Fijian and General Electors' communal seats. The tally included 83 per cent of all indigenous Fijian votes, 79 per cent of General Elector votes and 24 per cent of Indo-Fijian votes. The NFP on the other hand won 19 seats, winning 75 per cent of all Indo-Fijian votes and two per cent of indigenous Fijian votes. Six of their indigenous Fijian candidates lost their deposits (Norton 1994).

In the 1970s some of the contradictions mentioned earlier began to surface. Some nationalistic indigenous Fijians began to criticise Mara for being too pro-business, even pro-Indian, in order to maintain their support even at the cost of undermining indigenous interests. One of the critics of Mara was Sakeasi Butadroka, the then Assistant Minister for Commerce, Industry and Co-operatives, who had spent time working in rural indigenous Fijian communities as a cooperative officer, and who accused the Alliance leaders of favouring Indo-Fijians and undermining indigenous Fijian interests. Butadroka's fury was invoked by the revelation that an Indo-Fijian bus company was granted a licence ahead of the communally-owned bus company he was running in the Rewa Province. Butadroka was expelled by Mara from the Alliance Party in 1974 for his criticisms, and a year later in October 1975, he moved a motion in the House of Representatives that Indo-Fijians "be repatriated back to India and that their travelling expenses back home and compensation for their properties in the country be met by the British government" (Fiji, House of Representatives,

9 October 1975: 1104). The motion was not passed in its original form, as it was subsequently amended by Mara and the part relating to repatriation was deleted. The main thrust of the amended version thanked the Indo-Fijians for their contribution to Fiji. But the issue raised the fundamental question of socio-economic parity, a central focus of this book.[2] While the Alliance was fully aware of the issue of ethnic disparity, its approach was cautious, as it feared that an all-out affirmative action policy could antagonize both its Indo-Fijian supporters and the business community.

Butadroka was to haunt Mara in the next five years when, during the 1977 election, Butadroka polled an unprecedented 25% of the Fijian vote while the Indo-Fijian vote for the Alliance declined by 16%. The National Federation Party (NFP) won with a small majority and, for the first time, there was the possibility of an Indo-Fijian becoming Prime Minister. Of the total 52 seats, 24 were won by the Alliance Party, 26 by the NFP, 1 by Butadroka's Fijian Nationalist Party (FNP) and 1 by an independent. Interestingly, prior to this election, the Alliance government took a risk by implementing its 50-50 scholarship scheme, the first major educational affirmative action since independence. This meant that for all the government scholarships to the University of the South Pacific, 50% were to be for indigenous Fijians and 50% for other ethnic groups. This was strongly opposed by the Indo-Fijian community, who made up more than 50% of the Fiji population, and consequently that policy could have contributed to the decline in Indo-Fijian support for the Alliance Party.

Nevertheless, the educational affirmative action policy turned out to be one of the most successful development strategies of the Alliance government because it opened the floodgates for hundreds of indigenous students who otherwise would not have been able to go to university because of their socio-economic position and because they had lower grades than their Indo-Fijian counterparts. This led to the expansion of a Fijian professional and middle class in a significant way within a span of ten to twenty years.

From 1977 onwards the Alliance Party was targeted from both sides – from the indigenous Fijian nationalists, who thought that it was not doing enough for the indigenous people; and from the Indo-Fijians, who argued that it was biased against them. Moreover, the defeat of the Alliance Party during the first 1977 election was a direct challenge to its multiracial ideology and its claim to be the guardian of indigenous Fijian interest. However, a few days after the defeat of the Alliance Party the Governor General, Ratu Sir George Cakobau (an indigenous Fijian high chief) re-appointed Mara as Prime Minister, despite his party controlling a minority of seats in parliament. This was done in the interest

---

2   Butadroka, as a civil servant, had worked in the Co-operative Department and through his job he had first-hand experience of the socio-economic situation of indigenous Fijians in the rural areas.

of security and also because Mara commanded the respect of the house more than did Siddiq Koya, a Muslim and disputed leader of the NFP. The NFP was embroiled in an internal leadership crisis between Hindu-led and Muslim-led factions.[3]

Mara's minority government ruled for a mere five months before it was brought down by a vote of no confidence and fresh elections were called in September. The power struggle within the NFP had factionalised the party, and the Alliance Party won a resounding victory, taking 36 seats to the NFP's 15. The FNP failed to win a seat this time around and an independent candidate managed to win one seat. The FNP's significant losses were partly due to the imprisonment of its leader, Sakeasi Butadroka, for making statements "which were likely to incite racial antagonism and were therefore likely to prejudice public peace" (*Fiji Sun*, 16 September 1977). It could also be deduced that indigenous Fijians had "learnt" from the loss of the Alliance Party during the 1977 election, and were not prepared to see another politically costly split within their ranks that would lead to Indo-Fijians coming to power.

In the 1982 election the ethnic electoral pattern became more explicit, with 84.1% of Indo-Fijians voting for the NFP, and 85.6% of indigenous-Fijians voting for the Alliance.[4] But the economic conditions of the 1980s and the hard-line Alliance response to those conditions increasingly brought into question the legitimacy of Alliance hegemony. In the 1987 election the Alliance Party was defeated.

Alliance Party affirmative action policies

As a party which espoused multiracialism, the Alliance Party was faced with a number of obstacles as far as its affirmative action policies were concerned. First was political opposition from the Indo-Fijian community, which felt that the

---

3 With hindsight, it had been suggested by some that the action of the Governor General, in choosing Mara as Prime Minister, probably diffused a potential coup. Later in 1987, General Rabuka, who staged the 1987 military coups, said that when the Alliance Party lost the election in 1977, he was anticipating a possible military coup attempt.

4 The 1982 election was marred by allegations of foreign intervention and dirty politics. Desperate to win the election and avoid a repetition of the 1977 scenario, the Alliance Party hired Australian consultants to do research on the political situation in Fiji and to make recommendations as to the best election strategy. Two strategies in particular caused political controversy, leading to an official inquiry. These were: "to bribe the leader of one opposing political party; and to manipulate the criminal justice system to prevent the leader of another party from going forward as a candidate" (Wilkinson 1983: 9). The preoccupation with ethnic politics from independence to the 1980s had two interrelated effects; first, it helped to undermine the significance of class politics; and second, it increasingly caused "ethnicity fatigue" amongst grassroots voters. The ethnic hegemonic veil was beginning to wear thin as socio-economic conditions worsened. The Alliance Party was increasingly been seen as the party of the chiefs and the rich. This class opposition was to later emerge and make historical inroads into national politics, via the formation of the Fiji Labour Party.

preferential program was unfair to them. Second was the tactical and ideological problem of projecting affirmative action as a political necessity to address ethnic tension and hopefully tone down opposition. The third problem was whether indigenous Fijians were adaptable enough and ready to take full advantage of new opportunities, given that it was only as recently as 1966 that they were, for the first time, given full freedom of movement after being locked into the subsistence sector through the Native Regulations for much of the colonial period. The fourth obstacle was the logistical problems of implementing affirmative action.

The leaders of the Alliance Party were high officials in the colonial state, including Economic Development Officers, as we saw in the last chapter. They transferred the development thinking and practice they were used to during the colonial era as the basis for the post-independence indigenous development paradigm. As part of its developmental strategy, the Alliance government helped to perpetuate in the minds of indigenous Fijians a number of colonially-nurtured modernist ideologies that were to define the future trajectories of thinking on the subject of development for indigenous Fijians. These ideologies were *toso ki liu* (to move forward or progress) and *veivakatorocaketaki* (to uplift or develop). Both were based on the modernizationist ideological assumption that village life represented the old and archaic past and western economic values embedded in *veivakatorocaketaki* were to be embraced. The British were seen as agents of cultural enlightenment and British civilization, through the *vosa vakavalagi* (English language) and *i tovo vakavavalagi* (British or European culture), was perceived as the standard by which *toso ki liu* must be measured. Affirmative action for indigenous Fijians was articulated under the notion of *veivakatorocaketake ni i taukei* (Fijian development).

The concept of Fijian development encapsulated the *vakasama vou* (new or western ideas) which required *vuli vakavalagi* (western education) and *vakasama vakavalagi* (European thinking). The paternalistic British colonial hegemony had constructed an epistemological stratification which elevated British and European thinking and marginalized the indigenous Fijian world view in a way which undermined the sense of self-worth of indigenous Fijians. Whereas Indo-Fijians had a negative perception of the British, the British were seen by indigenous Fijians not as colonial oppressors but as agents of cultural enlightenment and political guarantors that would keep potential Indo-Fijian political ambitions in check. This reinforced British hegemony as well as strengthening the power of chiefs, who acted as the comprador class and as mediators of British hegemony. By the time of independence, unlike in other former colonies, there was no celebratory spirit but rather a sense of sadness amongst indigenous Fijians as the Union Jack was lowered. However, indigenous

Fijians had to come to terms with the new reality and the new buzzword was *veivakatorocaketaki*, which was believed to be the vehicle to catapult indigenous Fijians into the future.

Over time the meaning of *veivakatorocaketaki* was enlarged to include a number of variables such as the transformation of village life towards self-help, the building of infrastructure such as roads, seawalls, bridges and wharves and even the building of community halls, churches, chiefs' houses and church ministers' houses. It also included migration from rural to urban life and acquisition of European goods and various cultural traits. The degree of Europeaness defined the degree of *tosokokiliu*. Unfortunately, this unilinear developmental thinking, reinforced and encouraged by both the colonial and post-colonial states and embedded in post-colonial thinking about affirmative action, failed to capture the complexities of Fijian society in the global context; nor did it capture the complex cultural dynamics of the indigenous Fijian community and its basic needs. This led to failure of many post-colonial affirmative action policies, as we shall see later.

The term *veivakatorocaketaki* also embodied the indigenous Fijian perception of other ethnic groups. They saw themselves as located at the bottom of the economic heap compared to Indo-Fijian, Chinese and Europeans, who were seen as *vutuniyau* (affluent) and *torocake vakailavo* (developed). The perceived driving force for the *torocake* (progress) of other ethnic groups was based on both negative and positive stereotypes relating to assumed primordial ethno-cultural characteristics. For instance, at one level Indo-Fijians were perceived as *viavia levu* (disrespectful) and *kocokoco* (selfish), yet at another level they were considered *daucakacaka* (hardworking) and *gugumatua* (full of perseverance). The Chinese were often associated with business and were perceived as *mamaqi* (miserly) and *lawakica* (cunning), yet intelligent and more trustworthy than Indo-Fijians. The Europeans were perceived as *dau ni veivakararamataki* or bearers of civilization, development and modernity but were also capable of incalculable evil through their *vuku* (intelligence).

Understanding these epistemological realities is important in examining perceptions of development amongst indigenous Fijians and how these views shaped affirmative action policies before and after independence. However, let us not forget that the Alliance Party had been in power since the election under the first universal suffrage in 1966, even before independence in 1970; and many Alliance Party affirmative action policies since independence were a continuation of policies from the pre-independence era. Mara, as a senior civil servant during the colonial era who had worked in many rural areas, was passionate about indigenous Fijian development. To him, future political harmony and stability in Fiji lay in getting indigenous Fijians on the path to economic development.

In 1960 the government put into place a development plan for the coming five years, with a heavy emphasis on communications and agriculture. The underlying intention "was clearly to boost economic growth in the Fijian sector of the economy, as a means of reducing racial tensions and as a necessary condition for ultimate political independence" (Bayliss-Smith and Haynes 1988: 129). In 1965 Development Plan 5, 1966-1970 (DP5) was put in place. Its focus was on growth, with a shift from the emphasis on public sector capital as in previous years. At the same time, there was a relaxation of the rigid Fijian regulations, and the *galala* plantation system was enthusiastically encouraged in order to create a new society of indigenous Fijian peasants who were market oriented and free from restrictive communal obligations. Earlier in 1961 the Land Development Authority (LDA) was established to administer and finance a new land development scheme (Burns 1963).[5] This scheme was described by Watters thus:

> Here clearly, is the type of institution needed to promote the settlement of interior pockets of land by Fijians and others as independent farmers on secure tenancies. If such institutions can avoid the twin dangers of excessive paternalism and bureaucracy and their planning is technically sound, they could play a crucial role in rural development and accelerate the rate of social change in Fijian society (Watters 1969: 274).

The emphasis here was to mainstream affirmative action into the government's development plan. This was logistically effective because state resources could be easily "diverted" to indigenous Fijian rural projects through a national development framework; and it was politically clever because as part of the national economic plan it would not be seen as a separate indigenous Fijian project which would attract political flak. The idea of mainstreaming also related to the belief that progress involved rural-based indigenous Fijians being assimilated into the mainstream market economy. This notion was based on modernization discourse about the teleological path of development from traditional/rural to market/modern conditions.

About 500 new farmers were resettled by the LDA in 1964, mostly in Lomaivuna, on the main island of Viti Levu. This number doubled in 1965, and in 1967, as Watters (1969) recorded, 5140 new farms were created along new feeder roads, occupying a total area of 40,000 hectares. The Lomaivuna scheme involved commercial banana cultivation, while a scheme on the island of Taveuni targeted cocoa production. In less than a decade after it started, "this ambitious program

---

5   This is very similar to the Federal Land Development Agency (FELDA) in Malaysia to resettle Malays in rural areas for large scale agricultural production as we will see later.

quickly failed and collapsed altogether" (Brookfield 1979: 36). Just before independence in 1970, the LDA was abolished and its responsibilities were taken over by various government departments.

The failure of the LDA scheme was attributed to "falling yields, disease and hurricane damage" (Bayliss-Smith and Hayes 1988: 129).[6] The reasons for "falling yields" were linked simplistically to "communal obligations" (Bayliss-Smith and Haynes 1988: 130). Relocation from strict communal village life to independent entrepreneurial farming constituted a major social and psychological transition. In most cases, the new settlers recreated new communal kinship, based on families being from the same provinces or on other forms of traditional links.[7] In addition, many settlers saw their cash income as a way of meeting their communal obligations (communal fund-raising, provincial taxes, church levies, marriages, deaths etc.) back in their villages. This put pressure on many of them and greatly undermined their ability to accumulate wealth.

However, putting the blame purely on "culture" tends to over-simplify the process of transformation from subsistence life to the market economy. The "culture failure" theory prevalent amongst some economists (e.g. Ron Duncan 2007) argues from the neoliberal perspective that indigenous culture and entrepreneurship are incompatible and the former needs to be discarded if the latter is to survive. This view fails to appreciate the vast potential of indigenous culture in promoting entrepreneurial gains, as evident in many case studies in Fiji (Qalo 1997; Kingi 2006). The problem was not so much traditional culture as such but the lack of a process being in place to enhance entrepreneurial interests using both indigenous culture and market values in a mutually innovative way to enhance productivity. It has been proven that the two can co-exist, with one reinforcing rather than undermining the other, and there have been some amazing success stories of indigenous Fijian business which neoliberals have chosen to ignore. A model which revolved around enhancing the human capacity of the community for productivity rather than simply a capacity to serve the market could have worked.

Over the years, some indigenous Fijian businesses have done well by enhancing the capacity for production. To blame culture can unfortunately be interpreted by some as blaming an entire ethno-cultural group; and in the modern multicultural world to blame culture can be construed as dogmatic and ethnocentric. Nevertheless, the collapse of the LDA as an institutional enterprise did not necessarily mean the failure of the entire process because many of the

---

6   The establishment cost by the government was high, averaging £1,200. This included the cost of land clearance and planting, feeder roads and electricity supply. In addition to this was the cost of personal loans to settlers, most of which were never repaid (Ward 1965: 182-186).

7   Many of the settlers were from distant islands and provinces outside the places where the LDA schemes were located.

farmers, through government encouragement, remained as root crop, vegetable and *yaqona* farmers in a semi-subsistence way. Because many of the farmers were from the small islands such as those of the Lau Group, some of them saw the scheme not primarily as a money-making enterprise but as a chance to migrate from the small islands to Vitilevu, where educational and employment opportunities were available.

Towards the mid-1970s, as the euphoria of independence subsided, the government had to be seen to be committed to both national growth and indigenous development. There was demand for economic growth and import substitution and amongst the indigenous Fijian community the notion of *veivakatorocaketakini i Taukei* (Fijian development) was gaining currency within the rural communities and Fijian institutions. This idea was encapsulated Development Plan 6 (DP6) in 1970, which was strongly influenced by the Malaysian affirmative action plan in the form of the New Economic Policies (NEP), and which aimed to "improve distribution of incomes, including bridging of rural/urban and inter-ethnic disparities." (Quoted in Fiji Central Planning Office 1980: 4). DP6 emphasised "rural development", especially industries in which indigenous Fijians were most likely to be involved. By and large, rural development was associated with indigenous development, an approach based on the modernizationist notion of transformation of subsistence life into the market economy. This did not apply strictly to Indo-Fijians because, although most were rural-based, as sugar cane farmers, their lives revolved around the sugar industry and they were thus already mainstreamed into the market economy, although as poor cane producers. The rural development projects included pine planting, the Seaqaqa sugar cane project for indigenous Fijians and cattle projects in Uluisauvou and Yalalevu, both on the main island of Viti Levu. These rural development projects were continued by Development Plan 7 (1976-1980) (DP7), which emphasised expansion and redistribution. The affirmative action intent of DP7 is summed up in one of its objectives thus:

The main beneficiaries of policies aimed at achieving more equitable distribution of income and wealth will be the rural population generally and the Fijian population in particular. Powerful economic forces have tended to concentrate economic activity and hence prosperity in the urban centres – especially Suva and Lautoka. This concentration has tended to perpetuate existing business and commercial specialization along ethnic lines. A major objective in the Seventh Plan period and beyond will be to decentralize economic activity by location and broaden involvement by race and to enhance opportunities, material living standards and the social and cultural amenities of the rural areas (Fiji Central Planning Office 1975: 5).

This development strategy, which attempted to change the close structural association between ethnicity and socio-economic status or class, was borrowed directly from the Malaysian NEP. But unlike the Malaysian NEP, which was a massive social engineering undertaking involving politically-driven structural reconfiguration, the Fiji development strategy was a much softer program that operated purely at the policy level. Development Plan 8, 1981-85 (DP8) toned down the Fijian development strategy and focused more on diversification, generalized equity, self-help and the promotion of national unity. This was an interesting shift because, while the principles of equity and national unity were promoted, the ethnic factor was not made explicit, although it was assumed implicitly in the Plan's objectives. Diversification was to take the risky burden away from the Indo-Fijian-dominated sugar monoculture which, during the five years from 1975 to 1980, increased production by over 55%. Between 1970 and 1980 the contribution of sugar and its by-products to domestic exports rose from 66% to 81%; the share of sugar's contribution to GDP rose from 12% to 16%; and sugar's contribution to employment rose from less than 18% to over 22% of jobs (DP8 1980).[8] The Plan's emphasis was on primary industries because of the perception that indigenous Fijians were more at home with the land.

There was also the view that, given the preponderance of Indo-Fijians in the sugar cane farming sector, indigenous Fijians could learn agricultural skills and do equally well either in cane or other areas of farming. The idea was to transform the indigenous Fijian culture of communal subsistence into the competitive world of a market economy. This was assumed to be the secret of socio-economic progress and growth. Development Plan 9, 1986-1990 (DP9) totally de-ethnicized the development framework, with the main focus on "real economic growth" (Fiji Central Planning Office 1985: 8). This was the period of global recession caused by the oil shock, and structural adjustment policies (SAPs) were being introduced into Fiji.

Some indigenous Fijian rural development projects

While the Development Plans provided the macro-framework for socio-economic development, there was effort at the ground level to make indigenous Fijian development work, despite overwhelming odds. Some of these efforts

---

8 Development Plan 8 emphasised the need for more exports, as well as the expansion of domestic production as a part of the import substitution policy. Large-scale agricultural enterprises were encouraged with the direct involvement of a number of actors: private corporations; the Native Land Development Corporation; the government in co-operation with the landowners; groups of small holders, and groups of small holders organised into larger units. A key aspect of this participation was the involvement of the indigenous Fijians to ensure that they were able to 'free up' their land for development purposes. The involvement of the indigenous Fijians was intended to ensure that some of their land would be opened up for cultivation and also to have them directly involved in cultivation and management themselves.

were the Seaqaqa Sugar Cane Scheme (SSCS), the Yalavou Beef Scheme (YBS), the Native Land Development Corporation (NLDC) and the Farm Management Development Co-operative Association (FMCA).

The SSCS project started in 1974 through a loan from the World Bank. Initially it was part of an attempt to integrate smallholders into large projects as a way of improving the distribution of income to rural areas and decreasing the high rate of failure amongst individual farms. Undeveloped native land was opened up and subdivided to settle about 802 farmers, both indigenous Fijians and Indo-Fijians. Because of the government's intention for greater participation by indigenous Fijians in the sugar industry, 448 indigenous Fijians, compared to 339 Indo-Fijians, were selected for the scheme. The Fiji Development Bank (FDB) provided loans to individual farmers. The scheme was under the overall supervision and management of the Fiji Sugar Corporation (FSC), which provided technical support and which set the demanding target of 200,000 tons of cane to be harvested by 1980. This target was surpassed by 50% and the SSCS was hailed as an exemplary success. However, the predominance of sugar as a monoculture was contrary to the World Bank's expectation there would be mixed cropping:

> In addition to sugar cane, each farm is being planted with about 1 ac of mixed citrus and 0.1 ac of pineapples for the local market. Subsistence rice, root crops and vegetables would be grown on small plots... (World Bank 1976: 8).

The scale of the Seaqaqa scheme relative to Fiji's economy was indeed a massive undertaking which amounted to at least 10% of all government expenditure on economic services in the late 1970s. The loans by the FDB to the settlers within the same period accounted for 30% of the total agricultural loans portfolio (Fiji Bureau of Statistics 1983: 32).

One of the major concerns about the scheme was the relatively low performance of indigenous Fijian farmers compared to their Indo-Fijian counter-parts (Young and Gunasekera 1985). For instance, in 1981, a higher proportion of indigenous Fijians failed to produce enough cane to cover the credit allowance provided by the Fiji Sugar Corporation at the beginning of the season to cover input costs. The credit allowance, referred to as the Farm Basic Allowance (FBA), was calculated in terms of the amount of land the farmer had prepared and made ready for planting, and was expressed in terms of the anticipated production of cane to be delivered to the sugar mill in Labasa. Of all the Seaqaqa farmers, only 53% managed to meet their FBA repayments. Of the successful farmers, 32% were indigenous Fijians and 78% were Indo-Fijians (Young and Gunasekera 1985). Moreover, the reasons given were:

> Native Fijians were less interested participants and had to be actively recruited from the very beginning. They also suffered numerous failures as individuals, and more than two-thirds of all Native Fijians in the project did not meet their production quotas. Relatively poor entrepreneurial performance by Native Fijians is a phenomenon that has been noted consistently for decades. This is related to lack of knowledge about the capitalist economy and the pull of village communal obligations in using up their time and resources (Young and Gunasekera 1985: 10).

Although the observations above tend to be over simplistic, they do raise an important question regarding the inability of policy planners, most of whom were trained in mainstream economics, to create a model which allowed for mutual cross-fertilization between communal culture and entrepreneurship. The major strategy they used was to parachute subsistence indigenous Fijian farmers drawn from villages into the middle of the cash economy and hope that they survived through self-adaptation and even miracle. Indigenous Fijian farmers who settled on Seaqaqa maintained strong links with their original communities. They organised themselves into groups along provincial lines and there were expectations by their *koro*, *yasana* and relatives to contribute to communal fund-raising. Often there were psychological sanctions against non-commitment to these obligations in the form of allegations of being anti-*vanua*. Some indigenous Fijian farmers who could not cope sold their farms to Indo-Fijian farmers. To many of these indigenous Fijians, commercial farming life was a mere diversion from their less stressful semi-subsistence life in the village which they could always go back to, while for Indo-Fijian farmers, sugar cane farm life was all they had and they had to work hard to maintain it. This also accounted for the different attitudes and different levels of success in cane farming between indigenous Fijians and Indo-Fijian farmers.

Another significant factor about the Seaqaqa scheme was the mobilisation of communal labour for cane harvesting. Most of the cane cutters were recruited from villages in various provinces by the provincial councils to provide income, not for themselves, but for their Provincial Councils. Of the total number of cane cutters during the 1982 season, 1,988 (86.7%) were indigenous Fijians and 265 (13.3%) were Indo-Fijians. In terms of regional distribution, 70% were from the Northern Division; 26.8% were from the Eastern Division and 3.3% were from the Central Division. The workers received FJ$5 a day gross, but for those who were part of communal groups, "communal savings schemes absorbed a high proportion of this wage" (Bayliss-Smith and Haynes 1988:140).

The exploitative character of communally-organised labour was well illustrated by the case of the workers from Lau Province. A total of 236 were recruited by the Lau Provincial Council for the 1982 season. Transport was provided free for the islanders, who came from seven small islands in the province. The recruits came from the islands of Moala (3 villages), Vanuabalavu (3 villages), Kabara (1 village), Nayau (2 villages), Cicia (3 villages), Ono (1 village) and Matuku (1 village). As Table 3.1 shows, their gross pay averaged FJ$1.46 per person/day for the five-month season. Almost half of the wages went to living expenses and contributions to communal schemes, leaving FJ$0.83 for the cutters themselves. For the whole season, each of the 14 villages from which the workers originated gained on average FJ$727 in communal savings and only FJ$127 net for each worker. In other words, only 15% of the total amount of cash went to the individual workers and 85% went to the *vanua* (community).

Table 3.1 Gross and net pay of Lau Islanders recruited by Lau Provincial Council to cut cane at Seaqaqa, 1982 Season (FJ$)

Month (number of cutters)	Gross Pay	Accommodation Costs	Savings for Village Schemes	Net Pay Total	Net Pay Per Person
June (236)	7,940	2,260	2,260	3,420	14.50
July (236)	9,019	260	2,260	4,499	19.06
August (192)	9,139	1,510	1,870	5,759	30.00
September (193)	11,753	2,240	1,880	7,633	39.55
October (193)	9,102	1,910	1,910	5,282	27.37
Season's Total	46,953	10,180	10,180	26,593	25.33
Av.(per person)	1.46 (daily)	0.32 (daily)	727 (season)	0.83 (daily)	127 (season)

Source: Lau Provincial Council, *Lau 21/45 Cane Cutting*, File in District Office, Lakeba.

The distribution of income between the individual and the village community, as shown in the table above, clearly illustrates the point that communal obligations for cane workers were paramount over their individual accumulation. This was not so much due to the culture of the workers but to the way they were organized and the hegemonic institutional arrangement they worked under. The Lau Provincial Council was responsible for the entire logistical operation including recruitment, travel, work organization and allocation of pay. The Chairman of the Lau Provincial Council was Mara, the paramount chief of Lau and who was himself the Prime Minister and leader of the Alliance Party. Mara himself owned a cane farm in Seaqaqa and the use of cheap communal labour directly benefited him.

Thus the case of Seaqaqa, one of the Alliance government's flagship development projects as a form of affirmative action for indigenous Fijians, was one of the rare opportunities for indigenous Fijian and Indo-Fijian farmers to work side by side. While there was trans-ethnic engagement at one level on the farms, there was also the familiar communal segregation at another level. For instance, a separate farmers' association for indigenous Fijians, called the Seaqaqa Fijian Co-operative Society (SFCS) was set up and became the basis for their commercial solidarity. The formation of the SFCS was based on the assumption that as indigenous Fijians were new to commercial farming, it was prudent to form a co-operative, something rural indigenous Fijians were used to, to provide them with the necessary organizational, social and psychological support in a regimented farming environment. It exemplified the ambitious pursuit of the political imperative of Fijian development that relied on the deployment of a communal strategy to advance indigenous Fijian interests in a market economy.

As far as indigenous Fijian farmers were concerned, the Seaqaqa scheme was a mixed success. While there were failures, there were also success stories; but in the national scheme of things, indigenous Fijians were still in the minority as far as sugar production was concerned. Despite the Seaqaqa scheme, the proportion of sugar produced by indigenous Fijians remained stagnant. As Table 3.2 shows, in 1989 Indo-Fijians produced FJ$161.91 million (95%) worth of sugar while indigenous Fijians produced only FJ$25 million (0.5%). In 1993 the production figures were FJ$156.99 million (86%) for Indo-Fijians and FJ$22 million (0.5%) for indigenous Fijians (Fiji Sugar Corporation 1994).

Table 3.2 Sugar production by ethnicity, 1989-1993

	Indo-Fijian	Indigenous Fijian	Others	Total
	Value (FJ$m)	Value (FJ$m)	Value (FJ$m)	Value (FJ$m)
1989	161.91	25.27	3.34	190.52
1990	142.59	19.94	3.31	165.84
1991	144.14	23.05	4.82	172.02
1992	164.15	24.26	5.86	194.26
1993	156.99	22.81	2.19	182.01

Source: Fiji Sugar Corporation Industrial Statistics.

A common development strategy used in the 1970s and 1980s was the formation of producer co-operatives. In Chapter 2 we saw that one of the drawbacks of the co-operative society was the misconception that communal labour under the Fijian Regulations was compatible with co-operative society principles. This misconception continued into the post-colonial era. Thus Development Plan 7 of 1975 emphasised the formation of producer co-operatives to stimulate cash cropping as a tool of development policy for indigenous Fijians (Fiji Central Planning Office 1975). Thus one of the major initiatives was the setting up of the Farm Management Co-operative Association (FMCA) in 1978 with the support of the Ministry of Agriculture, Ministry of Co-operatives and the Ministry of Fijian Affairs and Rural Development. The objectives of the FMCA were along the lines of the strategic thrust of national agricultural development in Development Plan 8, which were: to provide management services to indigenous Fijian landowners who wished to pursue commercial development of their land; to ensure that land was developed on a sound commercial basis and was used in accordance with proper principles of land utilisation; to provide a training ground for indigenous Fijian land owners and young farm managers in agricultural and management skills; and to provide income for the indigenous Fijian land owners and employment for people living in rural areas (Fiji Central Planning Office 1980). The FDB provided capital support and financial management advice.

The FMCA scheme had mixed success. Its initial and main project, the Tailevu Dairy Co-operative, ended up accumulating debts and other projects too went the same way and had to struggle to survive. The 'failure' has been attributed to:

> ...a lack of focus of responsibility in the Native Fijian communal system, unskilled management, lack of financial accountability, and the subdivision of land into blocks that were farmed individually. The failure rate amongst Native Fijian block-holders was high as they lost interest in going it alone and went back to their villages (Young and Gunasekera 1982: 13).[9]

The communal tendency of indigenous Fijians has again been blamed as a major hindrance to accumulation. Of a similar scheme in Lovoni, Ovalau Island, Young (1984) noted that the ongoing power struggle between the village chief, who wanted political control of the co-operative, and the co-operative executives, who wanted to maintain a purely technocratic line of management, threatened to destroy the producer co-operative. Young also described how a co-operative farmer gave away six of his cows for a relative's wedding, without expressing any feeling of loss. This act of "generosity" was (and is) common amongst indigenous Fijian entrepreneurs. While they were encouraged to accumulate, they were also encouraged, in fact psychologically coerced at times, to respond promptly and obediently to communal obligations.

Another major project was the Yalavou Cattle Scheme (YBS), which was set up by the government in 1978 with Australian bilateral assistance of FJ$7 million. The mostly indigenous Fijian farmers were provided with 500-acre blocks in a 62,000 acre area of native land near Sigatoka in the South-western region. The farmers were nominated by the landowning groups and were gradually settled on the allocated blocks. By 1982, there was a total of 86 farmers raising cattle and goats. Some of the problems encountered in Yalavou were very similar to the problems in Seaqaqa. But in Yalavou, most of the farmers were from surrounding

---

9 However, there were other factors, such as the deregulation policies of the government in the 1980s, which saw the dramatic demise of many co-operative projects. Importation of cheaper New Zealand dairy products by Rewa Dairy, the main dairy manufacturer, made it difficult for the Tailevu Dairy Co-operative to compete.

villages and because of this they were still closely tied to their communities. The Yalavou scheme, despite its problems, continued to operate until August 1998, when it was temporarily closed due to unscrupulous business practices.

Perhaps one of the most ambitious Alliance initiatives, this time involving the Fijian Administration, was the setting up of the Native Land Development Corporation (NLDC) in 1974 as a commercial subsidiary of the Native Land Trust Board. The NLDC was to be involved in capital-intensive projects that were integrated into both the domestic and foreign market. It was to be involved in property management, real estate, merchandising and agriculture. The first NLDC project was a FJ$1.2 million, 1600-acre mechanised sugar cane plantation which was part of the larger Seaqaqa Cane Scheme. This was followed by a FJ$1.5 million investment supported by Australian aid for highly mechanised production of pigeon peas in Western Vanua Levu. The third project, worth FJ$1.5 million, was for horticultural production (mangoes and pawpaw) near the Nadi International Airport, for export. In addition the NLDC was involved in rice production.

All the NLDC projects failed and the NLDC debts had to be paid by the government. An important point to note is that the NLDC was in fact a neo-traditional institution clothed in capitalist garb. As an arm of the NLTB, itself a neo-traditional establishment, its political and economic direction was the prerogative of chiefs who were members of the NLTB board. The President of the NLTB was the Governor General, himself a high chief, and members of the board consisted of chiefs and indigenous Fijian technocrats loyal to the Alliance Party. This system of Alliance cronyism was temporarily "broken" when the Labour Party's Dr Bavadra became a board member while he was prime minister for a month before he was overthrown in a military coup in 1987. The NLDC embodied a dichotomy between communalism and accumulation. It also embodied a trade-off between commercial merit and communal cronyism. The collapse of the NLDC showed that communal capitalism contributed neither to private accumulation nor to communal wealth. Wealth was 'virtual' in that it was expressed in the form of communal prestige rather than in material manifestation.

However, contrary to existing stereotypes that indigenous Fijians were 'culturally' not capable of entrepreneurship, the problem needed to be contextualised in relation to the pressures exerted on indigenous Fijians by the socio-political power structure to maintain a communal way of life to 'protect' them from being 'undermined' by other ethnic groups. This provided legitimacy for communal mobilisation, even in the context of a competitive market economy. In other words, communalism was not necessarily a primordial cultural feature, but needs to be explained in a broader socio-political context of power relations and hegemony. Nevertheless, communal investment was encouraged at various levels of indigenous Fijian society. At the provincial level, the Alliance government sought to strengthen the Fijian Administration's economic capability by encouraging *yasana* investment. Some of the early Provincial Council investments were in the area of wholesale and retailing co-operatives, shipping, bus companies, copra production, piggeries, poultry farms, sugar cane and dairy farming and investment in existing companies belonging to other ethnic groups. As an example, in the 1970s the three Provinces of Cakaudrove, Bua and Macuata formed a company called CBM (Cakaudrove Bua Macuata), headed by the paramount chief and former President of Fiji, Ratu Sir Penaia Ganilau, with interests in diverse forms of investments. In addition, CBM bought 2.5% of the shares in a major local company, Stinson and Pearce Limited, owned by a European former Alliance Party Finance Minister. CBM's investment in the Ferry Freights Company, totalling FJ$150,000, was lost when the company collapsed.

The province of Tailevu invested FJ$56,000 in the now-liquidated Fiji Poultry Company and other agricultural projects. The Province of Rewa also invested in a bus company which was also liquidated. The province of Lau set up the Yatu Lau Company as its investment wing and began investment in bus companies and shipping, under the chairmanship of its paramount chief, Prime Minister Mara. The company still continues and is heavily involved in real estate. The Province of Kadavu also set up the Kadavu Development Company and later Kadavu Holdings and was involved in an inter-island ferry service which failed. It is now involved in real estate. Other Provinces were involved in similar communal investments. In the early days the directors of these companies were mostly chiefs. Traditional status rather than commercial sense became a natural qualification for company directorship. This changed over time as younger and more educated people began to take over running of these companies. Today, almost every province in Fiji has an investment company involved in major projects such as real estate, commercial farming, shipping and other enterprises.

Perhaps the most successful commercial affirmative action scheme of the Alliance government and the Fijian Administration was Fijian Holdings Company, formed in 1984 by the Great Council of Chiefs. It has now grown into one of the biggest companies in Fiji and remains as the flagship affirmative action project of the government and Fijian Administration. The company will be discussed in detail later. In the early days, the shareholders were limited to Fijian Administration institutions such as provinces, NLTB and the Fijian Affairs Board.[10] The provinces

---

10   Private shares were opened up in 1992, but only for those officially categorised as "Fijians"; that is if one is registered in the *Vola ni Kawa Bula*, the indigenous land and communal Fijian registration record, kept by the Native Land Commission (NLC).

collected their capital through communal collections (*soli-vakavanua*). It was the first real attempt at communal capitalism in Fiji (the communal mobilisation of resources for capitalist investment) on a large scale.

A significant feature of the NLDC and the provinces' approach to communal investment was the institutional 'collaboration' between the central government under the Alliance and the Fijian Administration institutions (NLDC and Provincial Councils in this case). Thus any development policy that involved the Fijian Administration institutions was, either deliberately or unconsciously, an extension of the Alliance government's communal and hegemonic design. Thus the communalist political and ideological strategy of maintaining the paramountcy of Fijian interest overshadowed the basic commercial rationale of generating material benefits. Indigenous Fijian failure in business was ascribed to a lack of resources for business success, such things as lack of capital and specific business skills; but the real cause was the influence of powerful social forces. As I will argue later when considering the case of the Fiji Development Bank's Commercial Loans to Fijians Scheme (CLFS), the problem was not capital, nor even skills, but the overall design of the process, including its conceptualization, implementation and monitoring. Communal investment itself led to de-skilling since it emphasised a collective but limited contribution by individuals rather than encouraging individual thrift and sharpening individual skills; and a lot of finance poured into indigenous Fijian business was diverted or undermined by communal pressures and obligations.

Nevertheless, the government was convinced that the three main reasons for "weak performance of Fijians" in business were: "deficiencies in business skills, a culture that is generally not conducive to business practices and achievement, and lack of capital" (Fiji Government 1993: 55). These 'excuses' missed the forest for the trees because, as I have argued earlier, the relations of production based on communalism discouraged the development of skills and the desire for accumulation. Also, the stereotypic, racist and self-defeating argument that blames "a culture that is not conducive to business" has become a sort of self-fulfilling prophecy which many indigenous Fijians themselves have been led to believe. My argument is that the 'culture' of the indigenous Fijians as an ethnic group was not the problem; rather, it was the pattern of communal hegemony that was imposed and reproduced deliberately from the political level and which, over the years, has permeated throughout various levels of society and permanently crystallised as traditional 'Fijian culture'. The ability to distinguish between ethnic (or Fijian) culture and political control disguised as ethnic 'culture' has become conceptually problematic and the source of current confusion.

Response to the failure of indigenous business

The consistent failure of indigenous Fijian business led to the formation of a Project Evaluation Unit (PEU) in the Ministry of Fijian Affairs in February 1974. The PEU's terms of reference included "evaluation of projects and requests for financial assistance, provision of management, accounting, and extension services, technical and economic feasibility studies and the identification of obstacles to the entry of Fijians into commerce and industry" (Fiji Government 1980: 23). In 1975, the unit changed its name to Business Opportunity and Management Advisory Service (BOMAS) and it was later moved and attached to the FDB, where it met its ultimate demise. It was later resurrected as the Client Advisory and Training Department (CATD) in the late 1980s.

For provision of capital, in 1974 the government asked the FDB to introduce a "soft loan" scheme, with a maximum of FJ$100,000, specifically to help indigenous Fijians engage in business. It was called the Commercial Loans for Fijians Scheme (CLFS) and part of the conditions of the soft loans were that the interest rate was subsidised by 1%, the bank's security requirement was relaxed, and there was a cash contribution of one-third of the value of the total project. But when the plan was revealed, it was strongly opposed by the Indo-Fijian-dominated Suva Chamber of Commerce, who saw it as "discriminatory and therefore contrary to the country's constitution" (Vusoniwailala 1976: 48). This led to controversy in the media which saw indigenous Fijian letter writers expressing nationalist sentiments under such headlines as "Indians Out of Fiji" and "They Don't Appreciate Fijians". One correspondent suggested that "by their opposition to governmental plans to improve the indigenous race's lot, the Indians of the Suva Chamber of Commerce showed the ingratitude of the Indians to the Fijians' hospitality" (*Fiji Sun*, 5 May 1975). Opposition to the special Fijian commercial scheme was due to Indo-Fijian businessmen seeing it as a competitive threat to their monopoly of the small business domain. The FDB project proposed to produce a class of indigenous Fijian entrepreneurs which could integrate into the Indo-Fijian-dominated business sector and break the cycle of an Indo-Fijian monopoly. The ethnic hostility it created was not surprising, as Indo-Fijian businessmen thought that state-subsidised business for indigenous Fijians was tantamount to unfair competition. Nevertheless, the project went ahead as the Alliance Party had promised its indigenous Fijian constituency.

While indigenous Fijians were being encouraged to enter agricultural production, the state itself was involved in direct capitalist production. By the 1980s, the state, under the Alliance government, had become directly involved in capitalist accumulation through its monopoly of the sugar industry, water supply, electricity, fish cannery, air services and forestry (Sutherland 1993;

Naidu 1989). It was also closely aligned to expatriate capital by subsiding the mining and tourism industry. Tourism not only benefited expatriate investors, it also generated wealth for a small group of chiefs, whose tribal land was leased to hotels, and most of whom had direct links with the Alliance Party hierarchy. Alliance elites and big business were closely linked. Some of the richest men in Fiji, such as Charles Stinson, Jim Ah Koy and Mahendra Patel, were closely linked to the Prime Minister, Mara. Mara was also known to have established a business empire of his own. The nationalist agitations of the 1970s and 1980s pointed out these business links as 'evidence' of the betrayal of the indigenous cause by Mara and the Alliance government. Despite attempts to serve the interests of indigenous Fijians through preferential policies, the positive impacts were not sufficient to create a visible indigenous bourgeois class and so satisfy the increasingly high expectations of indigenous Fijians.

It is true that the Alliance government's economic affirmative action policies for indigenous Fijians in the 1970s and 1980s were wide-ranging, but the success of those policies, so far as developing an indigenous Fijian entrepreneurial class was concerned, was mixed. Some individuals took advantage of the situation and succeeded, while most did not. This heightened frustration amongst indigenous Fijians; and someone had to be blamed. Nationalist conspiracy theorists pointed fingers at Indo-Fijians, and ultimately the Alliance Party, for allowing Indo-Fijians to thrive unchecked while indigenous Fijians were not provided with the same opportunities, despite the Alliance's pro-indigenous policies over the years. The nationalists argued that the Alliance's affirmative action policies were merely cosmetic exercises and that the real beneficiaries of Alliance policies were the indigenous Alliance elites and business elites of other ethnic groups. To bolster their political firepower, the nationalists joined forces with the militant unions and many joined the Fiji Labour Party when it was formed in 1985.

While the Alliance Party was being attacked by the nationalists from one side, it was also assaulted from the other side by militant unionism, starting in the 1970. Trade unions provided indigenous Fijian workers with an autonomous political space to express their new identity as members of the new proletarian class outside the confines of traditional loyalty. But for survival indigenous urban workers had to continually negotiate the multiple layers of loyalty, be they religious, political, cultural or professional, in an increasingly complex situation. The intensification of militancy within trade unions in the 1970s and 1980s was a direct consequence of the dramatic expansion of the capitalist economy after independence, through a shift from import-substitution to deregulation and export orientation and with it the increasingly unilateral control of the industrial relations machinery by the state and the restriction of workers' rights (Howard 1991). Increasing deregulation provided foreign and local capital the leverage to maximise profit while squeezing workers hard.

Ironically, it was the result of the seemingly contradictory policy of the Alliance government which, at one level, was encouraging communalism, yet at another, was promoting economic growth.

Threat to Alliance hegemony

Pro-indigenous policies were pursued within a dramatically changing economic and political landscape at a time when communal politics was coming under pressure and working-class consciousness was being articulated in a militant way. In the 1970s and 1980s there was a dramatic expansion of the indigenous Fijian urban working and professional classes which, despite the attempts of the indigenous elites and the Alliance government to keep them under their guardianship and within their orbit, had formed alliances with Indo-Fijian workers. This was to transform the Fiji political landscape forever. The working class, through the unions, was beginning to exert its power through industrial action and this posed a threat to the ruling Alliance Party. The consolidation of the economy led to the emergence of a more organised and articulate labour movement. In 1970 there were eight strikes involving 887 workers, resulting in 752 lost man-days; in 1971 there was a total of 28 strikes involving 4063 workers, resulting in the loss of 20,970 man-days. A year later, in 1972, there were 46 strikes involving 8,404 workers with a loss of 214,721 man-days. The 1973 figures were 19 strikes, involving 9,083 workers and a loss of 807,972 man-days (Reddy 1974: 11).

Most unions were multi-ethnic, except for the teachers' unions, which consisted of the predominantly indigenous Fijian Teachers Association (FTA) and the predominantly Indo-Fijian Fiji Teachers Union (FTU).[11] Urbanised indigenous Fijian workers (who numbered about 52% of union membership in the 1970s) were less susceptible to communal pressures than were their rural counterparts, and were readily inclined to join unions. Despite this, many of them were still loyal to their chiefs and still identified with the communal ethos. Communal loyalty recognised no geo-social boundary and encompassed both the rural and urban spheres yet, at the same time, was not total: workers would simultaneously show loyalty to their *vanua* and loyalty to their unions. The former provided them with their sense of ethno-cultural identity and the latter with their means of socio-economic survival. In fact as a result of urbanisation the urban centres increasingly became important for communal organisation. For instance, a large number of chiefs lived in the urban centres and conducted collections for communal investment.

---

11 The two teachers' unions later merged into the Fiji Teachers Confederation, but still maintained their distinctive ethnic identities.

Growing industrial unrest led to the enactment of the 1973 Trade Disputes Act to regulate union powers. But a more corporatist approach was put in place in 1976 with the formation of the Tripartite Forum, consisting of trade unions, employers and government representatives to collectively manage the industrial relations process (Kumar 1980).[12] The corporatist strategy collapsed in 1985 as a result of the government's unilateral imposition of a nation-wide wage freeze, recommended by the World Bank employment mission, which argued that Fiji's salaries were internationally uncompetitive and needed to be reduced to enhance export potential.[13] The IMF experts also thought that wages in Fiji were "15% too high" (Narsey 1985: 3).

During this period Fiji was reeling from the effect of the global economic crisis that enveloped the world economy in the 1980s. Fiji's economy was hit by a reduction in sugar production and lower returns for exported sugar and a decline in the tourism industry. Fiji's foreign debt increased by 754%, from FJ$35 million in 1970 to FJ$264 million in 1981. In 1979 alone, debt servicing constituted 18% of the annual budget. The state intervened harshly with 'rationalisation measures' such as pay cuts, redundancies of unestablished workers and the withdrawal of job guarantees for government-sponsored graduate teachers. This led to widespread protests, including a graduate teachers' hunger strike. In its 4-5 February 1985 Economic Summit the government justified the wage freeze thus:

> ...to create savings (of about $36 million) that can be used to spread the benefits of development more evenly among the population. The freeze should result in more money flowing into the banking system. This should make more finance available for loans-especially for projects that will boost industry, agriculture, export earnings and create jobs. It will encourage business to expand and invest. It should help to keep redundancies to a minimum or avoid it (Fiji Government 1985: 1)

The trade unions argued that the unilateral wage freeze was not only an extra burden on the workers but also a denial of democratic processes. They saw the freeze as direct state intervention on behalf of the capitalist class, an action which used workers as sacrificial lambs to facilitate private accumulation (Naidu 1986; Howard 1991).

Apart from the imposed neo-liberal reforms, Mara's government was increasingly becoming authoritarian and was moving more and more towards the right. Its

---

12 Despite this, some militant unions such as the Fiji Mine Workers Union (FMWU) continued to resort to industrial action. As a result of the 1977 FMWU strike, 700 workers lost their jobs and the union was de-registered. A common trend in the 1970s was that militant union leaders were quickly "tamed" and co-opted into the ruling Alliance Party in various capacities.

13 A 1982 World Bank-funded employment mission undertaken by the Institute of Development Studies (IDS), University of Sussex, made these recommendations.

foreign policy was being greatly influenced by the United States' Cold War agenda. An example was that, in 1982, under US pressure, Fiji banned Soviet ships from calling into Fiji ports and, at the same time, allowed previously banned United States nuclear powered and armed ships to come into Fiji ports.[14] Mara's government was seen by the radical unions as becoming increasingly despotic, with a powerful clique of chiefs and businessmen at the helm, mutually accommodating each other's interests and with an eye for union bashing. There were also allegations of corruption at the top which led to several scandals.[15]

Increasing authoritarianism at the national level was an indication of uneasiness about the growing opposition to Alliance hegemony, even from within the indigenous Fijian community. As Sutherland suggests, the "upper echelons of the Fijian community were worried that they were losing control over the Fijian masses" (Sutherland 1993: 179). So the Great Council of Chiefs in 1983 proposed a major reorganisation in the Fijian Administration. The last reorganisation was in the mid-1960s, when the Fijian regulations were withdrawn. But the resulting emancipation of indigenous Fijians was perceived by the Fijian power bloc as undermining its hegemony: "the abolition of the Fijian Regulations and the winding up of the Fijian judicial system, together with the non-enforcement of by-laws, meant that many of the decisions of the Provincial Councils were not pursued to their logical conclusion" (Fijian Affairs Board/Great Council of Chiefs 1985: 65). The Great Council of Chiefs wanted to strengthen communal authority at the provincial level as a means of controlling urban drift and an increase in crime amongst youth and, also, to maintain a disciplined communal workforce. Their concern was that the "line of authority from the Provincial Council to the [Fijian Affairs Board], the Great Council of Chiefs and the Minister of Fijian Affairs is clear and understood...[b]elow the Provincial Council the Fijians tended to wander from one authority to another" (Fijian Affairs Board/Great Council of Chiefs 1985: 68). The Cole Report which resulted from this review recommended the extension of the power and jurisdiction of the provincial administration (Cole 1984).[16] This effectively would have consolidated communal mobilisation at the provincial and grassroots level to maintain the Alliance's

---

14   This directly led to the formation of the Fiji Anti-Nuclear Group (FANG) by the trade unions, churches, students' unions and other civil groups.

15   A leading article in the *Fiji Sun* daily in 1985 titled "The Mara Empire" revealed the extent of wealth of Prime Minister Mara and his links with Fiji's leading businessmen. As a result, the *Fiji Sun* was sued by Mara for defamation.

16   Interestingly, the Cole Report was never implemented. The Alliance government announced one month before the 1987 election that it was going to be implemented. After the Alliance lost the election, the plan fizzled out. As late as 1994 Rabuka's government announced that it was going to implement the Report. This was met with opposition from many indigenous Fijians. The latest reorganisation of the Fijian Administration was made in 1998 when the Fijian Affairs Board was made independent from the Ministry of Fijian Affairs. We will discuss this later.

power base at that level. This was important for the Alliance's political influence and survival, to counter indigenous Fijian political 'dissent' in various forms, such as agitation through unionism in the urban areas.

Indeed the biggest threat to Alliance hegemony started when trade unions organised a 'Labour Summit' to counter the anti-union policies of the Alliance Party. An academic who presented a paper at the summit argued, in response to the wage freeze, that the "net effect must be that the wages and salaries freeze means a forced transfer/gift of what would have gone to employees as increments to their wages and salaries, into the ownership of the employers" (Narsey 1985: 4).[17] This trans-ethnic orientation, which put class struggle at the centre of the debate, set the tone for a new political paradigm. Thus the unions, in a later forum, accepted a resolution that a Labour Party be formed as a forum for the political mobilisation of workers of all ethnic groups, and to provide an alternative political organisation to counter the unilateral economic policy impositions of the ruling Alliance Party and the implicit support of the ineffective official opposition party (Naidu 1986). Both the ruling Alliance Party and the opposition NFP were seen to represent "bourgeois interests", underneath their explicit ethnic characters (Narsey 1985). They both advocated neo-liberal structural adjustment policies (SAP) and the curtailment of union power. The Alliance government had every reason to be wary, since the principles of the Labour Party were antithetical to communalism and neo-liberalism, the two major ideological foundations of the Alliance government. The NFP was also wary of the formation of the Labour Party because Labour's trans-ethnic appeal could undermine its fundamentally ethnic power base.

One of the significant developments at this crucial stage of political realignment was a split within the unions. In April 1985 the white-collar unions formed a confederation of public sector unions. It consisted of the Fiji Public Service Association (FPSA), the umbrella civil service union and largest union in Fiji, the two ethnic-based teachers' unions (now the Fiji Teachers Confederation) and ten others. The blue-collar unions, on the other hand, led by the Fiji Public Employees' Union (Fiji's second largest union) reacted to this by forming a confederation of their own. The split manifested the political and ideological contradiction that was to drive the unions apart; the blue-collar unions wanted to remain "apolitical" (Naidu 1986: 42) while the white-collar unions wanted a more confrontational and reformist strategy, achieved by forming the Fiji Labour Party (Howard 1991). The blue-collar workers' unions consisted mostly of casual and permanent manual labourers, whose bargaining positions were weakened by the insecurity of their jobs and the close political links of their leaders with

---

17 Dr. Waden Narsey, an IDS DPhil graduate, presented a paper titled, "The Wage Freeze and Development Plan: Contradictions in Fiji Government Policy," which provided the economic discourse that was to be the basis of the formation of the Fiji Labour Party.

the Alliance hierarchy. The largest blue-collar workers' union, the Fiji Public Employees' Union (FPEU), was led and controlled by indigenous Fijians who were closely aligned with the Alliance elites. The white-collar unions, given their resourcefulness and relatively independent political aspirations, were more disposed to contest state control; thus their desire to form the Fiji Labour Party. Despite opposition from the blue-collar union leaders, the decision to form the party was made on 9 May 1985, during the biennial conference of the Fiji Trade Union Congress (FTUC). The Fiji Labour Party was formally launched on 6 July 1985.

In a way, these developments were taken seriously by the Alliance government, which saw its indigenous Fijian power base being eroded by militant unionism. Its affirmative action policies were meant to keep the loyalty of indigenous Fijians intact. The focus on rural development-based affirmative action had minimal impact on urban indigenous Fijians, who were more independent and less amenable to chiefly control than were rural dwellers. In short, affirmative action as a means of communal hegemony and consolidation of indigenous loyalty was not working as well as was anticipated.

The emergence of the Fiji Labour Party (FLP) reconfigured the dynamics of political power and shifted the debate from the usual Fijian versus Indian dichotomy to one based on a claim to the legitimate guardianship of indigenous Fijians. This posed a direct threat to the Alliance's hegemony and at the same time gave the new FLP a sense of orientation into the new world of rhetorical and ideological warfare. Both parties wanted a share of indigenous support to enhance their legitimacy and their image. For the Alliance Party, indigenous Fijian support was crucial for its identity and survival; while the FLP needed to rebrand itself to shake off the image that it was an ethnically Indian party. The indigenous question became the battleground for political and ideological contestation as both sides accused the other of being "anti-Fijian", while reserving the claim to be "pro-Fijian" for themselves.

The FLP, led by Dr Timoci Bavadra, an indigenous Fijian medical doctor and unionist, fought the 1987 election in a Coalition with the predominantly Indo-Fijian National Federation Party (NFP). This happened despite consensus during an FLP general meeting in Lautoka that no coalition of any sort should be entered into with the NFP. With the new image of a multi-ethnic and clean party, the FLP was to distance itself from the NFP, which was tainted with an ethnic "Indian" image. In protest at the coalition, some withdrew support from the FLP, but the leadership of the party, spearheaded by powerful and uncompromising labour leaders and some left-leaning intellectuals, was determined to move ahead.

Contestation over indigenous development

The Coalition's main election messages were targeted at the "poor, weak and disadvantaged" and at the promotion of "multi-racialism" (National Federation Party-Labour Party Coalition 1987). Amongst the Coalition's concerns in this regard was the lack of economic progress of ordinary indigenous Fijians, which was blamed on neglect by the Alliance government, patronised by the chiefs and aligned with business.[18] As I have discussed earlier, the power base of the Alliance government, under Mara, was chiefly and dependent on communal hegemony and this was identified by the Coalition as the major factor responsible for indigenous Fijian economic backwardness. On the other hand, the Alliance pointed out that for sustenance of political stability, chiefly authority was crucial; and a multi-ethnic business elite was needed for economic growth and progress. While the FLP approach was based on an urban-based social democratic ideology, the Alliance Party had a more conservative position which encompassed a combination of interests including big business, the chiefly hierarchy and conservative communal values.

The rhetorical battle was taking place at a time when the Fiji economy was going through a recession and when indigenous Fijian participation in commerce had been improving, though not quickly enough. There was Indo-Fijian exclusive dominance in a range of economic sectors such as retail, wholesale, transport and the motor industry, amongst others, and they had the majority of practitioners in some professions.

Indo-Fijian businessmen had exclusive control of various sectors of the economy such as transportation, real estate, merchandizing and retail, to name a few; and at the same time there was no readily visible indigenous Fijian entrepreneurial class. Comparative figures provided by the Bureau of Statistics on 'economic activity' confirmed the socio-economic disparities. For instance, 23% of positions in the administrative and managerial category were occupied by indigenous Fijians, compared to 77% by Indo-Fijians. Among the clerical and related workers, 38% were indigenous Fijians and 62% were Indo-Fijians, while in the sales workers' category, 26% were indigenous Fijians and 74% were Indo-Fijians (Fiji Bureau of Statistics 1989: 52).

---

18   Other Coalition election pledges included: anti-corruption legislation; a leadership code; abolition of the *Official Secrets Act*; and enactment of a freedom of information act. The economic policies related to economic growth, better utilisation of resources, more jobs, a just wage, better working conditions, fair prices and easier access to finance. It also promised to work towards housing for all and better education, adequate health and nutrition at low cost, a fair deal for women and youth, greater assistance for the elderly, disabled and destitute and a physically safer society. It also promised to bring about "a fair and open government" (NFP-Labour Coalition Election Manifesto 1987).

However, towards the other end of the socio-economic continuum, 55% of those engaged in rural agriculture (both subsistence and cash), such as animal husbandry, forestry and fishing, were indigenous Fijians, compared to only 35% for Indo-Fijians. Clearly, the figures indicated a preponderance of Indo-Fijians in the 'middle class' socio-economic categories and of indigenous Fijians in rural primary production. Most rural indigenous Fijian producers were village-based semi-subsistence farmers, living within the communal setting. In fact only 10% of the independent 'rural settlements' for fully-fledged commercial farming outside the rural village and including *galal,* belonged to indigenous Fijians and 90% were owned by Indo-Fijians. To compound the problem, indigenous Fijians had a higher urban unemployment rate of 15.6% (compared to 9.7% for Indo-Fijians) and formed over 70% of the prison population (Adinkrah 1995).

Almost two decades after independence, it appeared that a lot still needed to be done in terms of affirmative action; but expectations of socio-economic progress amongst indigenous Fijians and their resentment of Indo-Fijian dominance in commerce had become a powerful political factor which could no longer be ignored. The FLP under Bavadra quickly exploited the situation to its advantage by blaming the Alliance government for the situation of the indigenous Fijians. Bavadra said:

> Ironically, the people who suffered most under the Alliance Government are the very people whose interests this government purports to champion, the native Fijians. By restricting the bulk of the Fijians to their communal lifestyle in the face of a rapidly advancing cash economy, the average Fijian has become more and more economically backward... This is particularly invidious when the leaders themselves have amassed huge personal wealth (Fiji Sun 17 April 1986: 4).

One of the most influential business links the Alliance elites had was with the Emperor Gold Mining Company at Vatukoula, which had, for years, been patronised by the Alliance through various forms of tax concessions and subsidy. Bavadra threatened to nationalise the mine if he came into power as a result of the extent of exploitation of workers and the raw deal the indigenous landowners of Nasomo were getting for their mined land (Emberson-Bain 1994). Bavadra also raised the question of liberalising the centralised authority of the Fijian Administration. In particular, he was concerned with empowering indigenous landowners by loosening the bureaucratic control of the NLTB on land:

> The NLTB must be democratised so that it comes to serve the interests of all Fijians and not just the privileged few and their business associates. In addition, more effort must be made to see to it that those whose land is

being used get more for their money out of the NLTB...The system must be rationalised so that all Fijians, not just a few, benefit more (Bavadra 1986: 74).

The Coalition promised to set up a Native Lands and Resources Commission to facilitate greater participation of ordinary indigenous Fijians in decision-making relating to the development and management of their land. This was not to undermine but to "work with the NLTB" (Sutherland 1993: 178). This approach had two interrelated prongs: a concern for the socio-economic conditions of indigenous Fijians; and an opposition to the dominant communal hegemony of the Fijian Administration and the chiefly establishment. This played into the hands of the Alliance demagogues, who used it to demonize the FLP as being anti-Fijian. There were personal attacks on Bavadra, accusing him of *liumuri* ("anti-Fijian" or "traitor") and a *nodra vakarawanika na Kaidia* or "stooge of the Indians" (Veitata 1987). The Alliance's use of racial scare-mongering alleging a possible Indo-Fijian 'take-over' of indigenous Fijian land and the 'suppression' of indigenous Fijian culture (if the Coalition came to power) was a common tactic during the election campaign.

The Alliance pointed to its pro-indigenous policies as evidence that it had the indigenous people at heart and declared that if the FLP came into power, all the affirmative action policies were going to be destroyed and the land and rights of indigenous Fijians were going to be taken away. Although indigenous land was solidly safeguarded by the tight provisions of the 1970 Constitution, which required 75% of the vote in both the House of Representatives and Senate and the assent of at least six of the Great Council of Chiefs' nominees in the Senate (Fiji Constitution 1970), there was still fear that these provisions could still be changed under a new regime.

Towards the coup

The victory of the Coalition in the 1987 election marked the first change in government since independence in 1970. In fact the Alliance had been in power since 1966 as part of the transition towards independence. Out of a total of 52 seats, the Coalition won 28 and the Alliance 24. Of the 28 Coalition seats, 19 were held by Indo-Fijians, 7 by indigenous Fijians and 2 by general electors. Although the Coalition fought and won the election on a multi-racial platform, the results still showed the dominance of communalism in Fiji's political culture. The Coalition won all the Indian communal seats. It also attracted 82% of the Indo-Fijian vote, compared to the 83% by the NFP in the 1982 election. At the same time the Alliance won all the Fijian communal seats and 78% of the indigenous Fijian votes. This was a decrease from 82% in the 1982 election. In the general communal seats, the Alliance support fell from 89% in 1982 to 82% in 1987. However, in four critical national seats the Coalition managed to draw enough indigenous Fijian support to win them the election.

A day after the historic victory, the *Fiji Times* editorialised:

> There have always been those who doubted the people of Fiji, who said we would never live together in harmony, never reconcile our differences. But yesterday the people spoke. Although coming from different religions, many backgrounds, we are yet one people. So the greater victory is for democracy (*The Fiji Times*, 13 April 1987: 6).

But this optimism was expressed too soon. Bavadra's newly installed government was condemned by Alliance supporters as an "Indian government" (*Matanitu ni Kaidia*) and Bavadra "an Indians' man". Ravuvu (1991: 89), an ardent Bavadra critic and nationalist ideologue, exemplified this sentiment when he said: "Fijians could be forgiven for concluding that Bavadra had risen to the top because he was the Indians' man. He was their choice, approved and appointed by their community". The ethnicist discourse became the dominant sound-bite, and fear-mongering of conspiracy for "Indian take-over" was rife:

> ...the Coalition victory in the 1987 elections seemed like a clever stunt performed with strings, mirrors and "democracy". The end result was that finally the Indians had got what they had long sought-control of the government and of the country (Ravuvu 1991: 87).

Immediately after Dr Bavadra's victory there were demonstrations on the streets of the main cities by the supporters of the Alliance Party and extremist nationalists. Corporations such as the Emperor Gold Mining Company allegedly funded some of these demonstrations. Led by the *Taukei* Movement (Indigenous People's Movement) the aim of the indigenous Fijian demonstrators was the removal of the 'Indian' government and the reinstatement of an indigenous government.

Increasingly, the situation deteriorated as spontaneous expressions of nationalism, fuelled by racial bigotry, spread like wild fire across the land. As I have observed elsewhere, this expression of nationalism, or *taukeism*,[19] was a lethal juxtaposition of various ideological components:

> *Taukeism* attempts to unite the Fijian community through the politicisation of culture, religion and race...a juxtaposition of racial, cultural, religious and warrior-machosist ideologies (Ratuva 1993: 59).

---

19 The term *taukei*, which means original owner of the soil or land, is normally used by indigenous Fijians as a dichotomy to the term *vulagi* or 'foreigner'– referring to Indians.

What is important to note at this stage is that communal hegemony was being mobilised to undermine liberal democracy. To maintain its formal control of the state apparatus, the Alliance government needed to consolidate its communal support and community elites needed the Alliance patronage for political prestige and power. The military, although theoretically "neutral" as an institutional security component of the state apparatus, had strong cultural and ideological links with the traditional power structure. This made it susceptible to manipulation by communalistic forces to serve the communalistic agenda ahead of the national interest (Sanday 1989).

The defeat of the Alliance Party in the 1987 election signified the limitations and crisis of the old hegemonic order, which could no longer sustain domination and legitimation by manufacturing consent through the use of communal appeals. In the case of the Alliance hegemony, while it still maintained the support of the majority of indigenous Fijians, the electoral system's numbers game had denied it the mandate to continue to rule. The Alliance Party had an important ally, the military, which was later deployed to achieve what the ballot box could not, to reassert its dominance. The nationalistic spontaneity following the April 1987 election and the large-scale anti-Coalition street protests and propaganda in the media by the Methodist Church and by nationalist activists provided the environment for military intervention on 14 May 1987.

4. The 1987 military coup: Affirmative action by the gun

Affirmative action became a much more intense political obsession after the 1987 military coup. In fact the term 'affirmative action' itself was first used after the coup. The coup provided the perfect justification for large-scale affirmative action because the supporters of the coup assumed that lack of socio-economic progress by indigenous Fijians had led to the rise of ethno-nationalism and the coup and that the only way to avoid another coup was to address socio-economic grievances through affirmative action.

The 1987 coup was an outward eruption of the undercurrent of ethno-political fissures that have characterized ethnic politics in Fiji since the colonial days and that were allowed to take a more volatile trajectory after independence through institutionalized ethnic compartmentalization. Under the guise of parliamentary democracy and ethnic balance, the constitution helped to legitimize separate representation, ethnicized party membership and ethnic competition for state power. Democracy became the means to communal contestation and the capture of state power rather than a framework to ensure social cohesion and national consciousness. That was not all. The high expectations of indigenous Fijians for a better socio-economic life after independence were not being met and the situation was worsened by the constant fear of Indo-Fijian political threat. Tension came to the surface as a result of the activities of particular individuals and groups in politics, the community and the church who were closely associated with the Alliance Party, and who took advantage of the situation to mobilize people under the rallying cry of "Fiji for the Fijians." Behind the ethno-nationalist front were some non-Fijian businessmen and professionals who either passively or actively supported the ethno-nationalist euphoria because they felt that their privileges, which were well protected under the Alliance government, were going to be lost under the new NFP-Labour government.

At the same time, the Fiji Labour Party and the NFP, confident of their electoral mandate, were oblivious to the rising ethno-political tension and the potential for future seismic transformations. The Labour Party leaders and ideologues assumed that the time was ripe in Fiji for class politics to displace communal politics and to create a multi-ethnic utopia for workers, peasants, the marginalized and the poor. The utopian ideology was that class consciousness had at last caught up with ethnic consciousness as a natural reaction to what was seen to be the Alliance Party's elitist, bourgeois, chiefly interests. While the Alliance emphasised the indigenous Fijian/Indo-Fijian dichotomy, the Fiji Labour Party attempted to down play ethnicity altogether and emphasised the 'rich versus poor' dichotomy. Both views were shown to have their own limitations as historical developments began to unfold. The reality was to be found somewhere in the middle. There was a complex interplay between class and ethnicity at different levels. The lack of socio-economic development amongst the rural and urban indigenous Fijian poor became a fertile breeding ground for ethno-nationalism. In times of crisis, socio-economic grievances were readily transformed into political anger and ethnic scapegoating. The visible wealth of Indo-Fijian business created potentially lethal political images amongst the poor and unemployed indigenous Fijians. This was a catalyst for communal dissatisfaction and mob violence, seen in street riots following the 1987 and 2000 coups during which Indo-Fijian shops were targeted by hordes of youths. The images of Indo-Fijian wealth fed into the realm of collective social psychology, especially in relation to the use of inter-communal stereotypes, to demonize the other in mutually dichotomous ways. Indigenous Fijians stereotyped Indo-Fijians as cunning, selfish and untrustworthy, always on the lookout to grab Fijian land using devious means. The Indo-Fijians stereotyped indigenous Fijians as lazy, dumb and lacking modern cultural dispositions. Both communities were well aware of each other's perception and have often 'accepted' them as 'normal'. At times these behavioural dispositions were internalized and even acted out. It was common for indigenous Fijians to lament their lack of work acumen and business proficiency compared to Indo-Fijians, Chinese or Europeans. Such lament was a classic case of a group internalizing the social mirror image projected by others, as symbolic interactionist sociologists would suggest. The collective impact on the collective social psychology of indigenous Fijians of the internalization of stereotypes was destructive. It gave them a sense of hopelessness and inadequacy, a psychological void which was readily filled by, and transformed into, ethno-nationalist agitation and anger.

The growing sense of grievance was given an ideological boost by the Methodist Church, which portrayed Indo-Fijians as heathens whose godless ways would invite the wrath of God on Fiji. The best way to appease God was to cleanse Fiji of the *lotu lasulasu* (worshipers of false gods) (Norton 1994). Religious bigotry was invoked to give greater legitimacy to ethno-political expressions of anger. The volatile mixture of socio-economic grievances, fear of an Indo-Fijian take over, fear of the loss of identity, fear of political disempowerment, belief in divine legitimacy and a negative perception of Indo-Fijian culture formed a lethal cocktail which was ready to explode once a trigger was provided. Whether real or perceived, these sentiments drove and projected ethno-nationalist rhetoric in a violent way.

Entry and retreat of the military

The military coup on 14 May 1987, led by Lt Col Sitiveni Rabuka, removed the Coalition from power and replaced it with a military government consisting of supporters of the Alliance Party. The coup broke the shell of democracy which was difficult to put together again and which spawned a coup culture that was to plague the country for the next two decades. The second coup on 15 September of the same year was an attempt by the military to avoid the formation of a multi-party coalition that was to be formed by leaders of the Alliance and the Coalition. One of the first priorities of the military regime was to secure control of state power through the reconfiguration of the military command by the removal of the commander and his chief of staff, the dissolution of parliament and the suspension of the constitution. A second priority was to restore indigenous interests through the Fijianization of the civil service and through aggressive affirmative action policies. For the military government, the ethnic strife and coups were evidence enough that more had to be done to address the issue of indigenous development. They saw the capture of state power by indigenous forces as an opportune time to push through their nationalist development philosophy.

The military was part of the bigger historical bloc consisting of a conglomeration of institutions such as the Alliance Party, the Great Council of Chiefs, the Fijian Affairs Board, the Native Land Trust Board, Provincial Councils, District Councils, Village Councils, the Methodist Church and various other indigenous Fijian cultural organizations. These diverse forces constituted a powerful establishment which had been nurtured by the British colonial state and which continued in power after independence. These were institutions which shaped the developmental trajectory, ideological dogma, and official identity of indigenous Fijians. They acted as institutional agents of cultural patronage and communal exclusivity. Over the years, indigenous Fijians had to negotiate and redefine their cultural identities, political rights, ideological disposition and sense of place in relation to the demands for unquestioned conformity to these institutions, while at the same time seeking alternative sets of values.

To legitimise the coup and its communal agenda, the post-coup regime had to put in place a constitution. Thus the 1990 Constitution was promulgated to entrench indigenous Fijian political paramountcy. It was a dramatic shift away from the 1970 Constitution, which had attempted to keep an ethnic balance in political representation. In the new constitution, the number of seats in Parliament was increased to 70; and of these 37 were for indigenous Fijians, 27 for Indo-Fijians and 5 for General Voters. The new Constitution provided that only indigenous Fijians were to be prime minister and president (Fiji Government. 1990a).

The 1990 Constitution was the cause of considerable political uncertainty amongst Indo-Fijians, who saw their political rights being undermined. Pressure came from various quarters, such as the Indo-Fijian community, certain 'liberal' indigenous Fijians and international organisations, for a review of Fiji's constitution. Even the World Bank suggested that one of the ways in which economic growth in Fiji could be restored, apart from the implementation of structural adjustment measures, was the resolution of the constitutional question. Increasingly the post-coup regime under Rabuka slowly gave way and the reform process was soon underway.

The review of the 1990 Constitution marked an important epoch in the post-coup era, because it signalled the 'retreat' of a communal monopoly of state power and the re-emergence of the multi-ethnic discourse at the centre of the political stage. One of the first requirements for the review was the setting up of a three-man Constitutional Review Commission (CRC) to review the 1990 Constitution and make recommendations.

The CRC was appointed in March 1995 by Mara, who became President after the death of President Ganilau in December 1993. A significant provision of the review was recognition of the "internationally recognised principles and standards of individual and group rights; guarantee full protection and promotion of the rights, interest and concerns of the indigenous Fijian and Rotuman people; have full regard for the rights, interests and concerns of all ethnic groups in Fiji" (Reeves, Vakatora and Lal 1996: 2).

The new constitution established two major frameworks for inter-ethnic concessions, which were to be the basis for a new state system: first, it ensured that the rights of all individuals, communities and groups were fully respected; second, it ensured the recognition of the paramountcy of Fijian interests as a protective principle continued to apply, so as to ensure that the interests of the Fijian community were not subordinated to the interests of other communities. The first of these frameworks was reflected in two ways: the delicate balancing of parliamentary seats and the consociationalist proposal of a multi-party and multi-ethnic Cabinet. The constitution provided for 71 seats; of these, 46 were to be elected through the communal franchise and 25 through the open franchise. Of the 46 communal franchise seats, 23 were to be for indigenous Fijians; 19 for Indo-Fijians, 1 for Rotumans and 3 for other ethnic groups. The 25 open seats were for unrestricted cross-ethnic voting. The consociationalist proposal established that, in forming the cabinet, "the Prime Minister must invite all parties whose membership in the House of Representatives comprise at least 10% of the total membership of the House to be represented in the Cabinet in proportion to their numbers in the House" (Fiji Government 1997: 107).

The second concession was made by ensuring that both the President and the Vice-President were appointed by the *Bose Levu Vakaturaga* (Great Council of Chiefs), thus guaranteeing that they would always be indigenous Fijians. Furthermore, other laws which safeguarded indigenous Fijian land and cultural rights such as the Fijian Affairs Act, Fijian Development Fund Act, Native Lands Act, Native Land Trust Act and Agricultural Landlord and Tenant Act were made difficult to amend. The Constitution also provided that where possible, "Parliament must make provision for the application of customary laws and for dispute resolution in accordance with traditional Fijian processes" (Fiji Government 1997: 139).

The third concession was the redefinition of the category of persons to be the recipients of affirmative action, entrenched in the 1990 Constitution as "Fijians and Rotumans", to a broader category of "disadvantaged". In other words, affirmative action was no longer exclusively associated with communalism and paramountcy of Fijian interest: it was to be extended trans-ethnically.

The military coup and coerced affirmative action

Was the coup itself a form of coerced affirmative action? In other words, was the coup designed to improve the well-being of indigenous Fijians? Ravuvu seemed to agree by suggesting that the coup had "the objective of defusing potential violence and creating a form of government which would ensure political paramountcy for the Fijians in their own land" (Ravuvu 1991: 89). But, as I have mentioned earlier, the notion of paramountcy of Fijian interest was not exactly in the best interest of the indigenous Fijians because it merely locked them into a communalistic schema, which retarded their commercial advancement and bonded them to a neo-traditional political and cultural structure. The coup was not 'progressive' (or affirmative) in the sense of economic or political emancipation, but a reactionary attempt to preserve and reproduce the old order (Sutherland 1993). Furthermore, the notion of paramountcy of Fijian interest, which the coup was said to preserve, was already entrenched in the virtually unchangeable provisions of the 1970 Constitution dealing with indigenous rights. In this regard the coup was totally unnecessary. While at face value the coup was 'preferential' (that is, biased towards indigenous Fijians), it was certainly not 'affirmative' in the sense of being progressive.[1] It was really after the coup that new affirmative action policies were drawn up. While the coup generally

---

1 At face value, if we stretch the definition of preferential treatment far enough, the coup, at least from the point of view of the supporters, was a pro-indigenous Fijian scheme, although illegal, aimed at "advancing Fijian rights". Even the real justifications for the coup by the coup-makers were not clear, as they began changing them as the circumstances demanded. But this is probably as far as the concept of preferential treatment could be comfortably applied. On the other hand, if we go beyond the face value, and consider the

had a reactionary basis in preserving the communal schema, some post-coup policies relating to affirmative action were to some extent 'progressive' in that there was a concerted drive towards economic advancement, as we shall later see. But on the other hand, even the 'progressive' affirmative action strategies, such as communal capitalism, still contained strong tendencies towards a narrow form of communalism.

Ravuvu further argued, in support of the coup, that: "It is imperative that Fijians must be given a special position in their country and that an element of positive discrimination be practised in favour of them for a period in education, politics, business development and other areas they are lagging behind" (Ravuvu 1991: 99). Again, while the 1970 Constitution had protected "special rights" for indigenous Fijians, the Alliance government (and even the colonial government) had also put in place a number of 'positive discrimination' measures in education and commerce. But the problem with these affirmative action policies (especially in commerce) was that they were conceptualised and implemented as part of an attempt to preserve communal cohesion and prestige rather than to advance individual entrepreneurship. Strangely, the coup had been justified on the basis that it would solve the problems which the pro-coup establishment created in the first place.

Furthermore, the economic crisis caused by the coup affected the entire population, including indigenous Fijians (Prasad 1988). For instance, according to Bryant (1993), in 1989 12% of indigenous Fijians lived below the poverty line, and this increased to 21% in 1991. This has been attributed largely to post-coup job redundancies, inflation and economic contractions generally (Barr 1990). Thus, both in political and economic terms, it is difficult to identify aspects of the coup that were 'affirmative' for indigenous Fijians.

1990 constitution and political affirmative action

The question posed above could also be asked in relation to the post-coup 1990 Constitution, itself a direct product of the 1987 military coup. Was the constitution a form of political affirmative action? This refers particularly to the notion that it was meant to protect the paramountcy of Fijian interest (through seat allocation, protection of political rights etc.). However, this should not be confused with the specific affirmative action provided for in the Constitutional, which will be dealt with separately and in more detail later.

political, ideological and economic implications of the coup, we see that the coup was in fact 'reactionary' so far as it tried to 'preserve' communalism and the old order which had kept indigenous Fijians within the confinement of communal stagnation, rather than a means to socio-economic progress.

For some, like Butadroka, the 1990 Constitution was the best protection for indigenous Fijian rights and a way to preserve Fijian unity. The major indigenous political party, the Soqosoqo ni Vakavulewa ni Taukei (SVT) echoed the same sentiments in its 1995 submission to the Fiji Constitution Review Commission (CRC), adding that the constitution had in fact united indigenous Fijians. However, the short seven-year history of the 1990 Constitution had instead seen increasing power struggles and factionalism amongst indigenous Fijian elites, instead of the communal cohesion which was originally anticipated by the pro-indigenous Fijian constitution. The power struggle between the leading traditional polities had origins in the pre-contact and colonial era (Routledge 1985). Of interest in this regard were the differences between eastern and western chiefdoms. Many western chiefs saw the coup as reaffirming eastern chiefly control and called for the formation of a separate confederacy to be called the *Yasayasa Vaka-Ra* Confederacy. The *Taukei* Movement, the extremist organisation which was responsible for the post-coup violence, also split up due to differences in strategy and eventually died a natural death.

The two most powerful men in the post-coup period, Mara and Rabuka, were consistently at loggerheads about how the post-coup state was to be administered. Both had tried to mobilise political support in different ways. Mara had a feudalistic and aloof approach to politics, based on his traditional appeal as a high chief and as a statesman of esteemed status in the Commonwealth when Prime Minister. He ran the Alliance Party, and later ruled the post-coup Interim Government in the same way he presided over his traditional subjects. That is, 'consensus' meant no dissent and unquestioned adherence to the *mana* of the chief. On the other hand, Rabuka, a professional soldier and a political novice in liberal democratic governance, relied entirely on his charisma and almost mystical appeal to indigenous Fijians as the 'hero' of the coup. He also relied on his links to the military and kept reminding his opponents of his political potency by occasionally issuing veiled threats of "repossession of power." Instead of working with Mara as deputy Prime Minister, Rabuka returned to the barracks as Commander of the Army. Within a few months he rocketed up the ranks from Lieutenant Colonel to Major General.

To reassert his power and undermine Rabuka's power base, Mara considerably reduced the military allocation in the 1991 budget and in June 1991 invited Rabuka and Rev. Lasaro, the leader of the fundamentalist Methodist group, to join his Cabinet. Both refused the offer, perhaps sensing that by accepting they would have come under Mara's direct control. On 8 June, Rabuka publicly denounced the Mara Cabinet and asked them to resign because "they have lost credibility" (*The Fiji Times*, June 9 1991: 1). He cited the continuing sugar industry crisis, Vatukoula gold mine strike, the unpopular VAT (Value Added Tax), and the formation of the new political party, the SVT, as evidence of the interim government's shortcomings. The sugar and gold mine disputes had been prolonged unnecessarily and no solution had been found; the imposition of the IMF-recommended VAT had provoked public dissatisfaction, while the formation of the SVT had factionalised the political loyalty of indigenous Fijians.[2] Rabuka argued that the formation of the SVT would open the way for the formation of other political parties, thus creating further factionalism amongst indigenous Fijians at a time when there was a need for unity. However, he later joined the party after succumbing to political pressure from members of the Great Council of Chiefs and also to avoid being politically isolated, and thus became its first leader.

The SVT was first conceived in July 1990 and was launched on 31 October 1991 as the political arm of the Great Council of Chiefs. It was meant to take the place of the Alliance Party, whose cohesion as a "multi-racial" party had been undermined by the wave of post-coup indigenous Fijian nationalism, which saw the Fijian Association (originally an arm of the Alliance Party) joining forces with the Fijian Nationalists and other nationalist groups. The new party, to fight the rough and tumble of party politics on behalf of the Great Council of Chiefs and indigenous Fijian community, was to have a new image, while retaining as paramount the interests of chiefs and indigenous Fijians. It aimed to "promote the interests of the indigenous Fijians, their advancement, the protection of their rights and interests and provide means of social, economic and political development in association with other ethnic communities in Fiji" (Soqosoqo ni Vakavulewa ni Taukei. 1991 Article 1.4: 1).[3]

So clearly, in this regard, the formation of the SVT was an attempt to preserve and perpetuate chiefly hegemony and communalism. This was further evident in its extensive use of Fijian Administration and state structures – in particular the Fijian Affairs Board, Great Council of Chiefs and Ministry of Fijian Affair's urban and rural network– to mobilise the indigenous Fijian masses, more than the Alliance did during its period of rule. Rabuka's power (in the context of

---

2   Meanwhile the overthrown Coalition suffered a serious setback as a result of the death of Bavadra of cancer. This led to a split down the middle within the Coalition, and the Labour Party and NFP went their own separate ways. The Labour Party mounted an extensive international campaign for the return to democracy in Fiji, but many Indo-Fijians opted to vote with their feet and left the country in large numbers. We will examine this in more detail later.

3   The formation of the SVT provoked a number of indigenous Fijian political parties traditionally opposed to the Alliance and later the coup makers to form a united commoners' front on 8 June 1991. The parties involved were the Fiji Labour Party, Fijian Conservative Party, Fijian Nationalist Party and All National Congress. The agenda for the meeting was, first, to discuss public issues such as the VAT, the Vatukoula Gold Mine strike and the sugar crisis and how to deal with them; and second, to form a common front to fight the SVT, which was seen as a chiefly party, in the next general election. It was also around the same time that a number of ethnic-Fijian nationalists, under the banner of *Kudru Na Vanua* (Rumble of the Land) had mooted the formation of a Fijian Commoners' Council to counter the hegemony of the Great Council of Chiefs. However, the formation of a Fijian Commoners' Front did not eventuate due to irreconcilable ideological differences between the participating political parties.

"democratic" politics) was established when he was elected leader of the SVT, ahead of Mara's wife, herself a high chief. Dissatisfied with Rabuka's leadership, a faction led by the late Josevata Kamikamica, former Co-deputy Prime Minister in Mara's Interim Government, left the SVT and formed a new political party called the Fijian Association.[4] As the first leader of the SVT, General Rabuka's status as a 'civilian' politician was confirmed and the stage was set for him to contest the 1992 election under the terms of the 1990 Constitution, which he helped create through the coup. As expected, because of the constitution's inherent bias towards an indigenous Fijian majority, the SVT won the 1992 general election with ease. The election was to be a political laundering process for Rabuka, whose return to centre stage had to be through the democratic process (although under an ethnocratic constitution) he overthrew four years earlier. The point that needs emphasis here is that the coup and its aftermath had in fact fractionalised indigenous Fijian politics even further than assumed. A power struggle within the indigenous Fijian hierarchy as to who should hold power in post-coup Fiji progressively deepened.

Another significant area of difference was the interpretation of the term "Fijian". The 1990 Constitution defined a "Fijian" in two ways: firstly, in terms of direct patrilineal blood link; and secondly, acceptance by one's *mataqali* for registration in the *Vola ni Kawabula,* the indigenous Fijian registry, outlining the pattern of land ownership inheritance and social hierarchy, based on the codified "traditional" social structure (Fiji Government. 1990a: 120). This provision was considered sexist and racist because it discriminated against those with indigenous Fijian mothers but with non-indigenous Fijian fathers.

The 1990 Constitution did not necessarily generate unity amongst indigenous Fijians (Madraiwiwi 1997). If the 1990 Constitution had in fact been meant to create communal cohesion, at least at the political leadership level, this was not to be the case. The 1990 Constitution remained a source of political and economic uncertainty, and as a result of both local and international pressure, it was eventually reviewed and replaced. The 1990 Constitution merely reaffirmed, although in a more dominant way, the paramountcy of Fijian interest already contained in the 1970 Constitution. However, it did provide for specific affirmative action provisions in economic development, civil service employment and education.

---

4   Kamikamica (who passed away in 1998) was an economic "realist" (supporter of the Structural Adjustment Programme). He also imposed the draconian Labour Decree mentioned in Chapter 4. But he was a political "liberal" who was more open to political change, compared to Rabuka, during the late 1980s and early 1990s. Rabuka's political transformation took place later towards the mid-1990s.

Affirmative action provisions of the 1990 constitution

As I have already stated, the specific affirmative action provisions of the 1990 Constitution dealing with socio-economic advancement should be distinguished here from the Constitution's 'political' affirmative role of promoting indigenous rights and unity. Although this may sound like splitting hairs, the distinction made is one between the 'higher' ideological aspects on the one hand and the more concrete prescriptions on the other.

The 1990 Constitution provided that "...Parliament shall, with the object of promoting and safeguarding the economic, social, educational, cultural, traditional and other interests of the Fijian and Rotuman people, enact laws for those objects and shall direct the Government to adopt any program or activity for the attainment of the said objects and the government shall duly comply with such directions" (Fiji Government. 1990a: Section 21). This provision was broad enough to give the government a free hand in giving directives to any state institution to carry out affirmative action policies. It was based on Article 153 of the Malaysian Constitution which vested power in the *Yang di-Pertuan* (President), acting on behalf of the Cabinet, to safeguard "the special position of the Malays and natives of any States of Sabah and Sarawak and the legitimate interests of other communities" (Malaysian Government. 1957: Article 153). Although various preferential policies for indigenous Fijians were already in place and were periodically mentioned in the various Government Development Plans in the 1970s and 1980s, it was deemed necessary by the post-coup government to have them entrenched more permanently in the Constitution. Apart from the constitutional provision itself, no laws were enacted to facilitate "those objects" mentioned. One of the reasons was that the post-coup SVT government did not have the legal expertise to draft affirmative action bills. In any case, fractionalisation within the SVT after the 1992 election would have made it difficult for the SVT to pass the controversial bills.

Perhaps the most specific affirmative action provision in the 1990 Constitution was the prescribed quotas for the public service. While Section 127 (10) provided equal opportunity for "citizens who are suitably qualified" and "fair treatment in the number and distribution of offices to which candidates of that community are appointed on entry", it contradicted itself by declaring that the Public Service Commission "shall ensure that each level of each department in the public service shall comprise not less than 50% Fijians and Rotumans and not less than 40% of the members of other communities" (Fiji Government. 1990a: 115). This was gazetted on 18 December 1990 as part of the Public Service Commission Regulations (Fiji Government 1990: 910).

Moreover, the interpretation of Section 21 created a dichotomy of opinions. The first interpretation was the 'nationalist' discourse, which insisted that being treated preferentially was an unquestionable right of indigenous Fijians as *Taukei* and therefore, it was argued, Section 21 was perfectly within the spirit of the international instruments relating to 'indigenous rights'. In its submission to the Fiji Constitution Review Commission (CRC) in 1995, the ruling SVT drew attention to what it interpreted as the "consistent" nature of Section 21 of Fiji's Constitution and Article 2(2) of the *Convention on the Elimination of all Forms of Racial Discrimination* to which the Republic of Fiji was a party (Soqosoqo ni Vakavulewa ni Taukei 1995: 95).

The second position was based on the 'liberal' discourse, which argued that Section 21 implied domination by indigenous Fijians rather than addressing their disadvantaged position. The best approach, in this view, was to address the socio-economic position of the 'disadvantaged', no matter what their ethnicity was. A class-based rather than an ethnicity-based approach was advocated. For instance, in response to Section 21, and the 1990 Constitution generally, the National Federation Party/Labour Party Coalition produced a booklet entitled *A Fraud on the Nation* where it argued that:

> There are disadvantaged people in all our communities, and our efforts should be directed to helping them all. Positive discrimination should be compatible with a democratic society; it should not vest paramount political power in any one community to the exclusion of others nor should it lead to the maintenance of separate systems for different racial groups. The remedial action must be proportionate, and related, to the need for it. The special provision must be temporary and should terminate after the objectives which justified them have been achieved. The constitution fails on all these tests (National Federation Party-Labour Party Coalition 1990: 8-9).

Along the same trend of thought, the Citizens' Constitutional Forum (CCF), a non-partisan and multi-ethnic civil society organisation, in its submission to the CRC recommended that affirmative action should not only address ethnic imbalance, but also the problems of the different disadvantaged social groups:

> The Constitution should recognise and encourage affirmative action for the poor and disadvantaged of all communities. Affirmative action policies should be researched in advance, carefully targeted, tested for cost effectiveness, transitional, time-limited and accountable (CCF 1995: 58).

The CRC opted for a synthesised version of the two discourses by emphasising benefits for "Fijian and Rotuman people", yet including "other ethnic communities" as well:

The Government of the Republic of Fiji Islands shall establish programmes which are reasonable and necessary to ensure for the Fijian and Rotuman people and other ethnic communities, and for women as well as men, and for all other disadvantaged citizens or groups of citizens, effective equality of access to;

(a) education and training;

(b) land and housing;

(c) participation in commerce and all aspects of service of the Republic of the Fiji Islands at all levels, and;

(d) other opportunities, amenities or services essential to an adequate standard of living (Reeves, *et al.* 1996: 699).

But the CRC dismissed the SVT argument about the compatibility of its position with the international instruments on indigenous rights, contending that the *Convention on the Elimination of All Forms of Racial Discrimination* talked about "special measures" to facilitate the protection, advancement and development of "certain racial groups and individuals belonging to them", for the purpose of ensuring equal "human rights and fundamental freedoms" through practices which "shall not be deemed racial discrimination" (Reeves, *et al.* 1996: 233). The SVT proposal merely helped to bolster the advancement of a politically dominant ethnic group, and marginalised others, and thus did not guarantee "human rights and fundamental freedoms" for other ethnic groups.

The CRC's recommendations were accepted after amendments by the Joint Parliamentary Select Committee (JPSC), set up by parliament to review and make recommendations to parliament on the CFC report. The JPSC consisted of representatives of all political parties (which were ethnically-based). The recommendations were unanimously accepted by parliament, although with some amendments, and incorporated into the new Constitution. The affirmative action provisions of the new Constitution, which became effective from 25 September 1998, provided that:

Parliament must make provision for programs designed to achieve for all groups or categories of persons who are disadvantaged effective equality of access to:

(a) education and training

(b) land and housing

(c) participation in commerce and in all levels and branches of service of the State (*Fiji Constitution (Amendment)*, Chapter 5, 1997: 82).

It went further to create provision for an Act that specified:

(a) the goals of the program and the person or groups it is intended to benefit;

(b) the means by which those persons or groups are to be assisted to achieve the goals;

(c) the performance indicators for judging the efficacy of the program in achieving the goals; and

(d) if the program is for the benefit of a group, the criteria for the selection of the members of the group who will be entitled to participate in the program (*Fiji Constitution (Amendment)*, Chapter 5, 1997: 82).

Clearly the change in the definition of designated groups, from "Fijian and Rotuman people" (1990 Constitution) to "all groups or categories of persons who are disadvantaged" (1997 Constitution) was a fundamental shift, reflective of the new reconciliatory and consociationalist arrangements suggested by the new Constitution.[5] Affirmative action has incorporated for a large and diverse group, defined not by ethnicity alone but by their being 'disadvantaged' in socio-economic terms.[6] The first attempt to operationalize the extended definition was when non-indigenous Fijian Melanesians, who were officially classified as 'others', were also eligible for special scholarships and loans under the CLFS in 1998.

The major shift in definition of the designated groups reflected the atmosphere of national reconciliation apparent in the 1997 Constitution. Despite this change, a number of affirmative action policies had already been in place since the coup and contained in the 1990 Constitution, which had a significant impact in terms

5   However, there are a number of outstanding issues in relation to this new definition, especially if legislation were to be enacted. How is the concept "disadvantaged" defined, and who should define it? Is the constitution referring to socio-economic (class) variables. If so, what are the variables and how do we objectively calculate and prioritise them? If the "disadvantaged" also refers to physical incapacity or political marginalisation, again how are these to be quantified and prioritised? Does it also include gender? If so, then another problem would be to disaggregate the "women" category into those who are really marginalised and those who are well to do and do not need affirmative action. If "disadvantaged" refers entirely to ethnic groups, how is that status to be justified? This is especially so given that ethnic groups are not homogeneous; there are fundamental differences between the "haves", who do not need affirmative action, and the "have nots", who do. As in India, there could be great difficulty in controlling abuse and false claims to being part of the designated category.

6   One of the very first gestures of this redefinition was the implementation of several affirmative measures by the government to ensure equitable treatment to members of the Melanesian (descendants of Solomon Islanders and Ni-Vanuatu who were brought to Fiji last century) and General Electors in Fiji on 9 September 1998. This included scholarships and other developmental funds for minorities such as Melanesians and others.

of ethnic balance and ethnic relations. These were in the areas of civil service employment, education and economic development. We shall now discuss each in turn.

Fijianization of the Civil Service

The 1990 Constitutional provision which prescribed that indigenous Fijians should not constitute "less than fifty per cent" of the civil service became the political mandate for large-scale ethnic discrimination in the civil service. After the coup, there was a process of deliberate displacement of Indo-Fijians in the civil service by the military regime, who did not trust their loyalty, or "ethnic reliability", as Enloe (1980) puts it. The "state security map" (again borrowing from Enloe) put the Indo-Fijians at the bottom of the list of ethnic reliability. The figures below show this trend quite clearly.

In 1986, just before the coup, of the total number of civil service staff, 52% were Indo-Fijians, 43% were indigenous Fijians and 5% belonged to other ethnic groups. The high turnover of Indo-Fijian staff after the coup (as shown in Table 4.1) dramatically altered the ethnic pattern. In 1987, of the total turnover, 79.5% were Indo-Fijians and Others, compared to 20.5% for indigenous Fijians; and in 1988 it was 68.2% and 31.8% respectively (PSC 1995). These figures were unusually higher than the average pre-coup turnover rate of 52% for indigenous Fijians and 48% for Indo-Fijians for 1986 and 1987 (Fiji Public Service Commission 1988).

Table 4.1 Civil service staff turnover, 1987-1994

Year	Fijian/Rotuman	%(of total)	Indian/Others	%(of total)	Total
1987	258	20.5	1003	79.5	1,261
1988	486	31.8	1041	68.2	1,527
1989	676	40.0	959	60	1,635
1990	532	48.8	560	51.2	1,092
1991	393	40.9	567	59.1	960
1992	740	52.6	666	47.4	1,406
1993	697	54.9	573	45.1	1,270
1994	701	58.6	497	41.4	1,198

Source: Fiji Public Service Commission 1995: 16.

However, by 1992 the rate of departure seemed to have 'normalised', with the figures for the two ethnic categories almost on par. The losses in the civil service were being made up by new appointments, which, as Table 4.2 shows, again favoured indigenous Fijians. From 1991 to 1994 indigenous Fijians constituted about 60% of the annual appointments. Prior to the coup, in 1985, new appointments to the civil service were 47% for indigenous Fijians and 53% for Indo-Fijians and others (Fiji Public Service Commission 1986).

Table 4.2 Civil service appointments, 1991-1994

Year	Fijian/Rotuman	%	Indian/Others	%	Total
1991	594	58.6	417	41.4	1011
1992	1182	58.0	857	42	2039
1993	892	57.7	657	42.3	1546
1994	631	57.2	472	42.8	1103

Source: Fiji Public Service Commission 1995:16.

The turnover and appointment rates were reflected in the ethnic distribution in the civil service from 1991 to 1994. As already stated, the ethnic proportions in the civil service were 52% for Indo-Fijians and 43% for indigenous Fijians before the coup in 1986, and five years later, in 1991, the proportion became 55.8% for indigenous Fijians and 44.2% for Indo-Fijians/Others (Fiji Public Service Commission 1995).[7] This pattern was more or less consistent from 1991 to 1994 (Table 4.3).

Table 4.3 Total number of staff in the civil service by ethnicity

Year	Fijian/Rotuman	%	Indian/Others	%	Total
1991	9,296	55.8	7,360	44.2	16,656
1992	9,682	56.6	7,429	43.4	17,111
1993	9,631	56.8	7,317	43.2	16,948
1994	9,709	57.2	7,261	42.8	16,970

Source: Fiji Public Service Commission 1995: 15.

The changes in ethnic proportions in the civil service within the ten years from 1985 to 1995 were significant. In 1985, the figures were: indigenous Fijians (46.4%), Indo-Fijians (48%), minorities and expatriates (5.6%). In 1995 the proportion for indigenous Fijians had increased to 57.32%, while that for Indo-Fijians had decreased to 38.57%, and minorities and expatriates decreased to 4.11% (Reeves, *et al.* 1996).

By 1997 only one of the ten heads of government departments was Indo-Fijian, compared to the relatively equal numbers prior to the coup. Most of those who left the civil service (about 80%) migrated. The migration pattern generally showed that in 1987 there was a net departure of 18,563, compared to 6,490

---

7   Note that the category here is Indian/Others. The proportion for Indo-Fijians alone will reduce slightly if we subtract the number for Others, who make up about 5% of the population.

in 1986 and 6,193 in 1985 (Chetty and Prasad 1993: 10). Of these, 78.1% were Indo-Fijians (compared to 41.2% in 1980), 6.0% indigenous Fijians and 12.5% Others. However, by 1989 the total number of Indo-Fijians migrating had declined to almost half the 1987 figures (about 7,412), but the proportion still stood at 79%. Altogether, an estimated 50,104 people migrated in the period 1987-1991, compared to 26,529 between 1982 and 1986. About 80% of these were Indo-Fijians (Chetty and Prasad 1993).

The job losses in the civil service and large-scale overseas migration of professional Indo-Fijians has been described as a result of 'ethnic cleansing' (*Daily Post*, 10 April 1999). Although not of the same degree and ferocity as, say, events in Kosovo or Rwanda, there was a definite trend of deliberate exclusion in politics and the civil service which impacted on people's sense of security. The "at least not less than 50%" constitutional quota for indigenous Fijians became the political mandate for the Fijianization of the civil service.

The loss of highly qualified civil servants and the increased promotion of indigenous Fijians may have undermined the quality of state service. Affirmative action in the civil service became an extension of the communal ascendancy which the 1990 Constitution entrenched. Control of the civil service by indigenous Fijians was considered necessary for political paramountcy.

Apart from the civil service, the two other important state apparatuses over which indigenous political control was deemed necessary were the military and the police. The military, as we have seen, has always been predominantly manned by indigenous Fijians. The police force's personnel in 1986 consisted of 50% indigenous Fijian, 47% Indo-Fijian and 3% Others; in 1995, the figures were 58% indigenous Fijians, 40% Indo-Fijians and 2% Others (Fiji Police Department 1996). After the coup, the Indo-Fijian Commissioner of the police force was removed, together with other senior officers of questionable loyalty. He was replaced by an indigenous Fijian, who later retired to give way to an army officer, Colonel Isikia Savua.

Affirmative action in this case had become a channel for ethno-nationalist demands. In this case, communalism went beyond its hegemonic tendency in manufacturing consent within the indigenous Fijian community and became the dominant ideology of the state. It became deployed as an ideological lever by the post-coup regime to marginalise Indo-Fijians in the name of paramountcy of Fijian interest. Thus a distinction should be made here between the two levels of communalism: between its role as a means of ideological and cultural spontaneity within the indigenous society; and, at the national level, as a politicised mode of ethnic domination. In a way, they were different sides of the same coin.

Educational affirmative action

As we have seen briefly in Chapter 3, affirmative action in education (the 50-50 scholarship rule) had been in existence since 1977. But after the coup, affirmative action in education intensified, with the government pouring more resources into the education of indigenous Fijians. The ethnic disparities within the educational system had been a matter of concern to the government. However, this disparity needs to be historically contextualised in terms of the communal approach to education in the early days.

During the colonial period a child's access to formal education was based largely on her of his parents' place in the colonial order, which in turn determined one's political status and socio-economic position. The earliest schools were set up for the children of colonial officials and white residents. This selective education approach was institutionalised under the 1916 Education Ordinance, which established a Department of Education.[8] In 1938, of the 442 schools in Fiji, 16 were exclusively for children of European and part-European origins, 346 were for indigenous Fijians, and 80 for Indo-Fijians (Whitehead 1981).[9] The standard of instruction in European schools was based on the New Zealand system of education, and they were staffed by qualified teachers from abroad, mainly from New Zealand.[10] In contrast, out of the 346 schools for indigenous Fijians, only 144 were eligible for government grant-in-aid. Most indigenous Fijian schools were sub-standard and had neither proper facilities nor properly qualified teachers. Only seven were government schools and of these only one had education up to secondary level, where 38 pupils were enrolled in 1938. The first indigenous Fijian secondary schools were exclusively for children of chiefs. This was part of the colonial agenda to reinforce the hegemonic role of the chiefly class in the colonial order. It was much later, in the 1950s, that some commoners were also allowed entry into these schools. As for Indo-Fijians, in 1938, of the 80 schools available to them, seven were government schools, and 66 were eligible for grant-in-aid. Only one of the schools had a secondary section. Only about a third of Indo-Fijian children attended school.

---

8   The 1916 Education Ordinance was later repealed and replaced by the Education Ordinance of 1929. Under both ordinances, the Education Board was provided with wide-ranging powers to control the registration and classification of schools and teachers, the instruction to be given, the standards to be maintained, and the qualifications and number of teachers required for various grades of schools. With these powers, the Education Board was provided with a mandate for educational segregation, allowing for schools to be registered and classified along ethnic lines, with separate schools for Europeans and part-Europeans, indigenous Fijians, Chinese and Indo-Fijians. This system continued throughout the colonial period and, to some degree, after independence.

9   The facilities provided by the schools varied, depending on the school's ethnic classification. European schools were freely supplied with books and stationery at cost price, except in the three government schools, where no fees were charged for primary classes, and £7.10s.0d for secondary classes.

10   Fiji's education system was based on the New Zealand system until 1988, when Fiji developed its own secondary curriculum.

The pattern of education in the post-war years was very similar. During the 1940s, 1950s and 1960s, school enrolment for indigenous Fijian and Indo-Fijian children increased considerably, and so did the government's gross expenditure on education, but the ethnic disparity in the distribution was still significant. In 1947, for instance, state educational expenditure per pupil was £7.9s.7d for European children, £3.10s.5d for Indo-Fijian children and only £2.19s.0d for indigenous Fijian children. This pattern continued throughout the colonial period until 1970, when Fiji became independent (Narayan 1984).

The apartheid-like ethnic separation of schools only helped to reproduce communal separation. The reproduction of values based on ethnic and class differentiation cloned a pattern of political behaviour consistent with the dominant hegemonic order. Robertson (1982: 89) noted that education played a role in the "preservation and modernisation of Fijian initiatives". Chiefs were seen as modernising agents and, at the same time, guardians of indigenous Fijian interest, through education. Oxford-educated high chief Sukuna insisted that the separation of the *turaga* (chiefs) from the *lewe ni vanua* (commoners) was a necessity and needed to be reproduced through education. An educated commoner intelligentsia would be potentially subversive by "undermining and confusing authority to their own ends" (quoted in Scarr 1980: 146). Hence early higher education was to be restricted to children of chiefs (Whitehead 1981), while education for commoners was geared towards vocational subjects such as farming, boat building, mechanics and handicrafts. As a result of a request by the Great Council of Chiefs, the Queen Victoria School, modelled on the British public boarding schools, was set up to educate sons of chiefs.[11] It was decided that instruction at the school was to be in English, while instruction in other indigenous Fijian schools was to be in the Fijian language. The chiefs had opposed but unsuccessfully the idea of commoners being taught in English during the period of im Thurn's reforms as well as land reform as we saw earlier in Chapter 2.

So was education based not only on ethnic (or horizontal) differentiation, it was also based on class (vertical) regimentation.[12] The process of 'vertical' regimentation in education reinforced communal hegemony, which emphasised

11 The Ratu Kadavulevu School (RKS) was set up later for the same purpose. The Adi Cakobau School was set up later for daughters of chiefs.
12 Apart from reinforcing and reproducing divergent ethnic consciousness, cultural education for ethnic Fijians and Indo-Fijians also locked them into a subordinate level of cultural hierarchy. The teaching of vernacular language and aspects of local culture were considered secondary – in fact, token modes of pedagogy. The primary mode of instruction was, and still is, English. It was, and still is, the only compulsory subject in the Fiji school system. English was not only a language, but a mode of articulation and reasoning. It was a total cultural mould, an instrument of cultural hegemony. One's degree of 'civilisation' and status in the community was determined by one's proficiency in the English language and familiarity with English high class cultural values (Personal communication with Ratu Mosese Tuisawau, a British-educated high chief). High chiefs, especially the educated ones, were usually considered to be the most 'civilised' because of their

the natural right of chiefs not only to lead but also to have preferential access to education. It was really only in the 1960s (as a result of the transition process) and more so in the 1970s that education was recognised as a right for ordinary indigenous Fijians.[13] This deliberate suppression of education for ordinary indigenous Fijians may give credit to the argument that communalism itself contributed to the relative retardation of indigenous Fijian education.

As independence drew closer, the difference in educational attainment between indigenous Fijians and Indo-Fijians was becoming a serious political concern, especially given the dominance of Indo-Fijians in other areas of society such as commerce. Affirmative action in education was first recommended by the Royal Commission of 1969, which suggested some "positive discrimination provisions" for indigenous Fijians. Much later, in 1977, the Alliance government put in place a 50-50 scholarship policy for tertiary education. In other words, indigenous Fijians would receive 50% of the scholarships and the Indo-Fijian and Other ethnic categories would receive 50%. This was the first attempt at imposing quotas. This policy was encapsulated in Development Plan 6, which was accepted by both the Alliance and the NFP in its passage in parliament. However, when the government attempted to implement the policy when granting scholarships, there were allegations of discrimination from the Indo-Fijian community. The reason for the allegations was that indigenous Fijian students could enter the University of the South Pacific's[14] Foundation (pre-degree) Science Programme with 216 marks out of 400, while Indo-Fijians had to score 261 marks. This, as we saw earlier, became a major election issue during the 1977 general election, which the Alliance Party lost (Ali 1982).

In the 1970s the Ministry of Fijian Affairs set up a Fijian education unit which worked collaboratively with the Ministry of Education to provide resources to indigenous Fijian schools, to provide scholarships and to monitor students' progress and achievements. Despite the preferential academic policies towards indigenous Fijian education, there was still little improvement compared to Indo-Fijians. Baba (1979) showed that the failure rate amongst indigenous

---

near-perfect imitation of British 'Oxford' English and of English upper-class cultural values and mannerisms. Some of these chiefs were educated at Oxford and were specially groomed by the colonial state to run Fiji and to continue to perpetuate British values after independence.

13   Even preferential choices (although not official) still allegedly persisted in the 1970s and 1980s. A controversial example was Prime Minister Mara's son, Ratu Finau, who in 1977 achieved a Grade 4 pass (the lowest was Grade 5) in the pre-degree Preliminary 2 programme at the University of the South Pacific. But he was awarded a law scholarship despite the fact that he did not achieve a Grade 2 pass (the highest being Grade 1), the minimum for a law scholarship. Several other children from chiefly families were allegedly given scholarships ahead of indigenous Fijian students who scored higher. Coincidentally, 1977 was also the year when the 50-50 policy allocation for scholarships was implemented.

14   The University of the South Pacific was set up in 1972 by 12 countries in the South Pacific as their main university. The countries are Fiji, Kiribati, Marshall Islands, Nauru, Niue, Solomon Islands, Tokelau, Tonga, Tuvalu, Vanuatu, Western Samoa and Federated States of Micronesia. It is based in Suva, Fiji's capital and has three campuses in Fiji, Vanuatu and Western Samoa.

Fijians at the University of the South Pacific was four times greater than that for Indo-Fijians. In 1980, only 20% of indigenous Fijians who sat the University Entrance Exam (UE) passed, compared to 33.4% of Indo-Fijians. This pattern was more or less consistent throughout the 1980s. Between 1980 and 1984, the annual average percentage of indigenous Fijian students who passed UE (i.e. those who passed compared to the total who sat) was 23%, compared to 26% for Indo-Fijians and 36% for Others.

In 1984, in response to this disparity in results by ethnicity, the Alliance government provided FJ$3.5 million towards Fijian education to upgrade indigenous Fijian educational facilities and resources (including teachers) at the primary and secondary school levels, and to provide scholarships for indigenous Fijian students. It was felt that providing assistance at an early stage of educational development was crucial in building up a solid educational base for indigenous Fijians. That made sense given the differential numbers in enrolment. For example, according to the 1986 census, of the total primary school enrolment of 67,426, there were 31,431 indigenous Fijians, 32,861 Indo-Fijians and 3,134 Others. In other words, indigenous Fijians constituted 46% of the total enrolment. (Fiji Bureau of Statistics 1989). At the same census, of the total secondary school enrolment, there were 17,582 indigenous Fijians compared to 21,727 for Indo-Fijians and 2,907 for Others. This time the proportion for indigenous Fijians was 41%, a relative decline of 5%. According to the Fiji Bureau of Statistics:

> [T]he larger differences in secondary enrolment between the two ethnic groups may in part be attributed to the unavailability of secondary schools in the rural areas. There were 55.0% of secondary schools in urban areas compared to 45.0% in rural areas. Comparatively, there was only 38.1% secondary enrolment in rural areas compared to 58.1% for primary enrolment (Fiji Bureau of Statistics 1989: 30).

Indigenous Fijian students were concentrated in the rural areas. At the 1986 Census, 67.3% of indigenous Fijians lived in rural areas, compared to 58.6% of Indo-Fijians. These figures were higher than the corresponding 1976 figures of 70% for indigenous Fijians and 60.5% for Indo-Fijians (Fiji Bureau of Statistics 1989: 13). This is evidence of the on-going impact of urbanisation on the demographics of the indigenous Fijian community. The uneven spatial distribution of schools was compounded by the higher failure rate for indigenous Fijian students in the Fiji Junior Examination in Form 4. The annual average failure rate for indigenous Fijians for this exam for the 5 years to 1995 was 20%, compared to 12% for other ethnic groups (Fiji Ministry of Education 1996: 57). Thus, a higher number of indigenous Fijian students dropped out before reaching the Fiji School Leaving Certificate level in Form 6.

After the coup, major affirmative action measures included a further annual grant of FJ$2 million for Fijian education, establishment of the Fijian Education Unit in the Ministry of Education and the development of Educational Media Centres in rural areas for indigenous Fijian schools. The aim was for the "development of basic education, particularly improvement of access to secondary education for rural students" (Fiji Ministry of Education 1993: 130). However, despite ambitious efforts by the post-coup regime, the educational disparity between indigenous Fijians and Indo-Fijians persisted. For instance, in the Fiji School Leaving Certificate Examination (which took the place of UE in 1988) the average annual pass rate (i.e., percentage of all those who passed) for indigenous Fijians from 1990 to 1995 was 38%, compared to 60% for Indo-Fijians.

In the area of enrolment, the pre-coup pattern still persisted. In 1996, of the total 142,116 primary school enrolment, indigenous Fijians made up 54%. But out of the total of 69,921 for secondary enrolment, indigenous Fijians only made up 45% (Fiji Ministry of Education 1996). There was a difference of 9%, more than double the difference of only 5% in 1986 (as we have seen), a year before the coup.

In terms of tertiary education, there was a steady increase in scholarships awarded to indigenous Fijians. Of the total number of university scholarships awarded by the Public Service Commission (PSC) from 1970 to 1974, 34% were awarded to indigenous Fijians; in the period 1975 to 1979, indigenous Fijians received 39%; in 1980 to 1984, 44%; in 1985 to 1989, 49%; and in the period 1990 to 1992, 52%. These allocations were increasingly disproportionate, given the fact that indigenous Fijians constituted only about one third of all students qualifying to enter university. In addition to this, an average of 62% of all in-service training scholarships were allocated to indigenous Fijians after the coup, compared to the roughly 50-50 ratio before the coup (Fiji Public Service Commission 1995). Apart from the PSC (a government institution), the Fijian Affairs Board [FAB] (a major Fijian Administration institution) also provided scholarships, but exclusively for indigenous Fijians. Between 1984 and 1988 the FAB awarded 1,181 local scholarships and 150 overseas scholarships; from 1989 to 1992 the local scholarships awarded increased dramatically to 1,719 and there were 108 overseas awards.

A World Bank Report estimated that about 75% of all indigenous Fijian students studying at the University of the South Pacific (USP) in Suva were sponsored, while at the same time, 78% of Indo-Fijians were private students. Yet the proportions of Indo-Fijians and indigenous Fijians at USP were roughly equal (World Bank 1993). The report commented on the lack of any practical criteria for awarding scholarships, and noted an "acknowledged bias" in favour of indigenous Fijians. The report cautioned:

> Given that indigenous Fijians comprise roughly only a third of all students qualifying to enter university, Government's reluctance to sponsor non-indigenous Fijians is clearly preventing qualified Indo-Fijians from entering university and artificially restricting the supply of graduates, where students do not have the private means to support themselves (World Bank 1993: xv).

Again, like the civil service affirmative action program, the pattern of affirmative action in education showed the extent to which the preferential award of scholarships had, instead of just advancing indigenous Fijian achievement, also undermined the rights of qualified Indo-Fijian students to university education. Educational affirmative action, in the context of communalism, as I have attempted to show, has meant the marginalisation of other ethnic groups. The ethnicization of what should be merit-based educational awards has continued to be an entrenched feature to reinforce the paramountcy of Fijian interests.

Economic affirmative action

While the 1990 Constitution provided the political framework for affirmative action, there were a number of initiatives that were put into place either immediately after the coup, before the promulgation of the Constitution, or afterwards. Compared to the post-colonial Alliance affirmative action policies, which were bundled together with the national rural development program, this time affirmative action was more specific in focus and intention. The first coherent economic affirmative action policies of the post-coup period were contained in a set of proposals called the *Nine Points Plan*. The plan was produced by the Fijian Initiative Group (FIG), which consisted of indigenous Fijian professionals, civil servants and entrepreneurs, which first met in 1988 (under the chairpersonship of Mara) and which became formalised in 1992. The proposals contained in the plan were: FJ$20 million equity was to be injected from the Fijian Affairs Board (FAB) to Fijian Holdings Company (FHC); a Unit Trust for Fijians was to be established; a Compulsory Savings Scheme (CSS) for Fijians was to be set up; Government concession to Fijian business was to be enhanced; a Management Advisory Services Department was to be established in the Fijian Affairs Board (FAB); and Fijians should have a minimum ownership of resource-based industries. Furthermore, certain sectors of the economy were to be reserved for indigenous Fijian investment; there should be ownership of a daily newspaper by indigenous Fijians; and the Fijian Affairs Board should be restructured and strengthened (Fijian Initiative Group 1992).

In response to the first proposal, the government allocated a FJ$20 million grant to Fijian Holdings via the Fijian Affairs Board. Cabinet also approved of the compulsory savings concept, although it was never implemented. The Fiji

Development Bank bought shares in the *Daily Post*, an indigenous Fijian-owned daily newspaper, which due to operational and financial problems, was bought by the Fiji Government in February 1999. The idea was that the government shares were to be sold later to indigenous Fijians. There was also, in the 1990s, an increased indigenous Fijian share of the Unit Trust of Fiji. In 1993 a New Zealand company, Hays Consultant, undertook a review of the FAB structure and made recommendations about making the FAB more independent of the Ministry of Fijian Affairs to make it more responsive to desirable changes. These recommendations were accepted and came into force in early 1999.

The main follow up to the *Nine Points Plan* was the *Ten Year Plan for Fijian Participation in Business (Ten Year Plan)*, authored by Laisenia Qarase, the Managing Director of the Fiji Development Bank (FDB), a leading proponent of ethnic Fijian affirmative action and later prime minister. It was commissioned by the United Nations Economic and Social Commission for Asia and the Pacific (ESCAP). The report, which was more comprehensive than the *Nine Points Plan*, suggested that the objective of affirmative action "should be the achievement of overall parity between Fijians and other communities in all spheres of activities within the shortest period of time possible" and should "ensure that indigenous Fijians achieve 50% ownership of the corporate sector and other business sectors by the year 2005" (Qarase 1994: 4) The five strategies suggested were: enactment of appropriate legislation with the object of promoting and safeguarding the interest of indigenous Fijians; reorganisation and strengthening of the Fijian Administration; accumulation of savings to provide investment capital; encouraging of indigenous Fijians in investment; and development of indigenous Fijian entrepreneurship, business education and training. These strategies merely reinforced the basic tenets of the *Nine Points Plan*, but the difference was the *Ten Year Plan's* sense of urgency and the specific target of 50% indigenous Fijian business ownership by the year 2005.

The *Ten Year Plan*, which later became the government blueprint for indigenous Fijian business, identified a number of government-controlled industries for privatisation, with government shares to be transferred to Fijian Holdings and other indigenous Fijian corporations. These included big monopolies such as Fiji Post and Telecom, Fiji International Telecommunications Limited (FINTEL); Fiji Forest Industries Limited (FFI); Fiji Pine Limited (FPL); Tropic Woods Limited (TWL); Pacific Fisheries Company (PAFCO); and National Bank of Fiji (NBF) the crisis-ridden state-owned bank.

A number of recommendations in the *Ten Year Plan* were promptly implemented. Some of these, similar to some of those implemented in the *Nine Points Plan*, included the reorganisation of the Fijian Administration, the expansion of Fijian Holdings Limited, the continuation of the Commercial Loans to Fijians Scheme, Unit Trust investment, the establishment of a Small Equity Fund within the

Ministry of Fijian Affairs and establishment of a management training scheme for indigenous Fijians in the private sector. The reorganisation of the Fijian Administration was based on the assumption that the modernisation process as required by affirmative action went hand-in-hand with the consolidation of communalism. By making the Fijian Affairs Board separate from the Ministry of Fijian Affairs, it was hoped that interference by the central government in the communal affairs of the Fijian Administration would be minimised, thus providing the latter with the necessary autonomy to streamline its communal organisational role and maintain cohesion within the indigenous Fijian community (Qarase 1995). However, on the other hand, in the drive for investment there were measures clearly designed to create a competitive indigenous Fijian "bourgeoisie."

As I have previously argued, the lack of a sizeable indigenous Fijian entrepreneurial class, to parallel the Indo-Fijian entrepreneurial class, was due to the emphasis on communal production in the colonial epoch and also during the period of Alliance rule. As Table 4.4 shows, towards the end of Alliance rule in 1986 there was a distinctive relationship between ethnicity and socio-economic status. About 60% of those working in agriculture, animal husbandry, and forestry and fishing were indigenous Fijians, compared to 40% for Indo-Fijians. There was a preponderance of indigenous Fijians in rural-based activities, operating on a small scale from villages. Indigenous Fijians also dominated in the service industries, the main activity being tourism. Most hotels were located on native land and they tended to employ local villagers (mostly as low-paid workers), as part of the agreement with landowners. However, on the other hand, Indo-Fijians and other ethnic groups dominated the professional, technical and related workers (55%), administrative and managerial (74%), clerical and related workers (62%) and sales (74%) categories.

Table 4.4 Occupational categories of economically active persons by ethnicity (Indians and Fijians only), 1986

Occupational Category	Fijians %	Indians %	Total
Professional, technical and related workers	45	54	15,574
Administrative and managerial	23	76	2,090
Clerical and Related workers	38	62	13,726
Sales workers	26	74	13,832
Service workers	60	40	14,479
Agriculture, animal husbandry, forestry workers and fishermen	60	40	102,614
Production, related workers, transport equipment operators and labourers	56	44	28,268
Workers not classified by occupation and unemployed	70	30	13,407
Total	**56**	**44**	**203,991**

Source: Calculated from Fiji Bureau of Statistics, 1989: 52.

Thus there was clearly ethnic disparity in the "middle class" categories. The conspicuously low representation of indigenous Fijians in the commercial sphere was evident in official company figures. For instance, between 1986 and 1987, just before the coup, of the 700 companies registered by the Registrar of Companies, only 15% belonged to indigenous Fijians, compared to 50% ownership by Indo-Fijians; 20% by Others and 15% joint venture by all the ethnic groups (Office of Registrar of Companies, 1997).

However, it is important to point out that, although on the whole Indo-Fijians dominated business, even within the Indo-Fijian community itself there were socio-economic differences. A survey compiled by Prasad (1978: 263) showed that, although Gujaratis constituted a tiny proportion of the Indo-Fijian population, they registered 153 of the 156 Indo-Fijian tailor/draper businesses, 35 of the 45 jewellery business, 22 of the 23 laundries, and all 13 of the bootmakers. Gujaratis registered 298 of the total 557 Fiji-Indian businesses. In comparison, non-Gujaratis tended to be dominant in the construction industry, with a 1:9 ratio. The same trend was evident in the transport industry, where non-Gujaratis registered 52 bus and taxi companies and Gujaratis only 2. All the butcheries were owned by non-Gujaratis (both Hindus and Muslims). Non-Gujaratis also dominated other services such as photography, film distribution and auto-servicing. The "general merchant" business category was shared between all Indo-Fijian groups (Gujarati 50, Punjabi free immigrants 18 and the rest 69). This pattern of ownership persisted into the 1980s, as shown in a survey by Kelly (1990). Kelly showed that while Gujaratis still dominated tailoring, jewellery, duty free and shoe making, they had also moved into hardware. Of the 14 major hardware outlets, 6 belonged to Gujaratis; but there were no Gujaratis in the construction industry.

The point I wish to make here is that disparity was not only inter-ethnic, it was also intra-ethnic. The inter-ethnic disparity tended to be over-emphasised, thus making it a contentious political issue. The preponderance of the Gujarati in 'visible' economic activities was the basis for the distorted perception that all Indo-Fijians were 'rich'. While there were identifiable inter-ethnic disparities, there were also intra-ethnic disparities. Class and ethnicity overlapped and cut across each other in various ways. But ethnic inequality has been emphasised because of the dominant perception in Fiji, which defines social relations fundamentally in ethnic terms.

Implementing post-coup economic affirmative action policies

After the military coups in 1987, the need to expand and consolidate an indigenous Fijian entrepreneurial class became an increasingly urgent political priority. The former Minister for Trade and Commerce, Berenado Vunibobo, suggested that "Fijian society must be prepared to accept changes if our people are to become part of the mainstream of the economic life of our country" (*Fiji Times*, 11 January 1990: 8). "Changes" in this case referred to adaptation to commercial life. This was necessary to serve two purposes: firstly to enable indigenous Fijians to have a greater share of the market; and secondly to dispel the stereotypic myth reproduced over the years that indigenous Fijians were not culturally oriented towards private enterprise. The indigenous Fijian elites made it a point to be seen to be actively promoting indigenous Fijian business in order to win political support. Thus the focus on capital accumulation by indigenous Fijians at the more 'visible' macro level was politically more important for the ruling elites than the hidden "very small informally-operated businesses, including people who sold cordial and home-made sweets outside urban schools, prepared cooked food for wharf and factory workers, operated grass-cutting contracts and sold in the municipal markets" (Chung, 1989: 193). Thus after the coup, emphasis was on investment in the area of finance and equity (as reflected in the *Nine Points Plan* and *Ten Year Plan*), a significant shift from the primary commodity production strategy of the 1970s and early 1980s. Both the *Nine Points Plan* and the *Ten Year Plan* were implemented in earnest. Some aspects of their implementation are outlined below.

One of the most important initiatives was the government grant of FJ$20 million to indigenous Fijian business in 1992. The grant was made to the Fijian Affairs Board, to buy "B" Class shares from Fijian Holdings Limited and hold them in trust for indigenous Fijians. These shares were to be sold to indigenous Fijian shareholders later. Since 1987, the operation of Fijian Holdings was aggressively extended to buy shares in many leading corporations in Fiji. Again, the involvement of the Fijian Affairs Board indicated the degree of importance put on the role of communal mobilisation, even in the realm of capitalist investment.

The post-coup government in 1989 provided two major concessions for the Commercial Loans to Fijians Scheme (CLFS), which was set up by the FDB in 1975 to assist indigenous Fijians in business. The concessions were: firstly, an increased subsidy of 5.5% per annum on loans up to FJ$200,000 under the scheme, giving an effective interest rate of 8% per annum to borrowers; and secondly, a cash grant equivalent to 10% of the fixed assets cost, with a maximum grant of FJ$20,000 for each project. Through government encouragement, loans under the CLFS increased dramatically after the coup. For instance, in the twelve years between 1975 and 1988 there were only 4,720 loans, totalling about FJ$25 million. But in the five years from 1989 to 1994, there were 6,189 loans totalling FJ$99 million. The upsurge in loan approval from 1989 reflected increased government concessions. Despite the initial optimism, CLFS had a high failure rate, with arrears averaging between 19% and 23%.

An area in which the quota system was significant was in the taxi business. The taxi business was always dominated by Indo-Fijians, as shown in Table 4.5. But on 22 October 1993 a ministerial directive stated that Indo-Fijians were not to be issued new permits. As the table shows, this significantly impacted on the ethnic distribution of taxi permits.

Table 4.5 Distribution of taxi permits by ethnicity

Year	Fijian	Indian	Others	Total
1988	272	2,265	49	2,586
1989	272	2,265	49	2,586
1990	289 (+17)	2,260 (-5)	37 (-12)	2,586
1991	399 (+110)	2,274 (+14)	37 (nil)	2,710 (+124)
1992	554 (+155)	2,279 (+5)	46 (+9)	2,879 (+169)
1993	748 (+194)	2,235 (-44)	107 (+61)	3,090 (+21)
15 June, 1994	988 (+240)	2,239 (+4)	124 (+17)	3,351 (+261)
16 August, 1994	1,100 (+112)	2,239	139 (+15)	3,478 (+127)
11 Nov, 1994	1,234 (+134)	2,239	153 (+14)	3,626 (+148)
31 Dec, 1994	1,289 (+55)	2,239	155 (+2)	3,683 (+57)

Source: Fiji Dept. of Road and Transport, 1994: 18.

The pattern of taxi ownership before the coup was roughly similar to that of 1988 and 1989 (Fiji Department of Road and Transport, 1994). After 1990 there was a deliberate policy to increase the issue of new permits to indigenous Fijians. In 1990, 17 new permits were issued, and this steadily increased over the years, so that by June, 1994 alone there was an increase of 240 in the number of new permits issued to indigenous Fijians since 1993. In comparison, the number of taxi permits issued to Indo-Fijians had declined from 2,265 in 1989 to 2,239 in June, 1994. As a result of the ministerial directive in 1993, no new permits were issued to Indo-Fijians from mid-1994 onwards. By the end of December 1994, 1,289 permits were held by indigenous Fijians compared to 2,239 held by Indo-Fijians. However, if the same average rate of increase continued, that is an average of 135 permits per month for indigenous Fijians and 0 permits per month for Indo-Fijians, the number of permits for both ethnic groups would be the same within 7 months from the end of December 1994.

The issue of taxi permits was a clear case of reverse discrimination where, while there was a genuine need to increase indigenous Fijians' share of the taxi business, there was at the same time a deliberate policy to minimise the Indo-Fijian share. Funding for new taxis for indigenous Fijians was provided by the CLFS, as mentioned earlier. But in 1995, CLFS funding for new permits was suspended due to the high rate of arrears.

One of the main indigenous Fijian commercial acquisitions was Fiji Television Limited (FTL). The government granted a 12-year exclusive television broadcast licence to FTL on the understanding that indigenous Fijian control of FTL would increase. In 1995, the main shareholders in FTL were FDB, 51%; Television New Zealand (TVNZ), 15%; Fiji Post and Telecom (FPTL), 14%; and the general public, 20%. The 51% of shares owned by FDB were held in trust on behalf of indigenous Fijians, represented by the 14 Provincial Councils (Qarase, 1994). The Provincial Councils owned Yasana Holdings Limited (YHL), a company established by the Fijian Affairs Board to look after provincial investment.

The Village Housing Scheme (VHS) was set up by the Fiji National Provident Fund (FNPF) in 1987 to provide homes for Fijians living in rural villages. A total of 27,373 applications amounting to FJ$53.91 million were approved and paid out (Fiji National Provident Fund, 1996: 8).

The Small Business Equity Scheme (SBES) was set up by the FNPF in 1990 to provide finance for small businesses, especially those owned by indigenous Fijians. Since it started, a total of 4,621 members were assisted, representing FJ$17.22 million in payments. In 1996, a total of 1,379 applications amounting to FJ$3.5 million were approved. Of these, indigenous Fijians submitted about 90% or 1,200 applications totalling F$2.76 million in payment. The details are shown in Table 4.6.

Table 4.6 Total Small Business Equity Scheme (SBES) Loans to 1996

Loan Type	Number	%	Amount (F$)	%
Transportation	54	3.9	183,071	5.2
Agriculture/Fishing	187	13.6	547,365	15.6
Retail/Wholesale	189	13.7	453,106	12.9
Small Industries	109	7.9	346,371	10.0
Equity Investments	722	52.3	1,189,717	34.0
Property Investments	49	3.6	540,110	15.4
Others	69	5.0	241,469	6.9
Total	**1,379**	**100**	**3,501,209**	**100**

Source: Fiji National Provident Fund, 1996: 8.

Apart from the above, indigenous Fijians were encouraged to join together (as *tokatoka*, *mataqali, tikina* and other forms of group) and set up companies, with the government's support. One such company was the Gaunavou Investments

Company Limited [GICL0 (Gaunavou translates as "modern times"). GICL (incorporated as a public company on 11 November 1994), was set up by the Suva City Fijian Urban Constituency branch of the ruling SVT "with the positive intention to start and promote indigenous Fijian enterprise and business activities" (*Daily Post*, 13 March 1999: 6). Amongst the shareholders were Prime Minister Rabuka and a number of government cabinet ministers. GICL, which was concerned with family-based shareholding, was meant to supplement Yasana Holdings (which dealt with provincial investments) and Fijian Holdings, which dealt with bigger shareholders.

In all of the above economic affirmative action projects, three main strategies could be identified. The first was the emphasis on communal investment, such as Fijian Holdings, Yasana Holdings and involvement of the Fijian Affairs Board; second was small scale of investment; and third was ethnic marginalisation as a result of strict quotas, as in the cased of taxi permits. The first two largely involved communal capitalism, a term introduced before, but which will be discussed in detail next. Communal capitalism was a re-adaptation of neo-traditional communalism in the new context of commerce, and as such posed a fundamental contradiction; on the one hand there was the need to create an independent indigenous Fijian entrepreneurial class, and on the other, the use of neo-traditional communal arrangement in this process. The latter provided an inhibiting environment for the former.

Communal capitalism

I define communal capitalism as a process whereby the communal system within the Fijian Administration was deployed to form commercial entities, and to collect and invest capital. Communal capitalism had a structure and a rationale. The structure followed exactly the same official structure as the Fijian Administration. It involved the *tokatoka, mataqali, koro, tikina, yasana*, and even the Fijian Affairs Board and Great Council of Chiefs. These various levels of socio-political organisations either had their own companies or were part of a collective commercial organisation under the *yasana* or Fijian Affairs Board. The rationale was that these communal groupings were to raise finance at different levels for the purpose of collective investment. The assumption was that capital investment was for the collective benefit of the *vanua*. For instance, capital for the provincial shares in Yasana Holdings or Fijian Holdings was collected from the 14 *yasanas* (provinces), who collected capital from the *tikinas*, who in turn collected from the *koros*. The *koro* collected its dues from the different *mataqalis* or *tokatokas*. Communal capitalism incorporated elements of both the communal semi-subsistence and individual capitalism modes. The resultant synthesis was a complex interplay between two systems, an "articulation" between the communal semi-subsistence and capitalist modes of production.

We could describe communal capitalism as, by and large, capitalist entrepreneurship operating within the framework of neo-traditional social relations. The chiefs were mostly made directors of provincial and local community-based companies and their blessing was sought in every investment endeavour. Invested capital was conceptualised as a communal entity that belonged to the *vanua*[15] or community and was symbolically epitomised in the chief. This mystifying appeal inspired individuals to selflessly provide capital through *soli-vakavanua* (community collection) in the name of the *vanua*. The significance of capital as an accumulative factor of production was undermined by loyalty to communal obligation towards the *vanua*. The overriding hegemony of the *vanua* as an ideological formation subsumed the identity of the individuals. Ownership of a company, for instance, was not seen primarily as a means towards accumulation but as an expression of political strength and prestige for the chiefs, acting on behalf of the community (personal communication with a group of Kadavu province villagers). So provinces were continually engaged in competition in their *soli-vakavanua* as a show of traditional rivalry for prestige rather than for the purpose of capital investment and competition in the market. Capital thus became part of the hegemonic mechanism by which chiefs were able to exert control over the *vanua* and individuals. Mismanagement and corruption by chiefs were considered an unquestioned part of their traditional privilege as head and guardian of the *vanua*. Recently, a number of chiefs, including the wife of the president, were legally challenged for abuse of the privileges described above. Many chiefs have, over the years, financially enriched themselves through this neo-traditional arrangement.

Given the contradictory demands of communal organisation and capitalist accumulation, there have been obvious challenges for indigenous Fijians to make headway in mainstream commerce. Despite the efforts directed at affirmative action up to 2000 there was insignificant progress in the commercial performance of indigenous Fijians.

Rural indigenous Fijians and affirmative action

The earliest forms of pro-indigenous development and affirmative action policies took place in rural areas during the colonial period and also during the post-colonial Alliance rule. A number of later affirmative action projects, based

---

15   The term *vanua* has a very ideological, political and spiritual dimension to it. It refers to the relationship between the land and people. It is a blanket term which refers to communal institutions, norms and values.

on communal capitalism (such as Fijian Holdings) directly involved villagers through *yasana* (provincial) shares. What we need to find out is, to what extent have the benefits of these affirmative action projects 'trickled' down to the villages in terms of socio-economic benefits over the years?

In 1986, for instance, about 36% of the "economically active" indigenous Fijians in the rural area were employed in the public or private sector and received a wage or salary. This ratio dropped slightly to 35% in 1989 (Fiji Bureau of Statistics, 1991). However, in 1995 it rose again to 37%. Table 4.7 shows that in 1995 the total number of economically active rural indigenous Fijians (who made up 30.2% of the total population) involved in commercial activities were as follows: 2.4% retailing; 17.2% cash cropping; 1.9% livestock; 3.2% fishing; 0.2% forestry; 1.7% service; 10.6% paid employment. In other words, only 37% had some form of steady cash income. Within a period of almost ten years, from 1986 to 1995, non-subsistence economic activity in the rural areas hardly increased. This was despite two decades of rural-targeted affirmative action.

Based on the above table, the percentage of indigenous Fijian villagers in business in relation to the total Fijian population (approximately 393,575) showed the following trend: retail (0.4%); manufacturing (0.005%); cash crop (2.86%); livestock (0.32%); fishing (0.5%); forestry (0.03%); service (2.7%); and paid employment (1.7%). This constitutes only about 6.19% of the total Fijian population. Also, as the table shows, economic disparity between provinces was very conspicuous, ranging from 18,107 people in businesses in Ba to 1,026 in Serua. Only 4 of the 14 provinces had more than 5,000 people in some form of business activity.

In rural areas, where communalism was still very strong, economic progress, as I have attempted to show above, had been virtually static, despite two decades of affirmative action which attempted to introduce commerce into village life. This contrasted with Malaysia, where the impact of affirmative action was felt within a short time. Indeed, the fact that indigenous Fijians congregated in communally organised villages inhibited their commercial development. For instance, figures show that in 1989, of the total 23,026 commercial farmers who lived in settlements outside communal villages, 20,398 (88.5%) were Indo-Fijians and 2,628 (11.4%) were indigenous Fijians (Fiji Bureau of Statistics, 1991).

Table 4.7 Village and settlements business types by provinces in 1995. Shows number of people

Province	No. of Villages	Retail	Manufacturing	Cash Crop	Live Stock	Fishing	Forestry	Service	Paid Employ	Subsist	Totals
Ba	112	156	0	979	239	330	88	49	2111	14155	18107
Bua	107	92	0	219	46	19	1	12	88	1892	2369
Cakaudrove	146	167	1	1888	84	275	4	58	301	1507	4285
Kadavu	90	113	0	4	7	50	0	19	150	2667	3010
Lau	119	140	4	848	3	75	1	22	458	2438	3989
Lomaiviti	107	95	0	610	2	65	0	13	595	1949	3329
Macuata	210	38	1	1542	65	523	31	641	554	603	3998
Nadroga	133	138	8	1629	198	136	2	0	794	52	2957
Naitasiri	146	121	0	423	94	2	0	1	329	4144	5114
Namosi	42	56	0	4	18	23	0	33	316	844	1294
Ra	202	112	0	1313	41	40	2	6	197	5206	6917
Rewa	55	91	1	684	171	194	1	141	520	601	2404
Serua	40	36	4	463	118	144	0	17	146	98	1026
Tailevu	143	194	3	682	178	194	3	84	394	5061	6793
Total	1652	1549	22	11288	1264	2070	133	1096	6953	41217	65592
Percentage	2.5	2.4	0.7	17.2	1.9	3.2	0.2	1.7	10.6	62.8	100

Source: Fiji Ministry of Fijian Affairs 1995. *Provincial Profile Project*: 64.

Has embourgeoisement worked?

The emphasis on creating and enlarging an indigenous Fijian middle class was part of an aggressive post-coup initiative. However, this enthusiasm was largely channelled towards communal capitalism. What that meant in reality was that indigenous Fijian business was to be embodied in indigenous-owned corporations such as Fijian Holdings, which would invest on behalf of indigenous Fijians. This undermined the competitiveness needed for individual enterprise and individual social mobility, thus retarding the expansion of an indigenous middle class. The insignificant change in the ethnic 'middle class' occupational categories for indigenous Fijians relative to Indo-Fijians in Table 4.8 for 1986 and 1996 appears to confirm this.

Although Table 4.8 shows an increase in the number of indigenous Fijians in the managerial category, from 487 in 1986 to 1,292 in 1996, the real significance of this was much less than it appeared to be. The increase in number by almost three times was due to two main reasons: firstly, the definition of managerial category in 1996 incorporated various other sub-categories which were not included in 1986; secondly, as we recall, there was an increase in the number of loans to indigenous Fijians by the CLFS from 1992 to 1996 and thus there was a proliferation of companies formed to formalise business ventures. But as we shall see later, a lot of these CLFS loans ended up in arrears or as bad debts. This would have exaggerated the total number of companies owned by indigenous Fijian.

Nevertheless, in general, the pattern of ethnic disparity in 1996 was almost the same as that ten years earlier. Indo-Fijians still dominated the managerial positions, with 76% of such positions being held by Indo-Fijians in 1986, increasing to 78% in 1996. Despite economic affirmative action measures, the ethnic gap had not closed: rather, it had slightly increased.

Table 4.8 Ethnic distribution of 'middle class' occupational categories, 1986 and 1996

Occupational Category	Fijian		Indian	
	1986	1996	1986	1996
Managerial	487 (23%)	1,292 (22%)	1,603 (76%)	4,548 (78%)
Professional and Technical	7,124 (45%)	13,699 (53%)	8,450 (54%)	12,351 (47%)
Total	7,611 (43)	14,981 (47%)	10,053 (57%)	16,899 (53%)

Source: Fiji Bureau of Statistics 1989; 1998.

The 1996 census report further disaggregated the managerial category into four sub-categories: director/chief executive; small business manager; specialist managers; and other department managers. The ethnic disparity within these categories is shown in Table 4.9. In all sub-categories, Indo-Fijians dominated, with between 60% and 82% of the total. The largest difference was for the chief executive position, in which there were 82% Indo-Fijians and 18% indigenous Fijians.

Table 4.9 Ethnic distribution of corporate managers' category, 1996[16]

Man. Category	Fijian (Number)	%	Indian (Number)	%
Directors/Chief Executives	196	18	879	82
Small business managers	568	20	2,344	80
Specialist managers	193	40	285	60
Other department managers	335	24	1,040	76
Total	1,292	22	4,548	78

Source: Fiji Bureau of Statistics 1998: 175.

The only area where there was a marked increase for indigenous Fijians was in the professional and technical category (as shown in Table 4.8). There was an increase in the number of indigenous Fijians in that category from 45% in 1986 to 53% in 1996. This relative increase was due mainly to two reasons: first was the large-scale migration of Indo-Fijian professionals after the 1987 coup; and second was the post-coup affirmative action in employment and education which led to the marginalisation of Indo-Fijians in the public service, as we saw earlier. Most indigenous professionals and technical experts were in the public sector (Fiji Bureau of Statistics 1998).

It is apparent that very little progress had been made in terms large-scale penetration of indigenous Fijians into the corporate sector, despite the concerted affirmative action drive. Other available figures tend to confirm this. As mentioned earlier, just before the 1987 coup only 15% of the companies registered by the Registrar of Companies belonged to indigenous Fijians, compared to 50% for Indo-Fijians, 20% by Others and 15% joint ventures by all other ethnic groups. In 1997, of the 101 local companies registered under the Tax Free Zones (TFZ) up to 1997, less than 10% were indigenous Fijian-owned. Of the 71 local companies in operation within the same period, in the TFZ only about 7 were indigenous Fijian-owned (Fiji Trade and Investment Board 1997).

Moreover, the post-coup state economy, especially after 1990, went through a period of contraction, and was not favourable for investment. Although the growth rate between 1989 and 1990 was a high 8%, it was followed by a period

---

16   The 1996 Census Report breaks down the corporate manager category into four sub-categories; directors and chief executives; small business managers; specialist managers; and other department managers.

of low growth. From 1991 to 1995 real per capita output growth averaged only 1% per year (World Bank 1995: 1). But despite this, the fact remains that this unfavourable investment climate affected everyone, including both Indo-Fijian and indigenous Fijians. Thus it cannot be seen as 'the' explanation for the continuing ethnic disparity in socio-economic performance.

Clearly, evidence showed insignificant improvement in the socio-economic situation of indigenous Fijians relative to Indo-Fijians between 1970 and the late 1990s, despite the exhaustive affirmative action measures. Indeed, the problem, as I have argued, needed to be understood in the broader sociological and political dimension, which requires an analysis of the interplay between socio-economic imperatives and the dictates of the dominant ideological and political processes rooted in the communal schema. Affirmative action and associated development policies have continuously been subsumed under communal hegemony, thus undermining intended socio-economic progress. But the prevailing belief in official circles tended to undermine attempts to come to terms with the fundamental cause of the problem, as reflected in Qarase's assertion:

> There is no doubt that the long-term security and stability of Fiji will depend, to a large extent, on the country's ability to close the gap that exists between Fijians and other ethnic groups in the various sectors mentioned. Closing the gap is a national problem and the solutions will require the support of all communities in Fiji. There is no time for debate on "why" and "how" Fijians are so far behind in Fiji's modern economy. Such a debate would mainly be irrelevant and futile (Qarase 1994: 4).

But stifling the debate on the "why" and "how" of the indigenous economic malaise continued to reproduce the problem. The problem was embedded in the socio-political and ideological schema of communalism. This is perhaps where Fiji and Malaysia differed in some respects. Affirmative action in Malaysia tried to promote individual rather than communal investment.

The Malaysian connection

Fiji, like other developing countries (e.g. South Africa, Namibia) had been obsessed with the Malaysian model of affirmative action, considered to be highly 'successful.' The business affirmative action strategy in Fiji, especially in relation to the development of indigenous investment and financial institutions, was based on the Malaysian model and this modelling intensified after the 1987 coup.

Fiji's links with Malaysia went back a long way. Relations were first established when the 1st Battalion of the Fiji Infantry Regiment was deployed in Malaysia (then called Malaya) from 1952-56 as part of the Commonwealth forces sent to suppress the communist insurgency during the "Malayan Emergency". The Malaya operation was politically significant because it reinforced the prevailing self-perception of indigenous Fijians as a "warrior race", to be deployed not only locally against Indo-Fijian trouble makers, but also internationally to support other indigenous peoples against "foreign" dominance (Nawadra 1995). The version of events Fijian soldiers were indoctrinated with was simple – to 'save' the indigenous Malays (*kai Maleya*) from the 'evil' communists (*komunisi*). In fact the term *komunisi,* like *kai Idia* (Indian), came to be associated with people of unscrupulous and arrogant behaviour within indigenous Fijian society.

Trained and ideologically conditioned in ethnic warfare at home, the Fijian soldiers perfectly fitted into their "liberating" role in Malaya against the largely Chinese communists. The Fijian soldiers' exploits have been mythologised in traditional dances *(meke)* and songs *(sere)*.[17] Significantly, many of the future leaders of Fiji, including the a Governor General and President, Ratu Penaia Ganilau (then a colonel and himself commander), and several members of the Alliance Party Cabinet, were officers in the deployed Fiji Battalion. This was where the political link was cemented, leading to Fiji's interest in 'importing' the Malaysian political model of consociationalism, which attempted to maintain national unity, yet provided for indigenous Malay political ascendancy. The Malaysian political model was seen as a desirable future alternative for Fiji after independence in 1970, but this idea was temporarily shelved after the May 1969 ethnic riots in Malaysia. During his reign as Prime Minister, Mara, himself a great fan of Malaysian politics, visited Malaysia to cement political and economic ties. Diplomatic ties between the two countries were established in 1977 and Malaysia set up its embassy in Fiji in 1984. In 1988, one year after the coup, Fiji set up its embassy in Kuala Lumpur.

The political and economic links between Fiji and Malaysia strengthened after the 1987 military coup. The coup was seen as a parallel event to the 1969 Malaysian race riots, after which indigenous Malaysian ascendancy was politically crystallised. Now that the coup had provided the platform for indigenous Fijian ascendancy, there was almost a sense of urgency to emulate the *Bumiputeraism* experience, as reflected in the words of the former ambassador to Malaysia, Dr Ahmed Ali, quoted in the Fiji Ministry of Information monthly bulletin, *Fiji Focus*:

---

17 *Bula Maleya* (Hello Malaya), one of the most popular songs in the South Pacific, was appropriated by Elvis Presley as the lyric for his song, *Drums of the Island.*

Fiji has much to learn from Malaysia... Fiji should also examine Malaysia's approach to elevating the socio-economic position of its *Bhumiputras* and securing them their political primacy. In addition Fiji could also draw from Malaysia's strategies for unity, its insistence on its own values, its religious and language policies – all these provide guidelines towards successful living in a multi-ethnic society (Fiji Ministry of Information. 1994: 39).

A bilateral agreement was put in place to facilitate trade promotion and training for Fiji citizens and in 1993 the Fiji Trades and Investment Board mounted a Fiji Week in Kuala Lumpur as a way of reinforcing trade links. In the mid 1990s Malaysia was Fiji's second largest importer of sugar, after the European Union. This accounted for 103 million tonnes of sugar annually through a long-term agreement.[18]

Malaysian corporate investment in Fiji was limited to Free Trade Zone (FTZ) manufacturing, tourism and finance. Some of the latest acquisitions included South Pacific Textile (Fiji) Ltd, employing 250 people; the SIA Cash and Carry – a joint venture with local employees operating a retail outlet for imported garment and fashion accessories and the Malaysian Bank/National Bank of Fiji partnership; and massive equity in the Carpenters Corporation, one of the largest wholesale and retail outlets in Fiji. In tourism, the Malaysian Berjaya Corporation owned the Berjaya Inn; Sateras Resources Limited owned the Tokatoka Resort near Nadi International Airport and the Suva Motor Inn in Suva; and the Malaysian Shangri-La owned the Mocambo Hotel and the Fijian Hotel, Fiji's largest five-star tourist resort at that time. In selling Fiji to Malaysian investors, Dr Ahmed Ali said:

...businessmen in both Malaysia and Fiji can tap the huge opportunities available in each other's countries...We want to welcome Malaysians to Fiji to do business and even share their knowledge and experience with us both in the public and private sectors. We also want to give something in return, not merely take (quoted in *Business Times* 1994: 10).

Part of the training program through the bilateral agreement was the sponsoring of the Chief Executive of Fijian Holdings Company to study affirmative action in Malaysia, in particular how the *Bumiputera* trust agency, National Equity Corporation (NEC), worked and how it could be emulated in Fijian Holdings.[19]

---

18 In 1993 the trade balance with Malaysia was between F$16-F$30 million surplus. Malaysia's exports to Fiji include yarn, rubber, telecommunication and electrical appliances.

19 NEC is one of Malaysia's leading investment institutions, set up by the Malaysian government to facilitate the *Bumiputera* participation in business. Through heavy government subsidy, and help from the Bumiputera Investment Foundation (which helps *Bumiputeras* to save money and develop entrepreneurship and investment skills), the corporation has been able to achieve a level of investment exceeding US$8.26 billion. The government assistance package includes general financial support of about US$1,475 million,

In August 1996, Gen. Rabuka visited Malaysia, where he expressed deep interest in "Malaysia's privatisation policy because it ensured indigenous participation in government-owned programs and assets" (*The Fiji Times*, 10 August 1996: 4) and took up Malaysia's offer to help in Fiji's privatisation program. But Rabuka was advised by Prime Minister Mahathir (who has been a leading campaigner for Fiji's re-admittance into the Commonwealth), that, while privatisation was important (Fiji had embarked on a major privatisation program), it was also important that "strict consideration must be given to ensuring that there is no direct sell-out of Government programs and assets" (quoted in *The Fiji Times*, 10 August 1996: 4). Rabuka's later visit to Malaysia was in September 1998, to coincide with the Commonwealth Games in Kuala Lumpur. During this trip, Rabuka was given a car by the Malaysian Prime Minister as a gift.

During the third Fiji/Malaysia bilateral meeting in Fiji in July 1997, Fiji's Foreign Minister reiterated what had become a recurrent rhetoric about Fiji's obsession with Malaysia:

> Fiji hopes to draw on the success of Malaysia in the last 20 years as a model at this crucial state in the nation's political history...Fiji realised that political stability was a requirement for economic growth. We should consider the Malaysian example as a very good pointer for us in the context (*Fiji Times*, July 3 1997: 3).

Perhaps the most controversial Malaysian involvement in Fiji was when the ruling SVT Party and the government employed Malaysian Federal judge, Zakaria Yatim, in the review of Fiji's 1990 Constitution. Yatim's role was to provide input based on the position of the *Bumiputera* provided in the Malaysian Constitution. He prepared the SVT submission to the CRC and also worked for the government as consultant for the Fijian Affairs Board and Prime Minister's office. Part of his contribution was to transplant the affirmative action provisions of the Malaysian constitution into the Fiji Constitution. Yatim's role was publicly criticised by the opposition parties as tantamount to "foreign intervention", and even in Australia, a judge said that he was "distressed to learn that an advisor to the Fijian leader was a Malaysian Constitutional expert", claiming that "The constitution of Malaysia was one of the most repressive constitutions one could imagine" (*Daily Post*, 17 June 1997: 3).

In adapting the Malaysian affirmative action model, Fiji was also faced with its own version of Malaysia's long-standing dilemma of reconciling the communal agenda and economic modernisation.

---

transfer of government shares at par to the corporation from forty profitable companies, a 14-year tax holiday and exemption from stamp duties and share transfer tax and use of government infrastructure and facilities to promote two unit trust schemes to mobilise the savings of Malays for investment (Fijian Holdings 1994: 11-12). Today Fijian Holdings Company operates as a miniature version of NEC.

5. Social engineering: Attempts to create an indigenous entrepreneurial class

The affirmative action policies after the 1987 coup was driven largely by the desire to "catch up" with the Indo-Fijian in the business sector by engaging indigenous Fijians in entrepreneurship to a greater degree. The creation of a vibrant indigenous middle class was a way of driving indigenous Fijian development forward to maintain ethnic balance and stability. Most of the affirmative action projects were targeted at urban, middle-class indigenous Fijians and hardly any was targeted at rural development for villages.

As we saw in the last chapter, the post-coup affirmative action programs prescribed under the *Nine Points Plan,* and later the *Ten Year Plan,* shifted the emphasis from primary production to large-scale financial investment, based on the *Bumiputera* model, to create an indigenous Fijian bourgeoisie to counteract the economic power of Indo-Fijians.

This chapter examines in detail some of the main post-coup affirmative action initiatives in the area of investment, focusing on the following: Fijian Holdings investment; Fiji Development Bank's Commercial Loans to Fijians Scheme; the Equity Investment Management Company Limited (EIMCOL) store scheme; the Fiji National Provident Fund Small Business Equity Scheme and National Bank of Fiji loans. In particular it will focus on communal capitalism and implications for the formation of an indigenous bourgeoisie generally.

Many of these projects were interrelated. All of them were collaborative initiatives between the government and Fijian institutions. Some of them, as we have seen in the last chapter, continued from the Alliance era, and were given an extra boost after the coup, while some were post-coup initiatives. However, for a number of reasons, many of these initiatives failed and left behind negative images of affirmative action.

Fijian Holdings Company

As we have seen, Fijian Holdings Company (FHC) was formed by the Great Council of Chiefs before the coup, but became the main focus of the drive towards indigenous capitalism after the coup. While it had played the role of facilitator of indigenous Fijian business since it started, it was aggressively expanded after 1987 in an attempt to capture a large segment of the corporate sector for indigenous Fijians.

In fact Fijian Holdings has its genesis back in 1970 after independence, when Prime Minister Mara approached the Australian multi-national Burns Philp Limited (BP) to help in the development of indigenous Fijian entrepreneurship through collaboration in business in the form of share acquisition. BP was the biggest company operating in Fiji and the South Pacific and had interests in shipping, butcheries, wholesale, retail, copra production, breweries, and automobiles, to name a few. Part of the agreement was for indigenous Fijians to be members of the company board of directors to accustom them to boardroom culture. Through this arrangement, it was hoped that, not only would the indigenous Fijians benefit financially from their investment, they would also receive the necessary training and acquire skills that would catapult them into the competitive world of business.

However, it was not until 16 February 1984 that the Great Council of Chiefs (GCC) decided to buy up to 50% in Burns Philp, under the following conditions: FJ$40 million was to be raised to buy shares from Burns Philp; Provincial Councils and other indigenous Fijian organisations were to be encouraged to collect their initial shares of FJ$1.5 million; a joint venture between the Fijian Affairs Board and Burns Philp was to be encouraged, and the Fiji government was to seek assistance from the Australian government for further financing; the Native Land Development Corporation (NLDC) was to be the holding company, and carry out negotiations with Burns Philp on the purchase of shares. While there was an urge to enter into capitalist investment, there was also a desire to do so within the patronising ambit of communal organisation.

Because the NLDC did not have the expertise and capacity to undertake such a high-risk business venture, it was decided to create a new entity to be called Fijian Holdings Limited (FHL). FHL was incorporated in 1984 with the following objectives:

> ...to increase Fijian participation in the commercial sector. The company achieves this through acquisition of equity in established, well-managed, profitable companies with excellent prospects for growth. It will: maintain a prudent and conservative approach to financial decision-making; Seek investments which have economically strategic significance; Endeavour to ensure the benefits from its investments are spread as widely as possible among the Fijian people; Promote the training of Fijian business executives, bearing in mind the need for attainment of high standards of professionalism, competitive performance and commercial skills (Fijian Holdings 1996: 3).

FHL's role was limited to the acquisition of equity. Its strategy was "to increase Fijian participation in the commercial economy...through acquisition of equity in established, well-managed, profitable companies with excellent prospects for growth", with "benefits spread as widely as possible among the Fijian people" (Fijian Holdings Limited 1994: 1). To ensure wide distribution of its benefits amongst indigenous Fijians, three types of shares were initially suggested; Provincial shares, Native Land Trust Board shares and Fijian Affairs Board shares.[1] Thus, as Table 5.1 shows, on 10 December 1984, when FHL was incorporated, the value of shares, distributed between the Provinces, Native Land Trust Board and Fijian Affairs Board, totalled more than FJ$1 million.

Table 5.1 Initial Fijian Holdings shares, December 1984

Shareholders	Amount ($F)
Ba Provincial Council	51,968.25
Bua Provincial Council	50,000.00
Kadavu Development Company	51,608.07
Lomaiviti Provincial Council	51,968.25
Macuata Provincial Council	51,968.25
Nadroga Provincial Council	51,968.25
Rewa Provincial Council	51,968.25
Lau Provincial Council	50,501.25
Naitasiri Provincial Co-operative	31,227.13
Cakaudrove Provincial Council	100,000.00
Fijian Affairs Board	101,968.25
Native Land Trust Board	500,000.00
Total	**1,145,145.95**

Note: At this stage, only 10 of the 14 Provinces had been allocated their shares. The Kadavu Development Company and the Naitasiri Provincial Co-operatives are owned by the Kadavu and Naitasiri Provinces respectively.

Source: Fijian Holdings Limited 1984.

The provinces without equity shares during the initial stage were Namosi, Ra, Serua and Tailevu, but later on they were also involved. Of the FJ$1,145,145.95

---

1   This approach was modelled along the lines of Malaysian state-established and supervised enterprises such as the National Equity Corporation (NEC), which held shares in trust on behalf of the *Bumiputeras*. But one of the fundamental differences was that the Malaysian investment institutions, although linked to statal political interference, were run by bureaucrats, operating within the capitalist entrepreneurial framework, outside the realm of traditional politics and culture. In the case of Fiji, traditional institutions were directly part of the investment projects. While Malaysian financial institutions held shares in trust for individual *Bumiputeras*, and were (and still are) ultimately accountable to the government, Fijian Holdings held shares in trust for neo-traditional/neo-colonial socio-political institutions (Fijian Affairs, Native Land Trust Board and Provinces), claiming to represent the legitimate interest of indigenous Fijians, and were ultimately responsible to the Great Council of Chiefs.

collected by the provinces, FJ$1million was used to purchase 1,000,000 "A Class" shares in a big company called Basic Industries Limited.[2] At this time there were no limited liability shareholdings.

The communal shares were based on two assumptions; first, indigenous Fijian elites were convinced that, after years of dependence on colonial paternalism and communal encapsulation, indigenous Fijians were not in a situation to independently pursue large-scale investment as individuals; secondly, it was assumed that communal shares represented the common interest of the *vanua* and thus had to be sustained at all cost. Thus communal shares became symbolic of two contradictory tendencies. On the one hand was the response to the modernisation imperative and on the other was the need to maintain communal socio-political cohesion.

Two proposals were later made to FHL as a way of expanding its investment: the first was that Fijian Holdings should buy majority shares in two companies, Fiji Industries Limited and Standard Concrete Industries Limited (both owned by Basic Industries Limited, a foreign company); the second option was that shares should be bought from the Carlton Brewery (Fiji) Limited.[3] The second option suggested that the state-subsidised Fiji Development Bank (FDB), which already had the capital, should act as a middle dealer by buying the shares, and then later sell them to FHL. This would solve the problem of raising initial capital and also ensure a smooth transition of equity sales.

The Great Council of Chiefs agreed to the proposals, and as a way forward, an action plan was drawn up by the FHL board to increase share capital from the Provincial Councils, the Fijian Affairs Board and the Native Land Trust Board to finance the purchase of shares from Basic Industries and Carlton Brewery.[4]

Fijian Holdings rapidly increased its investment and growth within a few years. In fact in 1985, a year after its inception, it was already paying dividends to shareholders. By 1992, profit after tax had reached FJ$2,752,554, after a downturn in 1987 and 1988 because of the effects of the military coup on the economy. The increase in investment and return was reflected in the rate

---

2   "A Class" shares are high dividend investments compared to low dividend "B Class" shares.
3   Carlton Brewery is an Australian multinational which brews Fiji Bitter (the only beer brewed in Fiji), Carlton Beer and Fosters Beer.
4   It was proposed that FJ$2 million was to be raised to buy shares in Basic Industries and FJ$4 million for Carlton Brewery, to top up the FJ$1million already collected, to make a total of FJ$5 million. A number of Provinces were not happy with the change in plan from investment in Burns Philip to investment in Basic Industries and Carlton Brewery, because they were not informed beforehand. The Board of Fijian Holdings considered the Burns Philip investment a risk because of its declining operations in Fiji, having sold most of its assets to W.R. Carpenters. The Methodist Church of Fiji, the largest and most politically powerful religious organisation objected to the Carlton Brewery shares, because of their association with liquor, drunkenness, crime and other forms of anti-social behaviour.

of dividends paid. As Table 5.2 shows, since 1985 the dividend increased substantially, except during the 1987 and 1988 period due to the disruption caused by the military coup.

Table 5.2 Fijian Holdings dividends paid, 1985-1992

Year	Dividend Rate (%)	Total Amount Paid (FJ$)
1985	10	119,500
1986	10	123,440
1987	10	123,440
1988	5	62,304
1989	10	124,609
1990/91	20	253,813
1992 (interim)	10	173,645
1992 (partly)	10	464,793
Total		**1,445,644**

Source: Fijian Holdings Limited 1993: 4.

Fijian Holding's communal investment strategy posed two fundamental problems: first, it was difficult to see how an indigenous Fijian bourgeois class could develop (as in Malaysia) if investment was restricted to communal institutions; second, there was the question of how redistribution of benefits to the people could take place. There was increasing pressure from leading indigenous Fijian bureaucrats and professionals not to restrict shares to the Fijian Administration institutions, and to open up shares to individuals. As a response to this pressure, the status of the company changed in 1992 from 'public' to 'private', to allow for private investment, either on an individual or group basis.

It was hoped the change would "greatly increase the number of shareholders and ... cater for individual Fijian investors, Fijian-owned companies and *tikina* councils",[5] so that the "benefits of Fijian Holdings' shareholdings are spread as widely as possible" (Fijian Holdings Limited 1993: 7-8). The ceiling for individual shares was put at FJ$10,000 and to ensure that only indigenous Fijians were to buy shares individual shareholders were confined to those registered in the *Vola ni Kawa Bula*, the kinship register, which officially defined a "Fijian". So while the restriction which guaranteed monopoly by communal investment was lifted, a further restriction, based on the ethnic background of individual investors, was imposed. This restriction was a direct application of the 1990 Constitution provision on pro-indigenous affirmative action and the controversial definition of the ethnic category, "Fijian".

---

5   A *tikina* is a district, which usually consists of several villages. Several *tikina* make up a *yasana* (province).

Moreover, the prescribed ceiling of FJ$10,000 was too low to yield a reasonably high return, especially for the aspiring indigenous Fijian entrepreneurs. The rules were changed overnight by the FHL board, who themselves had an interest in individual shares. We will deal with the acquisition of individual and associated problem shares later, but at this stage we need to examine the commercial operation of FHL and some of its dilemmas.

The dramatic expansion and consolidation of FHL in the 1990–1994 period was a result of the FJ$20 million interest-free loan provided by the post-coup government in 1989, under the *Nine Points Plan* affirmative action initiative. Paid-up capital grew from FJ$1.2 million in 1985 to FJ$27.5 million in 1994. The total assets rose from FJ$1.3 million in 1985 to FJ$36.3 million in 1994. The net value of assets increased from FJ$170,248 in 1985 to FJ$3.2 million in 1994. FHL dividend paid to shareholders was at 20% for "A Shares" and 5% for "B Shares". The "B Shares" were held in trust and invested for indigenous Fijians by the FAB from the FJ$20 million provided by the government as mentioned above. The dividend paid on these shares was to accumulate in a sinking fund to cater for the repayment of the FJ$20 million loan by the FAB to the government. It was anticipated that over time these shares would be sold to indigenous Fijian entrepreneurs.

By 1994, as Table 5.3 shows, FHL had an interest in nine major companies in Fiji.

Table 5.3 Details of Fijian Holdings Limited's investment portfolio, as at 30 June 1994

Company	No. of Shares	Shareholding (%)	Amount (FJD$)
Basic Industries Ltd:			
• Original	1,232,000	41	1,242,486
• Ex Pioneer	1,500,000	50	2,270,132
• Ex FDB	268,000	9	309,741
• Ex BP (FIL Shares)	1,050,000		1,050,000
• Hume Industries (Ex CSR)	2,000,000		2,000,000
Fiji Sugar Corporation (Ex Fiji Government)	4,732,100	13.2	2,860,557
Fijian Property Trust (Ex. FDB)	2,600,000	89.7	2,613,000
Carlton Brewery (Fiji) Ltd (Ex. FDB)	600,000	30.0	3,587,850
Unit Trust of Fiji	500,000	8.9	700,000
Motibhai & Company Ltd	2,000,000	100 (P)	2,007,125
Merchant Bank of Fiji Ltd (Ex. FDB)	1,428,500	50.0	1,435,643
Carpenters Properties Ltd (Ex. FDB)	3,000,001 2,000,000	30 20	3,021,657 2,010,000
Goodman Fielder Watties	2,000,000	100 (P)	2,003,757
Total			**27,111,948**

Source: Fijian Holdings Limited 1995; Fijian Holdings Limited 1996.

Table 5.4 shows the percentage of shares, profits and type of investment of FHL. The annual profitability of FHL was the impetus for aggressive expansion of its acquisition and investment diversification.

Table 5.4 Fijian Holdings investments, 1995

Company	Shares %	Profit (F$)	Types of Investment
Basic Industries Ltd	100	2.2 million	Manufacturing
Fijian Property Trust Ltd	89.7	not available	Real Estate
Carpenters Property Ltd	50.01	.808 million	Real Estate
Merchant Bank of Fiji	50	.870 million	Commercial, Personal Loans
Carlton Brewery Fiji Ltd	30.1	2.45 million	Beer Production
Goodman Fielder (Fiji) Ltd	100*	not available	Consumer Goods
Motibhai & Company Ltd	100*	3.91 million	Diverse Commercial interests
Fiji Sugar Corporation	12.8	12.3 million	Sugar Production
Unit Trust of Fiji	8.9	1.09 million	Capital Investment

* For Goodman Fielder, 100% is for the preference shares, and 10% for the ordinary shares. For Motibhai, 100% is for the preference shares.

Source: Fijian Holdings Limited 1995.

The pattern of FHL investment shown in Tables 5.3 and 5.4 indicated four tendencies. Firstly, in line with the *Ten Year Plan* for greater indigenous control of the corporate sector, FHL had progressively expanded into buying whole companies and majority equity. This was indicative of the degree of confidence it had generated with the financial and political support of the government and leading private sector businesses.

Secondly, faced with the reality of the market, FHL had to temporarily abandon its communal character and purchase shares from non-indigenous Fijian companies such as Motibhai Group, an Indo-Fijian company which had close links with the Mara regime. The rest were expatriate companies, except for the Unit Trust of Fiji and Fiji Sugar Corporation (FSC), which were public companies.

Thirdly, funding for the FHL shares came from two major sources, government and FDB. FDB itself was a para-statal institution, subsidised by the government, and headed by Laisenia Qarase, the author of the *Ten Year Plan*. Most of the shares, as shown in Table 5.4, were originally secured by the FDB and then sold later to FHL. The government contribution of FJ$20 million, as already stated, was held in trust by the FAB for future distribution. The direct link between the state and the communal schema was evident here. The link was not only political and ideological but also financial. However, on the one hand FHL had to rely on political patronage and financial support from the state, and on the other it relied on the private sector for investment. We have to remember that the state, at this time, was fundamentally an ethnocratic one, under the 1990 Constitution.

Fourthly, while the long-term beneficiaries of the FHL were supposedly the shareholders (communal and individual), the most immediate beneficiaries were the corporations in which FLH invested. FHL provided the badly needed capital to sustain some of those companies at a time when economic contraction had affected local investment. In other words, affirmative action was directly subsidising the operation of local and foreign companies such as Motibhai Group of Fiji and Carlton Brewery of Australia. Furthermore, some of these companies, such as Carlton Brewery, Basic Industries and Goodman Fielder, were monopolies which would be able to enjoy their dominance in the market through links with the indigenous Fijian elites and direct state patronage.[6]

Another issue of concern was the distribution of benefits from FHL shares. Again, here, we need to disaggregate between two levels of analysis: ideological discourse and empirical contextualisation. The first refers to the political justification for Fijian Holdings' operations, as reflected in Fijian Holdings' philosophy: "As a Fijian institution we have a responsibility for promoting and protecting the *commercial interests of the Fijian community* [my emphasis] and helping to secure its rightful place in the economic affairs of the nation" (Fijian Holdings Limited 1996: 1). The second level refers to the actual flow of economic benefits and socio-political implications of FHL's shareholdings. An empirical examination of the operations of Fijian Holdings is crucial in this regard.

Who 'controlled' Fijian Holdings Limited?

FHL was set up under the communal jurisdiction of the Great Council of Chiefs, with the direct involvement of the government. But how was this political mandate translated into commercial shares? Table 5.5 shows that in 1992 the total number of shares for the "A" category was 4,647,934, while the total for the "B" category was 20,000,000; with a combined total of 24,647,934 shares. Of this total, communal shares (which included shares held by NLTB, FAB, Provincial Councils and *Tikina* Councils) comprised 22,521,934 shares or 91% of the total of FHL shares. On the other hand, the individual shares (this included family and individual group shares) comprised 2,126,000 or 9% of the total FHL shares.

---

6   For some time Fijian Holdings executives have been trying to reverse some of the government's deregulation policies such as competition in cement and concrete manufacturing which has been monopolised by Basic Industries.

Table 5.5 Shareholding for Fijian Holdings Limited

Shareholders	A Class Shares	% A	B Class Shares	% B	Communal	Individual
Native Land Trust Board	500,000	10.75	-	-	x	
Fijian Affairs Board	100,000	2.1	20,000,000	100	x	
Ba Provincial Council	50,100	1.07	-	-	x	
Lomaiviti Provincial Council	55,100	1.18	-	-	x	
Nadroga Provincial Council	50,100	1.07	-	-	x	
Macuata Provincial Council	116,612	2.5	-	-	x	
Rewa Provincial Council	50,100	1.07	-	-	x	
Lau Provincial Council	50,100	1.07	-	-	x	
Cakaudrove Provincial Council	120,000	2.58	-	-	x	
Bua Provincial Council	50,100	1.07	-	-	x	
Koula Trust	40,000	0.86	-	-		x
Kadavu Development Company	50,100	1.07	-	-	x	
Naitasiri Province Co-op Ass Ltd	31,327	0.67	-	-	x	
Ra Provincial Council	50,100	1.07	-	-	x	
Tailevu Provincial Council	19,951	0.42	-	-	x	
Serua Provincial Council	10,100	0.21	-	-	x	
Namosi Provincial Council	10,660	0.22	-	-	x	
Cicia Plantation Co-op	400,000	8.6	-	-	x	
Nabukebuke Nailili Co Ltd	2,000	0.04	-	-	x	
5X Investment Ltd	100,000	2.1	-	-		x
KB Investments Ltd	100,000	2.1	-	-		x
Kubuna Holdings Ltd	5,000	0.1	-	-	x	
Kesaia Palu Vatu	1,000	0.02	-	-		x
Markin Investments Ltd	100,000	2.1	-	-		x
AWR Investments Ltd	10,000	0.21	-	-		x
Mavana Investments	200,000	4.3	-	-	x	
Bakani Investments	150,000	3.2	-	-		x
Q-Ten Investments	200,000	4.3	-	-		x
Kingfisher Enterprises Ltd	100,000	2.1	-	-		x
Vensalisi Investments Ltd	80,000	1.72	-	-		x
Stiks Investments Ltd	150,000	3.2	-	-		x
Duavata Holdings Ltd	150,000	3.2	-	-		x
Ratu Mara Education Trust Fund	300,000	6.4	-	-	x	
Vunikoro Investment Ltd	50,000	1.07	-	-	x	
Lana Investments Ltd	95,000	2.04	-	-		x
Nabuabua Holdings Ltd	100,000	2.1	-	-		x
Mualevu Tikina Holdings Ltd	100,000	2.1	-	-	x	
KYJ Investments Ltd	100,000	2.1	-	-		x
Baravi and Associates Ltd	100,000	2.1	-	-		x
M.B Investments Ltd	100,000	2.1	-	-		x
Kepa Investments Ltd	100,000	2.1	-	-	x	
Vunidogo Investments Ltd	100,000	2.1	-	-		x
Rukuruku Investments Ltd	50,484	1.08	-	-	x	
Taoi Investments Ltd	200,000	4.3	-	-		x
Rafire Investments Ltd	100,000	2.1	-	-		x
Rabuli Investment Ltd	50,000	1.07	-	-		x
Total	4,647,934	100	20,000,000	100	25	21

Source: Fijian Holdings Limited 1992.

Although there was a dominance of communal shares over individual shares, the value of the individual shares was far superior if one were to divide the communal provincial shares by the population of the provinces. The reality about the communal shares was that they did very little to enhance wealth distribution because not only was the return minimal, but also they were locked up in the communal institutions and very little, if any, value trickled down to the ordinary people.

Fijian Holdings and communal capitalism

Communal investment was one of the cornerstones of communal capitalism. Indeed, we have seen how communal capitalism became the dominant mode of investment in FHL (totalling 91% of total FHL shares). Communal investment within FHL occurred at various levels of communal organisation: the NLTB and FAB, provincial and *tikina* levels. Although under commercial law these bodies were legal entities in their own right, politically they were regarded as *dau ni veiqaravi* (servants) of the *vanua* and the Great Council of Chiefs. We now examine each of the main communal investors.

Native Land Trust Board (NLTB)

I wish to do three things here. First, to briefly explain the role and activities of the NLTB; second, to examine some of the contradictions it encountered as a communal institution attempting to be involved in commercial ventures; and third, to examine the implications of NLTB shares in FHL in the light of the broader socio-political context.

The biggest communal shareholder under the "A" Class shares (10.75%), NLTB was founded in 1940 by Sukuna, who described it "as a monument of trust in British rule, of confidence in its honesty and hopes for the future" (Native Land Trust Board 1975: 2). Its role was to administer indigenous Fijian land. The NLTB was to "provide the best services with the effective use of Native Land and other resources at our disposal to meet the expectations of our landowners, tenants, Government and other customers" (Native Land Trust Board 1995: 8). By 2000 the NLTB administered about 83% of the country's land, and of this 420,000 hectares are leased out to 24,700 tenants in agriculture, commerce, industry, tourism, and public and civil projects. From 1990 to 1994, through the NLTB indigenous Fijian landowners received about FJ$80.7 million worth of rentals, jobs, dividends, royalties and commercial ventures linked to land development.[7]

The NLTB's other role was to hold in trust and invest some funds for landowners. For instance, by 1987 FJ$1,837,907 worth of term deposits had been made for unclaimed funds at an interest rate ranging from 4.25% to 16.0%. In addition, the NLTB also administered a portfolio of shares in companies as trustees for landowners (Native Land Trust Board 1990). The respective landowning *mataqali* gave the NLTB the authority to reinvest royalties from leases or timber cutting concessions over native land. The companies for which the NLTB held shares in trust for landowners to December 1987 consisted of two timber companies and nine tourist development companies. The NLTB held a total of 464,444 shares in these various companies.

However, the NLTB's main dilemma has been the contradiction between its communal role as guardian of native land on one hand, and how it had used this role to enter into investment. The President of the NLTB was the Head of State, and the Chairman was the Minister for Fijian Affairs. Board members were carefully selected from the chiefly hierarchy and indigenous Fijian bureaucratic elite. Thus the heavily political and communalistic constitution of the board readily undermined some of its bureaucratic and commercial responsibilities.

To illustrate the above, in 1982 a grant of FJ$1,766,000, disbursed over three years, was received from the Australian government "to enable landowning units to participate in the development of the indigenous timber industry" (Native Land Trust Board 1990: 16). But the fund was diverted to financing a company, Kubuna/Fiji Forest Industry (FFI), and was used to purchase 7,000 redeemable preference shares of 50c each issued at a premium of FJ$49.50 each with a preferred dividend rate of 12.5% per annum (*The Review*, May 1997). The Kubuna/FFI Company had three components: the Kubuna Company, FFI and Westralian Forests Industries Ltd. The Kubuna Company belonged to the four provinces that made up the traditional Kubuna Confederacy.[8] The paramount

---

7   The mostly Indo-Fijian cane farmers' leases on indigenous Fijian-owned land began to expire in 1997. The leases, 30,000 in all, were administered by the NLTB. The original ten-year leases were issued under a 1967 ordinance and amended in 1977 to fall under the Agricultural and Landlord Tenants Act (ALTA). Leases were for 10 years, with a right to two 10-year extensions. As we noted earlier, 25% of lease money from native land was allocated to the NLTB for "administrative" purposes and the rest was distributed to landowners on the basis of their chiefly status and standing in the social hierarchy. This, together with the various investment and landowners' trust assets contributed to the NLTB's income, thus providing a source of its capital for Fijian Holdings shares.

8   In the traditional context there are three main confederacies (*matanitu*) in Fiji: Kubuna, Tovata and Burebasaga. They have their roots in the pre-colonial attempts to form centralised governments in Fiji by early European settlers and chiefs. A number of Provinces make up a Confederacy. These are based on traditional alliances between tribal polities. Today they still exist as a means of ceremonial and traditional mobilisation. In a way, the political loyalty of indigenous Fijians is diverse: they have loyalty to various levels of tribal

chief of the Kubuna Confederacy was Ratu Sir George Cakobau, former Governor General of Fiji and by virtue of that also President of the NLTB.[9] In charge of the financial operations of the company was the General Manager of the NLTB, Josevata Kamikamica, a member of the Kubuna Confederacy and thus subject of Ratu Sir George Cakobau. The FFI was a joint venture between CBM Holdings and Westralian Forest Industries, an Australian company, which provided the management and technical skills. CBM, owned by landowners of the three provinces of Cakaudrove, Bua and Macuata, was under the trusteeship of Ratu Sir Penaia Ganilau, the paramount chief of the three provinces, and also former President of Fiji, and successor to Ratu Sir George Cakobau, as Fiji's Governor General and President of the NLTB. Again, in 1989 a government-guaranteed loan was made from the European Investment Bank for purchase of FJ$1,575,986 worth of shares in FFI which The NLTB had almost identical arrangements with two other logging companies, the Pacific Lumber Company and Timbers (Fiji) Ltd. Public funds were diverted to fund their operations.[10] The 'latent beneficiaries', so to speak, were politically powerful individuals (both in the modern and traditional sense) who were able to exercise their authority in ways that would serve their communal or personal interests.

In another case, the NLTB purchased FJ$1,863,343 worth of shares from the Native Land Development Corporation (NLDC), an entity set up by the NLTB itself to develop native land for commercial purposes as part of the Alliance Party's affirmative action policy. Two loans were made to finance the operation of the NLDC: a loan worth 900,000 European Units of account from the European Economic Community (EEC) and a loan of FJ$1,380,000 from the Fiji government. The NLDC, which was headed by the Governor General's nephew, defaulted on its principal and interest payment for both loans, accumulating a total of FJ$1,656,330 in bad debt by 1989 (Native Land Trust Board1990: 17). In 1987, the NLDC was dissolved because of investment losses.

---

categories, loyalty to the Confederacy and loyalty to the state. The ownership of the collectively-owned ethnic Fijian companies theoretically belong to the "people" in the community, but the real power lies in the chief, since he "owns" the land and the "people". Chiefs are mostly made directors, shareholders, managers etc. "in the name of the people". Primordial servitude has been re-adapted to modern commercial exploitation.

9   As Governor General, he was Representative of the British Crown, Head of State and Chairman of the Native Land Trust Board. George Cakobau was the great great grandson of Seru Cakobau who along with other chiefs, ceded Fiji to Britain.

10   What enabled the NLTB to make arbitrary decisions in relation to indigenous Fijian land was the power it was vested with to grant logging licences and concessions on all Native Land under the Native Land Trust Act, which says that "The control of all Native Land shall be vested in the Board (NLTB) and all such land shall be administered by the board for the benefit of the Fijian owners" (Native Land Trust Act, Chapter 134). Granting of a logging licence by the NLTB does not require the consent of the members of the landowning unit, but if necessary the NLTB will carry out consultation. A concession is also a licence but is usually granted over a large area, usually to a major logging company, and over land owned by many owning units, and for a longer period than a standard licence. Most of the logging licences involving ethnic Fijian loggers were for joint-ventures with foreign companies.

The point I wish to raise here regarding the two cases above is that, because of the convergence of state power (through the Head of State, himself a high chief) and communalism in the operation of the NLTB, the distinction between state interest and communal interest became blurred. In fact state interest became subsumed under communal interest. Thus it was easy to channel and 'launder' money from bilateral and multi-lateral aid, meant for national purposes, into communal projects. The high chiefs who also had uncontested state power became agencies of communalisation through the NLTB. It was really this communal role which justified NLTB's investment in FHL.

NLTB's FHL investment was questionable on two grounds: first, NLTB's poor record in commercial ventures; and second, NLTB's investment of FJ$500,000 on behalf of landowners denied landowners the opportunity to be involved in direct investment on their own. Purely on commercial grounds, NLTB's record as a commercial entity has been disastrous. At the end of 1992, NLTB had an overdraft of FJ$14.8 million, increasing to FJ$16.1 million in 1993, and with FJ$4.4 million worth of cheques still pending presentation to the bank (*TheReview*, June 1997: 19). Losses had been recorded since 1986, and the accounts had not been audited since 1991. The unaudited figures showed an operating deficit of FJ$1.8 million in 1990, FJ$1.3 million in 1991 and FJ$1.6 million in 1992. By 1997, the NLTB was on the verge of bankruptcy, despite a substantial government annual subsidy of FJ$1 million and the 25% of the rent it received for collecting and distribution of lease monies. A major restructuring in 1998 to make it more commercially viable and salvage its operation saw almost half the workforce made redundant (*Daily Post*, 10 November 1998).

NLTB's commercial endeavours have been disastrous due to its inability to systematically and objectively reconcile commercial logic and the communal principles on which it was based. Its investment in FHL had two worrying implications. First, its paternalistic attitude in holding in trust landowner's funds for FHL investment would do little to enhance the entrepreneurial potential of landowners, who would do better as individual FHL shareholders. Thus, instead of encouraging entrepreneurship, NLTB's investment in FHL merely reinforced the pattern of economic dependence and paternalism that has been central to the communal schema since the colonial epoch. Second, the commission which NLTB generated from its FHL investment was ploughed back into sustaining the NLTB bureaucracy. Thus it is difficult to see how NLTB investment could in any way contribute to indigenous commercial "advancement".

Fijian Affairs Board (FAB)

The FAB was the largest shareholder in FHL with 100,000 "A" class shares (2.1%) and 20 million "B" class shares (100%). FJ$20 million was provided by the government under the *Nine Points Plan* to be invested in FHL and held in trust for indigenous Fijians. It was envisaged that the amount of shares would soon be dispersed and sold to other indigenous Fijian shareholders over time. This would depend on how much return the FAB's investment in FHL generated. As a low-interest investment portfolio, the "B" class shares were government guaranteed and the money borrowed to purchase them had to be repaid within 20 years without interest.

The FAB had a much broader role than did the NLTB. As the secretariat of the Fijian Administration, it was directly responsible to the Great Council of Chiefs. Although the FAB under the old structure was directly linked to the central state structure, the 1998 restructuring along the lines of the Hays Report meant that the FAB became independent of the state bureaucracy. This was a requirement of the *Nine Points Plan* and *Ten Year Plan* to ensure that, without interference by the state bureaucracy, especially with the expectation of a new multi-racial coalition under the new consociationalist arrangement, the FAB would be able to independently consolidate its program for indigenous advancement. Politically, this reform constituted a retrogressive step, reminiscent of the 1940s reform by Sukuna to consolidate communal hegemony.

In holding the FJ$20 million under trust, FAB was in fact acting as a trust agency for the government and for indigenous Fijians. Unlike in Malaysia, where *Bumiputera* trust agencies such as the National Equity Corporation (PNB) were fully-fledged financial institutions, FAB was not. As a purely communal institution serving the bureaucracy of the Fijian Administration, and without any experience or expertise in commercial matters, it would be difficult for the FAB to actualise its ideological mandate to serve the paramountcy of Fijian interest in ways that would be consistent with the requirements of modern commerce.

Provincial shares

As we have seen earlier, the total number of shares for the 14 provinces was 663,800 or 14% of the "A" Class shares. The provincial shares differed from both the NLTB and FAB shares because investment capital was collected directly from people through *soli vakavanua* (communal collection) at the various levels of communal mobilisation of communal capitalism.

The provinces, which were largely rural and whose population, in the main, lived a subsistence existence, were organised and administered under the Fijian Administration, through a mixture of state bureaucracy and communal socio-political arrangement. Capital for investment was generated through appeals to a communal sense of obligation to the chief and *vanua*. Provincial collection was through provincial taxation, which was meant entirely to sustain the provincial bureaucracy, and *soqo ni vanua* ("traditional" festivals), where there was a collective effort to mobilise members of a province both within and outside the village (those in urban areas and those who lived in other provinces). Some of the money collected through the latter was usually for "investment." Most *soqo ni vanua* were held in urban areas, especially Suva, because they would generate more money than if they were held in the village. These fund-raising festivals would be called by names which would project both a communal and 'modern' identity. Some examples were the *Bulou ni Ceva* (Lady of the South) for Kadavu Province, *Adi Tagimaucia* (Princess Tagimaucia, the name of a flower) for Cakaudrove Province and *Adi Natuicake* (Princess of the East) for Lau Province.[11]

Fund-raising in the *soqo ni vanua* would involve competition between various *tikina* or districts. Collection thus became a means of achieving communal honour and prestige. Part of the festivities would be ceremonial presentations as a means of showing communal solidarity with other *tikina,* with emphasis on kinship links. The *tikinas* collected money from the *koros*, which in turn collected money from the various *mataqalis* or *tokatokas*. The rank and file of the communal structure was actively involved in this process. Thus the *soqo ni vanua* had the purpose not only of collecting capital, but also, at a broader sociological level, to reaffirm communal cohesion and identity. The latter was important here because it had become a paramount priority, which in many cases undermined the commercial significance of the fund-raising. Money collected was no longer perceived purely in terms of monetary value but also in terms of *noda vei nanumi vakaveiwekani* (concern for each other as kinsfolk). The money collected was passed on to the Provincial Council bureaucrats who then worked out the investment technicalities with the relevant financial institutions and authorities on behalf of the people of the provinces.

Provincial investment had two fundamentally flawed assumptions. The first was the belief that the interest of the *vanua* or community directly translated into the interests of the individuals (*tamata yadudua*). Communal interest was symbolised in the chiefly authority. Thus, to provide generously to the community coffers was an expression of selflessness and communal solidarity. On the other hand, there was veiled psychological coercion: not being generous (*dau solisoli*) to communal *soli* (fund-raising) was considered "un-chiefly" (*tawa vakaturaga*) and "un-Fijian" (*tawa vakaitaukei*). At worst, there was the veiled threat of being punished by the supernatural *mana* of the *vanua* and *turaga* (chiefs) through disease or mishap. Thus, this ideological mystification, which underscored communal hegemony, made it easy for chiefs, bureaucrats and politicians to extract capital from indigenous Fijian peasants and urban workers.

---

11 The feminine gender names are because, as part of the fund-raising, there would also be a beauty queen competition to provide a festive mood.

The second assumption was similar to the neo-classical notion of the "trickle-down" effect of economic distribution, where it was assumed that the benefits of development would, in time, trickle down to the bottom from the top. In the context of provincial investment, villagers were told that the investment was for the *vanua* and thus for "their benefit". The investment details were not properly explained to the people at the grassroots level.[12] But analysis of the actual provincial investment figures in FHL throws into doubt the existence of "benefits" for villagers (Ratuva 2000).

The total number of shares held by the 14 provinces (with a total ethnic Fijian population of 394,999) was 663,800 in 1992, amounting to an average of 50,000 per province. That meant that the number of provincial shares per indigenous Fijian individual was only 1.68. Even if we calculated the number of shares in relation to the rural indigenous Fijian population, which was around 233,175, then the shares per head would amount to 2.84. Needless to say, an average of 2.84 shares (worth about FJ$1 each) was hardly sufficient to advance indigenous Fijian business. While large amounts of money have been extracted from the indigenous Fijian community for provincial investment, hardly any has trickled down in the form of improvement in the commercial sector in the provinces.

Fijian Holdings and private investment

Private investment in FHL started in September 1992, when FHL changed its status from being a public to being a private company. The total number of shares held by private investors for the 30 companies in 1992 was 2,126,000 or 9% of total FHL shares, and that figure has since grown.

The fundamental problem with private shares was that ownership was concentrated within a small group of influential state bureaucrats and professionals with established links with the state bureaucracy and banking fraternity. Sale of the private shares was opened without proper publicity and some individuals concerned were able to use inside information to form companies and snap up the limited individual shares available (*The Fiji Times*, 23 December 1992).

As evidence of the above, the Deputy General Manager of the National Bank of Fiji secured a loan of FJ$107,000, by mortgage, on 10 March 1992,

---

12 One of the strategies used previously in the provincial money collections was that people were told that money collected by individuals was to constitute their individual shares. Once individuals had collected the money, they were told that it would be culturally and legally proper that their shares were to be registered under their respective chiefs' names. Officially the shares belonged to the chiefs, who legally had the right to sell those shares and acquire new equities. This was indeed the case in respect of the Kadavu Provincial Council in 1993, where district chiefs became the legal trustees of the individual shares. In other words individual cash collections were transferred to legal ownership by the chiefs.

to buy Fijian Holdings shares for FJ$100,000. The company, KB Investments (Registration Number 9502), registered on 6 December 1991, provided two shares of FJ$1.00 each, while the National Bank of Fiji provided the rest. KB Investments received the bank loan only three months after it was set up. KB Investments, together with four individuals, also formed a company called the 5X Investments Limited, which secured a loan of FJ$75,000 from the National Bank of Fiji, to buy FJ$100,000 worth of Fijian Holdings shares. 5X Investments, with registration number 9515, was registered on 13 December 1991, seven days after the registration of KB Investments, and secured its bank loan on 27 January 1992, less than two months after it was registered. Owners of 5X Limited and KB Limited paid up only FJ$1.00 shares each. Another company, BIL, owned by the relatives of KB's director, secured a loan of FJ$120,000 from the FDB on 24 March (Korovulavula 1994).

In another case, Vensalisi Investment Limited (owned by the then Director of Public Prosecution and later Solicitor General, High Court Judge and diplomat, and also a board member of FHL) secured a loan of FJ$64,000 by debenture from the FDB to buy FJ$80,000 worth of shares from Fijian Holdings. This was just three months after the registration of the company (Registered Number 9613) on 6 February 1992. The FDB also provided Q-Ten Investments Ltd., a company owned by its own Managing Director, Laisenia Qarase (who was, we may recall, author of the *Ten Year Plan*), with two separate loans: one for FJ$112,400 on 2 August 1990, and the other for FJ$353,217.86 on 22 May 1992, using the same property as mortgage.[13] Q-Ten Investments Limited used some of the money to buy FJ$200,000 worth of shares from the FHL (Korovulavula 1994).

Qarase also used his privileged position to secure a loan of FJ$150,000 from the FDB for Mavana Investments Limited, a *tikina* company of which he was director and a shareholder. The loan was secured on 24 June 1992. This was a few days before the Minister for Foreign Affairs, Filipe Bole (a traditional kinsman of Qarase), received a loan of FJ$81,000 from the FDB on 2 July 1992 for Mualevu Tikina Holdings, a *tikina* company for which he was director and shareholder. Eight days later, the former Minister of Justice, Qoriniasi Bale, secured a loan of FJ$81,000 from the FDB for his Nabuabua Holdings. Mr Bale was later deregistered as a lawyer for defrauding clients of thousands of dollars.

Laisenia Qarase was a board member of FHL, and was also a board member and chairman of more than one dozen government and statutory bodies. He was also the chief business and financial advisor to the FAB and Great Council of Chiefs and was one of the brains behind the organisation, operation and logistics of FHL. A close associate of Laisenia Qarase, and Chief Executive of FHL, Sitiveni Weleilakeba, also secured a loan of FJ$120,000 from the FDB on 17 March 1992

---

13   The Certificate of title number for the property is C.T.14743.

to buy FHL shares for FJ$150,000 (Office of Registrar of Companies 1997). Qarase also approved an FDB loan for his brother to purchase one of Qarase's properties, originally purchased via an FDB mortgage (*Fiji Times*, 23 December 1992).

While the Great Council of Chiefs had tried to limit FHL investors to those indigenous Fijians registered in the *Vola ni Kawa Bula*, in a number of cases some non-indigenous Fijians, linked to the power elites, were also shareholders. Three such companies, Kingfisher Holdings Limited (with FJ$100,000 worth of shares in FHL), Nabuabua Holdings Limited (FJ$100,000) and Taoi Investments Limited (FJ$200,000) had, at a certain time, shareholders who were non-indigenous Fijians (Fijian Holdings Limited 1992). Taoi Investments Limited secured FJ$155,598.98 from the FDB on 25 April 1991, and bought FHL shares worth FJ$200,000 (Office of Registrar of Companies 1997). The General Manager of the Fiji Pine Commission and former Conservator of Forests registered a family company called KJY Investments Limited (Registered Number 9748) on 24 April 1992, which borrowed FJ$80,000 from the FDB to top up its FJ$100,000 share in e FHL (Korovulavula 1994).

The chairman of the FHL, Mr Lyle Cupit, was one of the most influential economic advisors to the Fiji government. He was a former Head of the Australian-based Carpenters Group of Companies, which for a long time controlled much of the wholesale, retailing, shipping, automobile, agriculture and real estate in Fiji (Fijian Holdings Limited 1995). He was also owner of one of Fiji's largest privately owned agricultural enterprises, Consolidated Agriculture Fiji Limited, and chairman of the government-owned Fiji Sugar Corporation and of the FHL-owned Basic Industries.[14]

There was a clear link between FHL investment and influential individuals in the state bureaucracy and the banking fraternity. The individuals concerned were able to take advantage of their intra-class privileged position to acquire loans from either the FDB or NBF for FHL investments. Thus, even within the context of communal capitalism, class factors (not in the traditional but in a bureaucratic and socio-economic sense) played a significant role in determining one's place in communal investment.

It appeared that affirmative action relating to FHL investment largely benefited individual indigenous Fijians who needed affirmative action the least. Most of those mentioned above were already well-to-do by virtue of their position in society. Affirmative action merely provided a further opportunity to accumulate

---

14   The Consolidated Agriculture Fiji Limited agricultural land in the Navua flats was destroyed by cyclone floods in January 1993. Amidst allegations of irregularities, corruption and political patronage, the flooded land was sold to the Fiji Government for FJD$7 million, for the purpose of "training" Fijian youths in farming skills (*Fiji Times*, July 4 1996). Most of the land, without the use of modern technology for clearing and development remained unused. In fact a lot of it was rendered unusable by the flood (*Daily Post*, May 2 1999).

more wealth. It was also clear that these individuals and the bank executives (FDB and NBF) from whom they acquired loans formed a close clique. The fact that loans were acquired within a very short time after the companies were registered and a few weeks or days before the FHL private shares became available raised suspicion about illegal "insider trading". It was clear that the direct beneficiaries of affirmative action (some of whom were mentioned earlier) were themselves members of the Fijian Initiative Group, which produced the *Nine Point Plan*. The generally suppressive political climate of the post-coup period discouraged any attempt at a political challenge to the above unethical practices.

Worse still, the indigenous Fijians at large were not informed of the decision to allow private investment. The "clique", as they came to be known, maintained virtual secrecy about the private shares sale and proceeded to acquire them themselves. In a Senate session, on 14 December 1992, Senator Korovulavula queried: "Shares to individuals were only opened to the public in September and I wonder how they (individuals) managed to secure those enormous loan facilities within such a short time" (*Fiji Times*, 15 December 1992).

In response to public criticism about conflict of interest, FDB General Manager Qarase said that all his loan applications were dealt with "strictly in accordance with the firm policies and practice of the bank" (*Fiji Times*, 21 December 1992). This did not lessen the barrage of criticism, well summed up by the *Fiji Times* editorial of 23 December 1992:

> But when you take a hard look at how Fijian Holdings Limited sold those shares last year to certain Fijian individuals and Fijian-owned companies, you must admit there's something not quite right about it… As it happened they (ordinary Fijians) lost out on a chance to boost their earning power because Fijian Holdings Limited didn't give them much of a chance to take up its offer to sell them shares…The money that got the company off the ground was public money. [T]he haste in which they were sought and finalised was rather unseeingly, involving mostly a small coterie of insiders, people working in financial institutions and bankers whose paths often cross in their line of work. (*Fiji Times*, 23 December 1992).

It was clear that it was rather difficult to see how investments by the NLTB, FAB and provinces could directly translate into the advancement of indigenous Fijian commercial life in material terms. By locking capital ownership within the communal institutions, under the mythological rhetoric of *vanua* ownership, there was very little chance of benefits "trickling down" to ordinary indigenous Fijians in ways that would improve their living standard. At the same time, as we have seen, the real individual beneficiaries of FHL private investment have been well-connected individuals using their knowledge of the financial market and official authority to monopolise the private shares. So the dilemma of FHL as the government's flagship affirmative action program was that it simply reproduced the communal system through communal capitalism and reinforced inequality by facilitating the dominant shares of a few indigenous elites. The situation was even more worrying when we consider the fact that in the *Ten Year Plan* there was an ambitious recommendation to "apply the FHL model in the forestry, fisheries, tourism and television sectors" (Qarase 1995: 2). In the next section we discuss other forms of economic affirmative action proposals prescribed by the *Nine Points Plan* and how they have been implemented.

However, as a result of the controversies, some of the individual investors sold their shares. Despite all these problems, FHL grew to become one of the biggest companies in Fiji, so that by 2008 it had assets totalling FJ$260.8 million and this increased by 13% to FJ$299.9 million in 2009 (Fijian Holdings Limited 2010). FHL investment ranges from 0.2% to 100% equity in companies, in a variety of areas.

After the coup in 2006 and the formation of the Fiji Independent Commission Against Corruption (FICAC), investigation into the affairs of Fijian Holdings was launched and Qarase was charged, convicted and jailed for 12 months for corruption on 13 August 2012.

Financial market investment

Both the *Nine Points Plan* and the *Ten Year Plan* were concerned with the lack of indigenous Fijian activity in the area of financial trading. As a result of a concerted drive towards financial market investment, there was increased investment in the Unit Trust of Fiji (UTF).

Set up by the Government in 1976, the UTF in the post-coup period was increasingly dominated by indigenous Fijian investors. The UTF accumulated capital through selling units and equity received was invested in shares, mortgages and government securities, amongst others. As shown in Table 5.6, from about 6 million units in 1992, UTF grew to about 7 million units in 1994. Based on these figures, the unit-holdings for indigenous Fijians represented 38.0% of the total unit holdings in 1992 and increased to 40% in 1994. This was a dramatic increase from 15% in 1986, before the coup. However, if we exclude the unit-holdings for the government and the Fiji National Provident Fund, a public institution, then indigenous Fijian unit holdings represent 60.5% of the total shareholding as at 30 September 1994.

Table 5.6 Unit Trust of Fiji: Distribution of unit holders

Unit Holders	1992	1993	1994
Govt. of Fiji	209,827	228,991	248,038
FNPF	2,059,135	2,059,135	2,059,135
Sugar Cane Growers	384,616	384,616	384,616
Fijian Dev. Fund Board	193,450	210,220	226,979
UTOF Ltd	74,869	74,869	74,869
Assns. & Groups	448,992	478,161	470,274
Individuals	1,179,465	1,045,254	1,627,991
Provincial Councils	298,614	348,475	252,599
Fijian Affairs Board	392,233	560,685	560,685
Fijian Holdings Ltd	500,000	500,000	500,000
National Mutual	301,449	327,581	360,319
Total	**6,024,650**	**6,217,987**	**6,765,505**

Source: Unit Trust of Fiji 1996.

Of the eleven major investment categories, four could be classified as indigenous Fijian communal investments. These were the Fijian Development Fund Board, Provincial Councils, FAB and FHL. Again, the pattern of communal capitalism clearly emerged. This becomes much clearer when we examine all the indigenous Fijian investments in detail as shown in Table 5.7.

Table 5.7 Unit holders by indigenous Fijians at 30 September 1994

Unit Holders	1992	1993	1994
Fijian Affairs Board	392,233	560,685	560,685
Fijian Dev. Fund Board	193,450	210,220	226,979
Fijian Holdings Ltd	500,000	500,000	500,000
Provincial Councils	181,423	308,627	227,415
Tikina Councils	114,933	193,860	83,296
Village	181,494	203,073	197,225
Individuals	746,675	573,369	907,087
Total	**2,310,208**	**2,549,834**	**2,702,687**

Source: Unit Trust of Fiji 1996.

Table 5.7 shows that unit-holdings for indigenous Fijians increased from FJ$2.3 million in 1992 (38% of total unit-holding) to FJ$2.7 million in 1994 (40% of total unit holding). In 1992, 70% of the total indigenous Fijian unit holders were communal institutions (consisting of FAB, Fijian Development Fund Board, Fijian Holdings, Provincial Councils, *Tikina* [district] Councils and Villages) and the rest were individual unit holders. In 1994, the figure was more or less the same. Again, the dominance of communal shareholding through the Fijian

Administration hierarchy indicated the extent to which the communal schema dominated the indigenous Fijian commercial ethos, even at the sophisticated level of financial trading.

So far we have looked at two cases of communal capitalism. Next we shall discuss two other cases of affirmative action (FDB and NBF), focusing, not so much on communal capitalism, although both banks were largely responsible for the controversial loans for private investments in FHL, but in commercial projects which, nevertheless, were linked to the broader processes of communalism and which seriously affected their operations. First we look at the FDB.

The Fiji Development Bank

We have seen that the FDB was responsible for funding major affirmative action projects such as FHL and rural commercial ventures. It was one of the first commercial institutions which the Fiji government mandated to assist "in the national endeavour to increase participation in the economy by indigenous Fijians and Rotumans" (Fiji Development Bank 1993: 7).[15] This was in line with FDB's mission statement to "provide finance, financial and advisory services to assist in the economic development of Fiji and in particular the development of agriculture, commerce and industry" (Fiji Development Bank 1997b: 7). Some of the agricultural schemes which the FDB helped to fund were the Seaqaqa Sugar Scheme and the Agricultural Co-operatives we saw earlier.

The two FDB projects which specifically targeted the promotion of indigenous Fijian commerce were the Fiji Commercial Loans to Fijian Scheme (CLFS) and the Fijian store scheme, referred to as Equity Investment Management Company Limited (EIMCOL).

---

15   The Fiji Development Bank itself was set up on 1 July 1967, under the 1967 Fiji Development Bank Act to take over the role of the Agricultural and Industrial Loans Board, set up in 1951. It is a semi-autonomous statutory body, with a board of directors appointed by the Minister of Finance. The bank is subsidised by the government, as it is seen as the government's most important development vehicle. The specific objectives of the bank, apart from allowing special provision for indigenous Fijian participation in commerce, are to attain a well-balanced lending program in Fiji's main economic sectors, to acquire equity in selected commercial enterprises for eventual purchase by individuals and institutional investors in Fiji, to plan and develop supervised lending schemes to promote rural prosperity, to diversify Fiji's financing facilities, and to utilise modern technology to enhance the efficiency and effectiveness of the bank's operation.

Commercial Loans to Fijian Scheme

When the Commercial Loans to Fijian Scheme (CLFS) started in 1974, there was criticism from the Indo-Fijian business community, which saw it as a form of discrimination. Further concessions were granted after the 1987 coup to facilitate easier access and repayment, as we discussed earlier.

The post-coup regime asked the FDB to review the soft loan policies for indigenous Fijians, and consequently the ceiling was raised from FJ$100,000 to FJ$200,000, and the interest subsidy was increased from 1% to 5.5% per annum. Furthermore, if the loan involved the purchase of fixed assets, the government would provide 10% of the cost. This change in policy led to a dramatic increase in lending to FJ$45.4 million in the period between 1989 and 1991, an average of FJ$3 million a month. By the end of 1991, 8,497 loans valued at FJ$71.8 million had been made. This was at the height of the "lending boom", when the economy was experiencing a healthy growth rate of 8%; but towards the middle of the 1990s the Fiji economy experienced a major slow down, which affected the FDB's operation. By 1996, the amount administered under this scheme was FJ$66.9 million. This made up 20.3% of the number and 27.2% of the value of the bank's total loan portfolio. Table 5.8 shows the total amount and number of commercial loans made by the FDB to indigenous Fijians under CLFS from the period 1990 to1995.

Table 5.8 Commercial Loans to Fijians Scheme (CLFS) approvals, amount (F$000) and number of loans (in bracket)

	1990/91	1991/92	1992/93	1993/94	1994/95
Portfolio					
Transportation	8,321 (597)	4,395 (463)	5,658 (439)	3,572 (391)	2,975 (285)
Real Estate	8,004 (112)	5,186 (52)	3,777 (44)	10,625 (70)	14,810 (64)
Invest/Finance	0 (0)	2,200 (21)	2,710 (52)	524 (11)	1,832 (116)
Retail/Wholesale	0 (0)	0 (0)	2,463 (328)	1,898 (352)	1,754 (222)
Commercial	2,959 (725)	3,542 (419)	744 (59)	319 (33)	859 (34)
Timber	510 (16)	866 (15)	627 (11)	295 (11)	857 (12)
Tourism	146 (8)	688 (17)	323 (17)	110 (11)	127 (13)
Manufacturing	1,766 (59)	3,131 (24)	260 (23)	298 (20)	877 (19)
Construction	390 (13)	124 (8)	36 (7)	148 (7)	243 (6)
Total	**22,096 (1,530)**	**20,132 (1,019)**	**16,598 (980)**	**17,789 (906)**	**24,334 (771)**

Source: Fiji Development Bank 1997a: 13.

The table shows a general decrease in the number of loans (but not in the amount) from 1990 to 1995. This was due to the economic slowdown after 1989-1990, the peak growth period. Also, the FDB began to carefully monitor its loans because of a high rate of "non-performance". However, the significant increase in amount (despite the decrease in number) during the 1994/95 period was due to the dramatic increase in the real estate portfolio as a result of two huge communal investment loans for two high-rise office blocks in downtown Suva, for the Rewa Province (the province in which Suva City is located) and Suvavou, the traditional owners of the land on which Suva City is built.

The investment/financial institutions portfolio needs special mention here because of its links with FHL. A sizeable amount of this portfolio was invested in FHL. Loans for this portfolio started in the 1991/92 period, the same time at which FHL opened up equity to private investment, as we saw earlier. The CLFS loans became an important source of capital for FHL and for Unit Trust of Fiji private investment. The amount lent varied considerably, and in many cases depended on the socio-economic status of the clients. Two loan-size categories (100,000-250,000 and 250,000-500,000), as shown in Table 5.9, consisted of seven clients only. These included the Managing Director of the Fiji Development Bank himself and other members of the "clique" (mentioned earlier in this chapter) which controlled the individual shares in FHL.

Table 5.9 Financial institutions portfolio

Loan Size Category (FJ$)	Number of Loans	Value (FJD$)
0-10,000	74	282,838
10,001-20,000	20	199,126
20,001-300,000	7	142,811
30,001-50,000	16	302,780
50,001-100,000	41	2,120,457
100,001-250,000	6	490,645
250,000-500,000	1	298,820

Source: Fiji Development Bank 1997a.

The government subsidy to CLFS was substantial, as it was part of the government's economic affirmative action policy and was used to ensure that the Fiji Development Bank continued to remain afloat, despite the loan concessions. From 1985 to 1994 a total of FJ$9,352,321 worth of subsidy and FJ$1,838,156 worth of guarantee was provided by government. These were in addition to the annual subsidy the government provided the FDB.[16] Although CLFS loans were

---

16 It should be noted that the FDB's CLFS was a totally different portfolio to the normal bank commercial loan. From 1992 to 1996, of the FJ$248.3 million worth of loans approved, loans worth FJ$164.6 million were normal commercial loans, while loans worth FJ$83.7 million were for CLFS, a ratio of about 2:1. In other words, about half of the total FDB loan portfolio was for indigenous Fijian affirmative action.

strictly for indigenous Fijians, political imperatives were beginning to dictate otherwise. The SVT government had formed a Coalition government with the General Electors Party after the 1992 election and, as part of the political concessions involved, CLFS loans were extended to other ethnic minorities under the "General" or "Others" ethnic classification in 1993. Table 5.10 shows the CLFS loans approval, by ethnicity, with the general electors loans totalling more than FJ$1 million in 1994 and close to FJ$2 million in 1996, although the number of loans was still relatively small.

Table 5.10 CLFS loans approval by ethnic classification

Ethnicity	1994		1995		1996	
	Number	F$000	Number	F$000	Number	F$000
Fijian/Rotuman	754	15,140	564	27,710	195	18,351
General Electors	45	1,241	38	1,798	7	197,000
Total	799	16,381	602	28,508	202	18,545

Source: Fiji Development Bank Board Paper No. 11/397(28 February 1997): Annual Review for Commercial Loans to Fijians, Rotumans and General Electors.

The inclusion of the general electors (who consisted of Chinese, Europeans, part-Europeans and Pacific Islanders) in the CLFS may have been a useful political lever to ensure that the SVT-General Voters Party Coalition remained cohesive at a time when indigenous support was divided between Rabuka's SVT, Kamikamica's Fijian Association Party (FAP) and Butadroka's Fijian Nationalist Party (FNP). Further concessions for general electors were provided just before the 1999 election in the form of scholarships and an increase in the CLFS ceiling to FJ$200,000. This occurred after the coalition between the SVT and the United General Party (UGP), a new party for general electors, was formed.

One of the key features of the CLFS loans was regional inequality in the distribution pattern. Most of the loans went to urban or semi-urban localities and very few went to the rural areas. More than 50% of the loans were concentrated in Suva, the capital city. The loans practically reinforced existing wealth maldistribution and helped to worsen regional wealth disparity.

Despite its noble intentions, CLFS was based on the vacuous assumption that merely increasing the capital input into indigenous Fijian business would in some way generate commercial success. This view has been consistently perpetuated in the *Ten Year Plan* and even various FDB Annual Reports from 1994 to 1996. This was the reason for the increase in the ceiling in 1988. It was assumed that the lack of commercial enthusiasm of indigenous Fijians could be addressed by quantitatively expanding the loan portfolio. However, the socio-economic and political climate of investment was far more complex, as FDB itself later realised in some of its assessment reports. One of the problems was that

CLFS clients did not have the necessary skills to fully implement the business plans which accompanied the loans. This problem had been recognised much earlier in the 1960s and 1970s. The communal encapsulation and marginalisation of indigenous Fijians from mainstream commerce largely contributed to this. Ironically, despite recognition of the problem, there was an almost deliberate attempt to perpetuate it through encouragement of communal capitalism.

The CLFS crisis: Affirmative action in question

By the middle of the 1990s, the ambitious plan for wide capital disbursement under CLFS was beginning to feel the strain of increased arrears. Clearly there has been a high level of non-performance in the CLFS over the years. The level of non-performance for the CLFS portfolio was 45.28% for 1994, 42.41% in 1995 and 34.06% in 1996. The level of write-offs increased from 17% in 1994 to 21.59% in 1995 and 23.63% in 1996 (Fiji Development Bank 1996b).

One of the most popular loans was in the real estate portfolio. This needs some discussion here because, not only did real estate constitute the greatest amount in terms of disbursement, it was also considered to be the most easily identifiable in terms of visible evidence of indigenous progress. Also, there was a view that real estate did not involve much commercial ingenuity but rather that it was a passive form of investment which involved no more than putting one's property up for rent and waiting for money to flow in. This seemed attractive to many indigenous Fijians. After the military coups in 1987, the cost of residential houses slumped as a result of the dramatic downturn in the immediate post-coup economy and massive emigration by Indo-Fijians. A large number of expatriates were recruited to fill vacancies left by the large number of professionals who had migrated and these provided a growing market for the real estate business.

In 1989, in an attempt to encourage indigenous Fijians to invest in property, the government provided grants for fixed asset loans. This led to a dramatic increase in real estate loans. This initiative was withdrawn in 1991, after just two years of implementation, due to declining commercial performance. This resulted in a decline in real estate loans by 50%. However, in 1993 the number of real estate loans went up again because of the Fiji National Provident Fund's (FNPF) newly-introduced Small Business Equity Scheme (SBES).[17] The SBES was another form of commercial affirmative action, meant to enable indigenous Fijians to produce

---

17   The Fiji National Provident Fund (FNPF), the national life saving scheme, was established to take the place of the pension scheme, first introduced by the colonial state. While pension funds can be collected only after retirement, FNPF money can be used to buy residential houses, pay for education or for investment purposes.

the necessary equity contribution.[18] Some of these loans were used to make up the equity for real estate loans from the FDB, and this accounted for the increase in the number of real estate loans by more than 60% (Fiji Development Bank 1994a).

However, by the mid-1990s the real estate portfolio was beginning to face problems. On 25 July 1996 a paper to review the CLFC real estate performance was commissioned and its findings painted the doomsday scenario that there was a "nation-wide low" and that real estate loans performance was "deteriorating" (Fiji Development Bank 1996c). It recommended that measures be put in place before the situation worsened. Records showed that the total CLFS real estate sector collections decreased by 18.47% from 60.65% in June 1995 to 42.18% as at March 1996 (Fiji Development Bank 1996c). By 30 June 1996 the CLFS debt had accumulated to FJ$34.5 million. A significant number of debts were unserviceable. The crisis was not limited to the CLFS, but affected the FDB's real estate portfolio in general, which posed a serious threat to the lending capacity of the bank because as at 31 March 1996 the real estate portfolio made up FJ$116.98 million of FDB's total loan portfolio of FJ$326.9 million – almost half of the total loan portfolio.

The reasons for this mounting debt and portfolio decline were, firstly, the oversupply of executive homes, due to the early rush after the coup by indigenous Fijians to buy homes for investments.[19] There was no systematic survey of the real estate market before the loans floodgates were opened. Secondly, in the case of Suva, where most of the debtors concentrated, there was competition with non-indigenous investors who had built luxurious flats around the city area and many expatriates had moved in to occupy them as they were much cheaper, safer from crime (compared to the middle-class suburbs) and more convenient for travelling to work, for shopping, and to other city centre facilities.

Given the extent of the real estate portfolio crisis, the FDB review team recommended that:

(1) Loans for executive house rental be discouraged until December 1996 to new applicants.

---

18   The SBES for transport purposes, like taxis and boats, were suspended in 1993. This affected some of the indigenous-Fijian business proposals already in the pipeline. A classic example was when hundreds of the urban working population of Kadavu, one of the 14 provinces, were asked by the provincial business wing, the Kadavu Development Company (KDC), to contribute certain portions of their FNPF savings to the cost of the company's inter-island ferry. Many filled and signed the forms they were provided, to approve deductions from their FNPF, but were disappointed when the scheme fell through. In sociological terms, the KDC's approach to acquiring capital is a common method by ethnic-Fijian elites to manipulate primordial relations, loyalties and institutions to serve certain commercial interests.

19   On the other hand, the decline in the number of real estate loans to Indo-Fijians, as with other types of loans, was due to the political uncertainty in Fiji, and also because of the uncertainty about the soon-to-expire Agricultural Landlord and Tenants Act (ALTA), on which most Indo-Fijian farmers relied for their livelihood.

(2) Lending for live-in residential property should continue. But care was to be exercised to ensure that only those with secure employment were to be considered, and direct deductions were to be "pursued with intensity".

(3) Emphasis was to be placed on collection and rehabilitation of poorly performing accounts (Fiji Development Bank 1996c: 2).

Despite the crisis besetting the CLFS real estate portfolio, two large loans were made in 1995 to two indigenous Fijian companies which had close connections with the government and chiefly support. The first loan, worth FJ$3 million, was made to the Rewa Provincial Council, and the second, worth FJ$2 million, was made to Nadonumai Holdings Limited, belonging to the people of Suvavou. Suva, the capital city, was situated in Rewa province. The paramount traditional chief of Rewa was Adi Lala, the wife of the President of the Republic and former Prime Minister, Ratu Sir Kamisese Mara. The Managing Director of the FDB at the time of the loans, Qarase, came from the same province as Mara. Nadonumai Holdings Limited was owned by the original settlers of Suva, who were relocated by the British colonial state to a new settlement, called Suvavou (new Suva) to clear the Suva peninsula for a new capital for Fiji in 1882.[20] Despite attempts by the Suvavou people to be paid compensation by the colonial and post-colonial states, it was not until 1994 that the Rabuka government gave the Suvavou people a goodwill gesture by providing them with a piece of land and FJ$2 million loan, to be topped up by the FDB, to build an office block in downtown Suva. Both these loans, clearly facilitated by state patronage, increased the real estate loans figure in 1995, despite the decrease in the number of loans. Part of the deal was that the two buildings were to be rented by government departments. The two high-profile loans were politically significant because, as two of the very few indigenous Fijian-owned high-rise buildings in Suva, they symbolised indigenous Fijian real estate "success" in a highly visible way. They also symbolised the shift towards "think big" indigenous projects, as in Malaysia, through purchase of high-cost assets. Importantly, the two building were communally owned and symbolised the strong political links between the FDB and the ruling power elites and were an example of how affirmative action resources could be readily disbursed along political lines.

The real estate portfolio was not the only one in trouble. Another review of working capital loans for the retailing and wholesaling sectors of the CLFS, dated 22 March 1994, noted with dismay that 80.4% by number and 41% by value of the total working capital loans for retailing and wholesaling were

---

20 The first capital of Fiji, Levuka town on the island of Ovalau, was the scene of the British take-over ceremony on 10 October 1874. In 1882 the capital shifted to Suva, the current capital, because it had more space for expansion, unlike Levuka, which was surrounded by hills.

outstanding. This unusually high degree of "non-performance" was blamed on "market problems" and "misuse of funds" (Fiji Development Bank 1994b: 6), so the review recommended that the loans in this particular portfolio be frozen. The "market problems" were partly because retailing and wholesaling had been traditionally the monopoly of Indo-Fijians, and it was very difficult make inroads into these domains. The problem of "misuse of funds" was blamed on diversion of funds to communal obligations. The case of the EIMCOL projects, as we shall see later, bore testimony to these two problems.

As the crisis deepened, there was a sharp decline in CLFS approvals in 1996, both in terms of numbers and value. By 31 December 1996, 2,023 accounts valued at FJ$68.72 million were still outstanding. Up to the same period, real estate constituted 57.95% by value, but Retail /Wholesale and Transport/ Communication made up the majority in terms of number of loans, with 30.65% and 31.34% respectively.[21] These outstanding loans varied in terms of size. The most difficult loans to recover were smaller loans (0-10,000), because a lot of the small businesses set up through these loans were not commercially viable and could not compete with bigger and better established businesses (Fiji Development Bank 1996a).

By 1996 the sectors with deteriorating performance, in terms of percentage of outstanding loans to total size of the portfolio were infrastructure/construction (32.5% in 1995 to 87.7% in 1996), tourism (14.4% in 1995 to 41.5% in 1996) and wholesale/retail/restaurant (51.8% in 1995 to 54.9% in 1996) (Fiji Development Bank 1997b). The poor performance of the wholesale/retail sector was due to five major loans totalling FJ$2.3 million to Tropikana Industries Limited and four EIMCOL companies, all of which suffered financial difficulties and had to close down. The best-performing loans were in the financial institutional portfolio (as we saw earlier), most of which were used to buy Fijian Holdings Limited shares.

By June 1996 the number of loans had drastically declined by 50%, but the value of approvals went down by only 0.29%. The decline in the number of loans was due to two reasons; firstly, FDB had to suspend lending for retail, wholesale and transport projects; and secondly, two large loans were made for high-rise commercial buildings in Suva, as we have seen. While this increased the amount loaned, it actually reduced the number of loans in the real estate portfolio.

---

21   However, the FDB had some consolation in 1996. The arrears in terms of percentage to the total portfolio decreased from 25.34% to 20.48%. There was also a slight decrease in the percentage of the loan provision in relation to the CLFS from 9.13% to 7.93%. The non-performing accounts percentage to portfolio decreased from 44.28% to 25.74%. The write-offs portfolio decreased from 7.45% to 6.74%. These "decreases" were due largely to the combined effects of cleaning-up exercises, approval of quality loans and imposition of certain policy restrictions.

FDB's solution to the CLFS's problems was to introduce loan restrictions. These were not positive steps to remedy the crisis but interventionist policies to punish current and potential customers and salvage the CLFS from its ultimate demise and, perhaps, save FDB from public ridicule and political backlash. For instance, as far back as May 1991 the fixed asset grant was suspended. In July 1995, working capital loans for retail and wholesale, together with loans for the purchase of road freight transport vehicles (RFTV) with a weight of 2 tonnes or less were also suspended. In December of the same year, taxi loans to new clients in the central and eastern regions were suspended as well. However, all these suspensions were for the duration of one year, pending improvement in financial conditions. Further loan suspensions, some extensions from expired 1996 suspensions, were carried out in 1996. These were: loans for purchase of RFTV with a weight of 2 tonnes or less, extended to July 1997; all forms of purchase of RFTV of 3 tonnes capacity; lending for executive rental homes (discouraged), working capital loans for retail/wholesale extended to September 1997; new loans (to new clients) of FJ$10,000 or less for any purpose under the Wholesale/Retail sector for 1 year to September 1997; taxi loans in the central and eastern regions, extended to December 1997.

In terminating lending for certain projects, the FDB explained that:

> The FDB believes, however, that it is prudent banking practice to terminate lending in specific sectors when there is clear evidence that many clients in those sectors are getting into difficulties. To continue lending would be to ignore the warning signals and create even greater difficulties for the Bank and customers. The suspension period gives the Bank an opportunity to improve supervision of poorly performing accounts and to rehabilitate them. Resumption of lending is dependent on the outcome of performance reviews (Fiji Development Bank 1997a: 13).

Various internal reviews were critical of the CLFS performance. For instance, the reviews for 1994 and 1996 were far from being encouraging.[22] A 1994 review confirmed what was generally felt:

> One disturbing fact still remains that even after 18 years from inception of this scheme, Fijians and Rotumans have not really ventured into manufacturing, tourism and construction type of business. They prefer to invest in those projects that do not require much entrepreneurial and technical skills (Fiji Development Bank 1994a: 4).

---

22   Review performance of the FDB Commercial Loans to Fijian Scheme (CLFS) is undertaken every year or so, not by an independent body, but by the research section of the FDB, to determine its effectiveness and viability over time, and also to make recommendations. It is usually undertaken upon request by the Ministry of Finance, and the findings are submitted to the FDB Board, who are all appointees of the Minister for Finance.

This observation is very significant because it shows that while the problem had been identified by the FDB, it failed to look for appropriate solutions to address the problem. The 1994 FDB Annual Review of CLFS (different from the one earlier quoted) identified a number of problems, which directly implicated the commercially inhibiting influence of communalism: lack of proper planning, lack of cash control, lack of stock control, lack of business exposure, no business contacts and lack of knowledge of legal and other requirements necessary to set up business (Fiji Development Bank 1994b).

My intention in outlining these details is to illustrate in an empirical way the wide gap between political rhetoric in favour of indigenous affirmative action at one level and the concrete problems of implementation at the operationalization level. This survey is also relevant in terms of making the point that, contrary to prevailing reasoning that lack of capital was to be blamed for indigenous Fijian economic backwardness (Sutherland 1998), the problem was more fundamental. It was the inability to utilise available capital due to lack of innovative ideas about how to generate the maximum out of the existing communal life of indigenous Fijians. As a source of development funds the FDB was the most important institutional vehicle for economic affirmative action by the government and Fijian Administration, but it was confronted with a number of problems which were to threaten its capacity to carry out this mandate. First, it did not provide the necessary entrepreneurial skills to enable CLFS clients to compete with the established business. The training they were provided was merely for operating business accounts rather than how to manage a business in a competitive economic climate by forging business links and networks,. The FDB's policy was geared towards 'delivering the goods' in the form of loans, and there was little emphasis on capacity building and empowerment to enable clients to independently and creatively pursue their business. Second, there was no thorough sociological assessment of the possible contradictions between traditional cultural obligations and commercial practices that would undermine the viability of the business. In many ways, CLFS clients were still strongly attached to communal demands such as communal collections. Ironically, while at the political level there was encouragement of CLFS loans for individual entrepreneurship, there were also expectations that recipients remained loyal to their *yasana, tikina, koro, mataqali* and *tokatoka* and were obliged to contribute to communal demands (personal communication with a number of CLFS clients). There was also commitment to one's kinship obligation which demanded the free offering of resources such as food.

Equity Investment Management Company Limited (EIMCOL)

The Equity Investment Management Company Limited (EIMCOL) was set up in 1990 as a successor to the Business Opportunity and Management Advisory Service (BOMAS), set up in 1975 to "work solely with the Fijians", and to help them in their endeavour to enter the commercial world (Hailey 1992: 12).[23]

EIMCOL, unlike the CLFS, was not directly part of the FDB's portfolio but was a semi-autonomous project, established in 1990, and administered and facilitated by the FDB after BOMAS, originally attached to the FAB, collapsed.[24] The aim was to "assist Fijians and Rotumans enter the retail trade…long-term venture designed to school the participants in the commercial disciplines of retailing" (Qarase 1995: 21). The EIMCOL project was to be a national show piece for the FDB by producing indigenous Fijian supermarket managers. Unlike the CLFS projects, where clients ran their own business, EIMCOL stores were to be run directly by FDB. The idea was based on the Papua New Guinea (PNG) *Stret Pasin Store* (Street Fashion Store) model, where PNG nationals served as trainees in small Chinese shops, learning basic knowledge and skills of retailing at a micro level. In many ways, the PNG project served its purpose initially, but as a result of the general social unrest and lawlessness, retailing declined dramatically. The FDB sent one of its senior executives to PNG to study the project and, upon his return, enthusiastically recommended its implementation in Fiji. But instead of starting small by training clients for small retailing activities, the FDB embarked on a "think big" project by training supermarket managers. Applicants were restricted to indigenous Fijians and Rotumans, who were vetted and put on a training program with Carpenters Group, a major corporation with links to FHL, for six months.[25]

Upon completion of training, the successful "trainee managers" (as they were officially called) were allocated a supermarket each to run but were directly accountable to the FDB. The supermarkets were owned by a series of EIMCOL limited liability companies (i.e. each shop was owned by an EIMCOL company),

---

23   BOMAS had a very short life. It was first under the Ministry of Fijian Affairs and later it came under the Fiji Development Bank. Its role was fundamentally to train ethnic Fijians in the basics of entrepreneurial skills, to enable them to become independent business people. BOMAS failed because it was "inappropriate, poorly planned, under-funded, and starved of resources and qualified staff" (see Hailey 1992).

24   The EIMCOL was approved by Cabinet in December 1988 and the government committed itself to a FJ$3 million grant to the project. On 20 May 1989, the position of manager was advertised and EIMCOL was registered two months later. The Directors of EIMCOL were Laisenia Qarase, FDB Managing Director; Harry Kiss, former Director of the Ports Authority of Fiji; Tevita Vugakoto, FDB's General Manager Administration and Special Projects and Jone Tabuya, General Manager, EIMCOL.

25   A Post and Telecommunication technical officer, with inappropriate qualifications, was appointed training officer, but his appointment was later terminated due to incompetence. A General Manager was also appointed on 20 May 1989, who was later sacked after EIMCOL went into a crisis.

with the FDB and government as shareholders and funders. The government contributed one-third (FJ$3 million) and the FDB two thirds, (FJ$6 million) of the interest-free loan. EIMCOL management monitored the performance and provided instructions and supervision occasionally. Ownership of the shop was to be transferred to the trainee after 15 years, or earlier, depending on the completion of the full loan repayment. By 1992, nine shops, located mainly around the capital, Suva, had been purchased at different prices, and were run by EIMCOL trainee managers.

Within two years of its beginning, EIMCOL began to go through a series of crises, which led to its collapse. On 31 December 1991, the General Manager was sacked and was replaced. In late 1992 three EIMCOL supermarkets (Natokawaqa, Navua and Bureta Street)[26] were closed, and on 17 September 1993, the remaining six supermarkets were sold to the store managers, despite the FDB's initial promise that ownership would not be transferred until satisfactory payment of the loans had been made. The supermarkets were sold at prices that were far above the original prices. By 1996, all the EIMCOL supermarkets had been sold and EIMCOL as a commercial project collapsed. It threatened to bring down the FDB's pro-indigenous Fijian commercial program and, more importantly, given its high profile as a "model" for indigenous Fijian business, it was a major political blow to the government's affirmative action program. This, together with other factors, contributed to the forced resignation of Mr. Qarase as Managing Director of the FDB in 1997.[27]

Although it was not part of the plan, the reason given by the FDB for selling the shops was that the managers wanted to run the shops themselves. But one thing was clear, the transfer of ownership at an early stage meant that the FDB was going to be free of the cumulative liabilities it had created itself. The managers were to be ultimately responsible for the inevitable crisis, but the FDB was not to escape responsibility altogether as legal and political challenges were mounted against it.

The collapse of the EIMCOL scheme was the result of a number of interrelated reasons. While in principle the EIMCOL project looked viable, FDB's ambitious haste to concretise the idea was driven more by the political need to show the indigenous Fijians, and in particular the Great Council of Chiefs and the Fijian Administration, to whom Qarase was directly responsible as financial advisor, that the prevailing sentiments for affirmative action could be satisfied and that something concrete was being done. As the leading development institution in

---

26 The Natokawaqa supermarket was closed three months after its purchase because the sale was declared null and void since it was still under legal proceedings with a caveat by an interested party.

27 In July 1997 Isoa Kaloumaira, General Manager Finance, Planning, Research and Marketing was appointed Managing Director of the FDB to take the place of Laisenia Qarase, who became General Manager of the Merchant Bank of Fiji, another subsidiary of Fijian Holdings Limited.

the country, the FDB felt that it had both the political and moral responsibility to be at the forefront of facilitating the indigenous Fijians' participation in commerce. The FDB could not provide the appropriate managerial and commercial skills and knowledge, backed by relevant logistical systems. The general manager and training officer initially appointed to EIMCOL had neither the experience nor the expertise in the sort of commercial venture that EIMCOL was intended to carry out. Training for trainee managers in the initial stages was less than commendable. For instance, on 18 November 1992 the trainee managers, disgusted with the EIMCOL management, wrote a letter to the Prime Minister, where, amongst other things, they pointed out that:

> During training, the trainees spent most of the time doing practical labour work and very little time was spent on identifying the elements of real business, like working out prices, controlling cash flow, controlling creditors and debtors and identifying real sources and markets. As a result of these, the trainees, after acquiring their individual shops took a longer time to adjust/orientate themselves to the commercial environment. Overall, the managers underwent very poor training and were not prepared well for what they encountered. They were led to believe that they would be running small retail outlets. Instead they were given supermarkets to run. They were not prepared to run supermarkets. They were out of their depths and most had to improvise to survive (*Fiji Times*, 18 November 1992: 5).

Furthermore, purchase of the supermarkets was made without due consideration of some basic socio-economic factors such as location, consumer market and potential competition. Most, if not all, of the EIMCOL supermarkets were located close to established and thriving Indo-Fijian-owned supermarkets and retail shops, which were selling goods at considerably lower prices. EIMCOL did not have an import arm or a central buying house from where the supermarkets could buy goods cheaply and instead they had to purchase bulk goods from Indo-Fijian supermarkets. One of the supermarkets was designated as the buying and distribution centre. Due to their higher retail prices compared to their competitors the EIMCOL supermarkets could not survive for long. In a lot of cases the supermarkets allocated were in such bad shape that trainee managers had to spend a lot of time and funds on repairing plant, equipment, fixtures and fittings.

As a result of the wide publicity of the EIMCOL crisis, bordering on a national scandal, the FDB became defensive, and shifted the blame to the trainee managers. In a strongly worded letter to the editor of *The Fiji Times*, Qarase insisted that the manager trainees were to be blamed because of their lack of commitment and for flouting basic commercial rules. He said that "as students and trainees they appear to be adopting a 'we know best' attitude instead of applying themselves to learning the basics of their business" (*The Fiji Times*, 19 November 1992: 5). The "blaming the victim" syndrome adopted by Qarase was further deployed in an advertisement in *The Fiji Times*, while referring to the initial sacking of two supermarket managers:

> In both the cases referred to in the recent media publicity, the managers concerned failed to follow the rules. They were not totally committed. Their appointments were terminated due to consistent mismanagement, failure to abide by the principles of business and continuing breaches of their terms and conditions of employment. Both managers had ample opportunity of over two years to learn and to improve their performance. They had the benefit of intensive, concentrated training covering many aspects of retailing, combined with hands-on experience. They knew that the scheme was about performance and those who did not perform to a satisfactory level were dropped. They did not perform... We had a number of meetings with them to discuss their problems. It made no difference. They continued to break the commercial rules and to demonstrate their lack of discipline. The FDB had no choice but to terminate their appointments. At the end of the day, the Bank has a fundamental responsibility to safeguard taxpayers' funds under its stewardship (The Fiji Times, 28 November 1992).

Politicians also joined in the controversy. Senator Manu Korovulavula, an indigenous Fijian Senator and businessman, addressed the Senate and charged:

> They (FDB) are bankers who do not have any exposure to food merchandising business, more so in the scale of supermarket. How then can they justifiably say they can teach people what and how they should carry out their work, when they themselves do not really know, because they had no such training or relative past work experience (Korovulavula, *Speech to Senate*, 12 July 1994: 5).

Senator Korovulavula suggested that any form of commercial affirmative action for indigenous Fijians should include the contribution of Indo-Fijians and other races:

> The Government of the day, perhaps, is not aware of or advised that a considerable number of successful businessmen, in particular the Indians, on account of the solo Fijian efforts to enter and participate in business, with respect stood aside and observed with deep regret the series of Fijian business failures. In silence there are those who do care for the Fijians to be successful in business too. They might feel that it might be unbecoming of them if they offered their assistance that might not be welcomed for political conservative orientation. Humans as we

are, it would be unnatural to think that every person in Fiji is ready and willing to help the less fortunate, who struggle each day to make ends meet (Korovulavula, *Speech to the Fiji Senate,* 12 July 1994: 5).

The Fiji Senate passed a motion, "That this house expresses deep concern at the past method of commercial management adopted by the Equity Investment Company Limited (EIMCOL), with regard to the disbursement of FJ$3 million grant by Government" (Fiji Parliament. 1994). The collapse of the EIMCOL caused a major political stir which saw Indo-Fijian political leaders calling for a total review of the wastage of public resources through indigenous-Fijian affirmative action.

One of the consequences of the collapse of the EIMCOL was ethnic scapegoating. The leader of the indigenous group *Kudru na Vanua* (Rumble of the Land) told the author that "the failure of Fijian business is a result of *Vere Vakaidia* (Indian conspiracy)". Based more on perception than reality, ethnic scapegoating diverted attention from the real issues that needed addressing.

The National Bank of Fiji (NBF): Hand-outs and coup payoffs

After the 1987 military coup there was forced "Fijianization" of a number of institutions (such as in the civil service, as we have seen). Amongst them was the National Bank of Fiji. Unlike the FDB, the National Bank of Fiji (NBF) did not have a formal government mandate to put in place affirmative action programs for indigenous Fijians. But after the military coups in 1987, the post-coup regime unilaterally imposed pro-indigenous measures in the NBF which later had drastic consequences.[28]

After he staged the coup the then Lt Colonel (now Major General) Rabuka unilaterally appointed Visanti Makrava, a Rotuman (politically classified as indigenous), an NBF branch manager (Samabula Branch), to become the Chief Manager of NBF, without the knowledge of the NBF board or the Minister of

---

28 Until 1999, NBF was a 100% Fiji government-owned bank, set up as a fully commercial bank in 1974, under the NBF Act, which suggests that the NBF's financial role should be undertaken in the "national interest". The term 'national interest' being ideologically loaded, it became the convenient justification for the complex commercial and socio-political mess it ended up with. The pro-ethnic-Fijian agenda was not formally prescribed but was part of the post-coup political design, subtly infused into the psyche of the bank management by the military regime. The post-coup political climate, characterised by firmly entrenched ethnic polarisation, nationalist passion for permanent ethnic-Fijian paramountcy and rhetorical opposition to what was seen as Indo-Fijian dominance of the economy, was the perfect setting and created a fertile atmosphere for the bank's unwritten political agenda.

Finance.[29] The "appointment" took place in typical military junta style. Makrava and a group of M16-toting soldiers entered the NBF headquarters and told the then Chief Manager, Gordon Ryan, an Australian expatriate, seconded by the Commonwealth Bank of Australia, to vacate his office because he (Makarava) had been appointed by Rabuka as NBF Chief Manager. Makarava himself had complained to Rabuka about the expatriate managers "on holiday" in Fiji, and the need to localise the top management positions. This was more than welcomed by the military, which in fact became the first beneficiaries of the gunpoint localisation. They were provided with special bank facilities, including preferential loans. In the name of indigenous well-being, unsecured loans were "handed out" liberally to supporters of the coup (*The Review*, July 1995).

Makrava handpicked a number of indigenous Fijians and Rotumans for the top management positions, despite their lack of experience and expertise. But within a few years the bank was enveloped in crisis. In 1994, the Auditor General reported that approval limits were being exceeded, repayments were irregular, loans were repaid from overdrawn personal accounts, loans were not reviewed or monitored, and there was no insurance cover for some loan securities (Fiji Office of Auditor General 1994). Loans were made available liberally to family members, friends and those with powerful political connections and in many cases securities were not provided. For instance, the NBF branch on Makarava's home island of Rotuma had about FJ$400,000 in deposits and F$13 million in loans. This was a loan to deposit ratio of more than 300%. This compared unfavourably with the ratio of 50% for Nadi, Fiji's fastest growing urban centre.

Many loans were given under political pressure. A Korean logging company, Taveuni Woo Il, in which the former President, Ratu Sir Penaia Ganilau, had a 33% shareholding , with a further 20% of shares held by the Cakaudrove Provincial Council, and with a paid-up capital of FJ$1.5 million, owed more than FJ$5 million on security of about FJ$1.4 million. There were many other loans that were approved under political duress. The former Deputy Chief Manager, Kalivati Bakani, admitted that the political pressure, though indirect, ensured that "you got the message" (*The Review*, July 1995: 21).

Post-coup propaganda convinced many indigenous Fijians that the bank had indeed been "recaptured" from expatriates to serve their commercial interests. Many withdrew their accounts from other expatriate banks like the Australian WESTPAC and the trans-Tasman Australia New Zealand Bank (ANZ) and joined NBF and its newly introduced NBF Group Insurance Scheme (GIS).[30] This mass

---

29   The Minister of Finance was directly responsible for the National Bank of Fiji. He appointed the members of the Board. At the time of Visanti Makarava's "appointment" as Chief Manager, the Minister of Finance was the late Josua Cavalevu.

30   This involved individuals joining an insurance scheme as part of a collective professional or social group, with relatively generous loan conditions.

exodus was partly an attraction to the relatively liberal conditions of the NBF loans and partly a feeling of patriotism whipped up by the coup makers that investment in NBF was politically good for indigenous Fijians.

By 1995, when the NBF problem became a public scandal, the NBF had paid-up capital of a mere FJ$15 million. By 30 June 1995, it had FJ$450 million in deposits, against FJ$390 million worth of loans, despite the Reserve Bank of Fiji directive that loan growth be contained at FJD$355 million, as a condition for the FJ$15 million government sinking fund deposits and its own funds. Doubtful loans were estimated by the accounting firm Aidney-Dickson to be FJ$93 million, while the World Bank's estimate was FJ$120 million (*The Review*, July 1995). Worse still, there was a liquidity shortfall of over FJ$70 million. Due to this, overnight borrowings were around FJ$15-20 million in December 1993, reaching FJ$70 million in 1995. The crisis was so deep that the newly appointed Minister of Finance, Berenado Vunibobo, said that, "The National Bank of Fiji is, for all intents and purposes, insolvent", and angrily said that he "was shocked. [I]t is fundamentally flawed" (*The Review*, July 1995:16). More than FJ$300 million in bad debt had been incurred, and the bank began borrowing about FJ$80 million a day to maintain liquidity.

Ironically, things began to swing back in a full circle. In 1995 the new Minister of Finance quickly moved to remove top bank executives (mostly indigenous Fijians promoted or planted there during the coup) and brought in expatriate bankers to clear up the mess. The list of bad debtors printed by the *Fiji Times* read like a "Who's Who" list, headed by President Mara. It included Prime Minister General Rabuka's companies, chiefs, government ministers, senior army officers, senior civil servants and selected coup supporters. Individual debtors and families who were part of the Fijian political and military elite owed up to FJ$1 million each. The decision by the government to lay off National Bank of Fiji workers as part of the recovery measures led to a nation-wide strike by the Bank Employees Association. A compromise was reached whereby workers were to be given a handsome retirement package.[31]

Perhaps the coup was able to inspire a sense of an entrepreneurial urge amongst indigenous Fijian elites as they saw a chance to take advantage of their unrestricted power and access to state resources to unilaterally push through some of their communal aspirations. But the means was irregular and the process was not directed and managed in a way that made commercial sense. Some loans were political payoffs to those who played a significant role in the coups. A

---

31   Towards the end of 1996, criminal charges of corruption were laid against a number of leading figures in the loan scandal. Of these, two were government ministers (Mr. Ovini Bokini, former Minister for Lands and Mr. Koresi Matatolu, former Minister for Agriculture). The accused included Makrava, the sacked Chief Manager of the National Bank of Fiji, and other business people. Mr. Bokini faced 32 charges of corruption. Investigations into these charges mysteriously fizzled out as a result of political pressure.

number of people who were responsible for the ethnic beatings and burning in the streets of Suva were allegedly given loans up to FJ$500,000 without security (*Fiji Times*, 10 August 1995). Many others who played important roles in the coup were likewise allegedly "rewarded" by the NBF.

At the height of the political controversy surrounding the scandal, General Rabuka defended himself by saying that NBF Chief Manager, Makrava, as his appointee, had done a lot for the indigenous Fijians, and those who were criticising him were conspiring against indigenous Fijian interests.

The crisis of the NBF loans, some of which were for "commercial" and some for "personal" purposes, was due to a number of factors. It can be easily argued that the main "blame" had to be located within the whole politics of communalism itself, which led to the take-over of the bank and the imposition of preferential loans. The laxity in repayment, borne of the feeling that the NBF had become a communal bank of some sort, made the situation worse. The main difference between the NBF and the other affirmative action policies (FHL, UTF, CLFS and EIMCOL) was that while the shortcomings of the other ones had to do with their communal approach to investment, the NBF fiasco was based on unsystematic and coerced communal disbursement of public funds.[32] The entire indigenous Fijian state elite was caught up in the fiasco. It was a blatant case of greed, ethical irresponsibility and criminalization of the state never before seen in the history of Fiji. While the financial loss to the economy was substantial and reversible in the short term, the psychological impact to the indigenous Fijian community in terms of diminished self-esteem and reinforcement of anti-indigenous reputation and stereotypes as commercially incapable would linger on.

The failure of many affirmative action projects contributed to friction and division within the indigenous Fijian community as manifested at the political level. During the 1999 general election, the ruling SVT Party under Rabuka lost the election to a Fiji Labour Party-led coalition and for the first time an Indo-Fijian became prime minister of Fiji. This contributed to Fiji's third coup a year later.

---

32   In March 1999, the NBF was privatised. The majority share (51%) was purchased by Colonial Life Mutual Assurance.

6. Appeasement, scams and tension: Affirmative action programs, 1999 to 2006

Affirmative action programs between 1999, after the FLP-led coalition came to power, and the 2006 coup can be understood in terms of three major trends. The first was the failed appeasement strategy by the FLP-led coalition under Prime Minister Mahendra Chaudhry (1999 to 2000); the second was the use of affirmative action as a conflict resolution mechanism and associated scams (2000-2001); and the third was attempted reconciliation and tension leading to the 2006 coup (2002 to 2006).

The dominant feature of the first period was the urgent attempt by the Labour-led coalition to mobilize indigenous Fijian support through the public proclamation of its support for affirmative action: a desperate move to win acceptance in a hostile and volatile political environment. When Chaudhry's coalition came to power in 1999 it was faced with two seemingly contradictory tasks – first was the urgent need to appease indigenous Fijians by promising to continue with special measures for them while at the same time addressing the interests of Indo-Fijians who voted overwhelmingly for the FLP. This involved a very fine and potentially fragile balancing act to satisfy two communities with different expectations. The appeasement effort did not work because indigenous ethno-nationalists were determined to destabilize Chaudhry's government, until it was removed in a coup in May 2000.

The second phase of affirmative action, carried out by the military-appointed interim government under Laisenia Qarase between the May 2000 coup and August 2001 election, was meant to lessen ethno-political tension in the wake of the 2000 upheaval. However, it was beset by irregularities, corruption and manipulation for electoral gain by the interim ministers. Scams led to the suspension of the affirmative action program as investigations continued into millions of dollars' worth of fraud. The strategic approach to implement affirmative action initiatives to help take Fiji out of the political doldrums was tainted by abuse of power and lack of proper government purchasing procedures. Paradoxically, the scams did not deter indigenous Fijian voters from voting overwhelmingly for Qarase's Soqosoqo Duavata Lewenivanua Party (S DL) during the 2001 election.

The third phase, between 2001 and 2006, was dominated by the SDL's use of affirmative action as part of its broader national reconciliation program. Although the victory of the SDL during the 2001 election provided Qarase's pro-indigenous policies the boost and legitimacy they needed in the wake of the embarrassing scams, the political climate had changed and the military, which supported affirmative action policies immediately after the 2000 coup to help quell tension, was vehemently opposed to some of Qarase's bold policies, such as the Qoliqoli Bill and Reconciliation, Tolerance and Unity Bill (RTUB). The tensions which followed culminated in the overthrow of Qarase's government by the military on 6 December 2006.

Appeasement and the 2000 coup

In 1999 Mahendra Chaudhry was appointed Fiji's first Indo-Fijian prime minister after the victory of the Labour-led coalition. This was the first election under the 1997 Constitution which prescribed the alternative voting (AV) system which gave voters the option to either vote "above the line" for the preferred political party (which have already exchanged preferences amongst themselves) or "below the line" for their preferred candidates numbered in order of priority. The AV system was meant to avoid dominance by a single party thus forcing formation of a coalition government as a way of moderating extremist parties and creating middle ground politics. However, the results of the 1999 election did not reflect this expectation. The FLP won all 19 Indo-Fijian communal seats and 18 of the 25 open seats. The NFP, under Jai Ram Reddy, which went into the election by forming a "moderate" alliance with the SVT, under Sitiveni Rabuka, did not win any seat after losing a total of 20. Reddy's alliance with Rabuka was seen by Indo-Fijians as an act of betrayal and Chaudhry was quick to take advantage of this. The SVT, in power since the 1992 election, won only 8 seats and lost 24. The details of the election results are shown in Table 6.1.

Table 6.1 Results of the 1999 election

Party	Votes	%	Seats	+ /-
Fiji Labour Party	231,946	32.2	37	+30
Soqosoqo ni Vakavulewa ni Taukei	143,177	19.9	8	-24
National Federation Party	104,985	14.6	0	-20
Fijian Association Party	72,907	10.1	10	+5
Christian Democratic Alliance	70,153	9.7	3	New
Nationalist Vanua Tako Lavo Party	31,587	4.4	2	New
Party of National Unity	28,874	4.0	4	New
United General Party	10,144	1.4	2	New
United National Labour Party	3,963	0.6	0	New
Coalition of Independent Nationals	2,405	0.3	0	New
Lio 'On Famör Rotuma Party	1,982	0.3	0	New
Party of the Truth	234	0.0	0	New
Farmers and General Workers Coalition Party	197	0.0	0	New
Viti Levu Dynamic Multiracial Democratic Party	124	0.0	0	New
Natural Law Party	109	0.0	0	New
Nationalist Democratic Party	13	0.0	0	New
Independents	17,382	2.4	5	+4
Invalid/blank votes	39,567	-	-	-
Total	**399,759**	**100**	**71**	**+1**

Source: Fiji Election Office 1999.

The SVT's election loss can be attributed directly to a shift in indigenous Fijian support to emerging parties such as the Fijian Association Party (FAP) ,which won 10 seats; the Christian Democratic Alliance (CDA), 3 seats; the Nationalist Vanua Tako Lavo Party (NVTLP), 2 seats; and the Party of National Unity (PANU), 2 seats. Division within the ranks of indigenous Fijians was of significant advantage to the Fiji Labour Party, which formed a coalition government with the FAP, led by Kuini Speed, Bavadra's former wife, and the CDA, which was set up with the blessing of the President, Ratu Sir Kamisese Mara. Of the 18 cabinet posts, 11 were allocated to indigenous Fijians, a move which was generally interpreted as Chaudhry's tactical manoeuvre to appease indigenous Fijians.

In response to threats of violence and destabilization, one of the very first tasks for Chaudhry when he became prime minister was to allay fears that he would revoke existing affirmative action programs. The first assurance was provided by the president, Ratu Sir Kamisese Mara, who during his speech to open parliament on 15 June 1999 emphasised the Labour-led coalition's commitment to safeguarding and protecting the rights and interests of the indigenous people of Fiji as enshrined in the constitution (Mara 1999). In his address to the GCC in the same month Chaudhry proclaimed in no uncertain terms that the Labour-led coalition fully recognized the unique and special position of indigenous Fijians and Rotumans and emphasized continued assistance in the areas of education, land, housing and participation in business. He promised the chiefs that $5 million would be set aside for indigenous Fijian education. He also expressed concern about the low success rate of indigenous business and one of the solutions he offered was injection of funds for more training and management support and guidance (Chaudhry 1999).

As a way of winning popular support, the coalition devised a pro-poor economic policy, which was contained in the 2000 national budget announced at the end of 1999. The budget emphasised the importance of the social service sector, notably education, social welfare, poverty alleviation, healthcare and micro-enterprise initiatives for those who wanted to start their own business. There was also a proposal for the removal of Value Added Tax (VAT) on some basic food items as well as reduced housing rates, electricity and water rates (Fiji Government 1999). There was an increase in Family Assistance Allowance by $1.5 million to $5.6 million. In addition, the Housing Authority interest rate for those with income below $6,500 was reduced from 11.5% to 6% and over time the interest rate for those with a salary above $6,500 would be decreased progressively. The Coalition also introduced the Student Loan Scheme to enable children from poor families to attend tertiary institutions. The government also put a stop to some privatization initiatives and started a review of the rice quota for import and export.

Buoyed by the popular pro-poor policies, the coalition government started treading on more politically sensitive ground. For instance, they set up a commission of inquiry to carry out an investigation into the government tendering process of the privatisation deals, corrupt practices within the civil service, tax evasion practices of prominent indigenous Fijian and Indo-Fijian businessmen and the tendering process for the mahogany forest harvesting and Y2K computer systems upgrade contracts, of which it was alleged that thousands of dollars changed hands between big companies and prominent indigenous Fijians. Some of these issues were very closely tied up with affirmative action, especially with regards to government tenders in favour of indigenous Fijian contractors. Opponents interpreted these moves as Chaudhry's attempt to deepen his hegemonic control of the state system, weaken the power of the business community and above all indirectly undermine affirmative action despite his public rhetoric about support for indigenous interests. This sentiment, often coloured by nationalist overtones, was echoed by George Speight, the self-styled leader of the 2000 coup, when he wrote to the GCC after his illegal instalment as prime minister in May 2000 that "before the People's Coalition Party came to power, Mr Chaudhry was a leading opposition spokesperson, who was always critical of affirmative action in favour of the indigenous community" and he "made sure when he came to power that this affirmative action, in favour of the indigenous community was removed" (Speight 2000).

Chaudhry's own uncompromising approach and his choice to ignore political advice regarding indigenous sentiments were probably his greatest enemies. Despite being warned by the president not to touch land issues, Chaudhry was adamant that land reform was a priority. One of the coalition's very first initiatives was the establishment of the Land Use Commission (LUC), first proposed by the Bavadra government to oversee the development of indigenous Fijian land. As part of the initiative he invited a number of chiefs to accompany him to Sarawak in Malaysia to observe aspects of development of native land and how these could provide relevant lessons for indigenous Fijians. He also recommended that some of the powers of the NLTB be curtailed and transferred to the LUC.

Although there were some good ideas behind the land reform project as far as encouraging indigenous entrepreneurship was concerned, politically and culturally, tinkering with the land system, even minimally, was a taboo issue. In the midst of the controversies and opposition, Chaudhry, who previously had minimal links with indigenous Fijian chiefs, used the Malaysian trip as well as patronage of selected chiefs not linked to nationalist groups to consolidate his position. For instance he diverted a FJ$175,000 grant from the Government of Taiwan to build the house of Sairusi Nagagavoka, a prominent chief from Ba

Province (where Chaudhry was born), who happened to be a close friend as well (*Fiji Times*, 24 February 2008). This was quickly branded as buying loyalty and as corruption and did little to enhance his public relations efforts.

Suspicions were further aroused when the government's farming assistance to cane farmers was introduced. Cane farmers who were displaced were given $28,000 upon vacating the land to move to other areas of their choice, while the indigenous Fijian farmers who replaced the displaced Indo-Fijian farmers were not given any assistance at all. A total of 708 applications were received and 206 of these were approved. Of the approved applications, 14 were from indigenous Fijians who received a total of $392,000 and 192 were from Indo-Fijians who received a total of $5,204,000. In his speech to parliament on 21 November 2001 Qarase referred to this as evidence of Chaudhry's ethnic bias and disdain of indigenous interest (Qarase 2001). The farming assistance formula was subsequently altered by the SDL government after the 2001 election – the new formula awarded $10,000 equally to both outgoing farmers, who were mostly Indo-Fijians, and incoming farmers, who were mostly indigenous Fijians.

Apart from sugar, rice was also a significant agricultural commodity targeted by the Labour-led coalition as a priority. The allocation of $4.5 million for the opening of the Rewa Rice mill was an attempt to resurrect an ailing industry as well as to provide cheaper rice for customers. Opposition to this plan came from rice importers such as Punjas Limited, owned by a very influential Gujarati family, and nationalists who saw it as another move mostly in favour of Indo-Fijian rice farmers.

Indigenous nationalists painted almost every Chaudhry policy on land and development as anti-indigenous and pro-Indo-Fijian. This fuelled ethnic and religious prejudices and a wave of ethno-nationalist grievances and protests reminiscent of 1987. As the situation became desperate Chaudhry made a public appeal in his last public speech a week before his government was toppled: "Let me remind those people who are protesting today...the rights and interests of our indigenous community – the Fijians and Rotumans take precedence over the rights and interests of other communities" (Lal and Pretes 2008: 141). In the same speech he made an emotional plea to appease indigenous landowners:

> Another reason for agricultural development is that land in this country is largely owned by our Fijian brothers and sisters. Now much of that land is lying idle and underdeveloped except in the sugar cane belt. A lot of other land is not put to productive use. The government's strategies are to see that by investing money in agriculture that we will encourage our Fijian brothers and sisters to develop their land so that they can benefit from that development (Lal and Pretes 2008: 140).

These words fell on deaf ears as the protests and acts of destabilization continued, reaching a climax on 19 May 2000 as thousands of indigenous Fijians marched through central Suva City. The protest culminated in street riots, looting and burning in the CBD. The march coincided with the taking over of parliament by members of the elite Counter-Revolutionary Warfare unit (CRW) from the Fiji Military and a number of politicians and activists led by George Speight.

The president, Mara, whose daughter was amongst those taken hostage, denounced the coup and declared a state of emergency. On 29 May the military asked him to *vakatikitiki* (move aside) as it suspended the constitution and assumed control of political power through martial law. The members of the government were held for 56 days and were released after the Muanikau Accord between Speight and his group and the military was signed, with the promise of amnesty for the former upon return of all weapons to the military. After Speight's men released the hostages and returned most of the weapons, they were promptly arrested at the Kalabu Primary School where they converged to set up a new base after they left parliament. The leaders were tried and some, including Speight, were imprisoned.

Support for indigenous Fijian affirmative action was Chaudhry's trump card for appeasing indigenous Fijians. The hope of doing so diminished as a result of the coalition's other controversial policies (such as proposals for land reform, farming assistance and an inquiry into corruption, amongst others) which were deemed to be anti-indigenous. The failure to sway indigenous Fijians was worsened by Chaudhry's strong-headed and uncompromising approach to governance and politics and his refusal to listen to advice from indigenous Fijian leaders or heed warnings of impending instability from close advisers.

Conflict resolution and scams: Revisiting 1987

In the wake of the 2000 coup, an interim government was set up by the military under the leadership of Laisenia Qarase. One of Qarase's first projects was the creation of a new affirmative action framework for indigenous Fijians to address the grievances which inspired the 2000 political upheaval. The responsibility entrusted to Qarase's interim government was quite a difficult one, given the failure of past affirmative action programs and the fluid and tense political climate in the wake of the 2000 coup. The economy was in free fall, tourism had declined drastically, agriculture and manufacturing had been disrupted, unemployment skyrocketed in an unprecedented way and ethnic distrust had worsened considerably. To make matters worse, the constitution was suspended, the institutions of the state had been paralysed and people's confidence in state security had been seriously compromised as a result of widespread violence at the time of the coup and the threat of further violence in the following months.

The interim government was faced with two major dilemmas. First, what was the most convenient way to rebuild the state institutions and inter-communal trust without being seen to be politically partial? Second, what was the best way to rebuild the national economy while at the same time recognizing that indigenous development interests were critical for stability and had to be tackled immediately? The interim government thought it wise, given the still reverberating chorus of ethno-nationalism and its potential for further destabilization, to address the issue of indigenous Fijian development head on. The first task was to devise an affirmative action framework in the form of two major documents, namely the *Blueprint for the Protection of Fijian & Rotuman Rights and Interests* (Blueprint) and the *20–year Development Plan (2001 – 2020) for the Enhancement of Participation of Indigenous Fijians and Rotumans in the Socio-economic Development of Fiji,* commonly known as the 20 Year Plan (20YP).

The Blueprint

The Blueprint identified some crucial areas for indigenous development, especially "issues which have been of great concern to indigenous Fijians and Rotumans regarding the security of their rights and interests as the indigenous communities in Fiji, and also the advancement and acceleration of their development, so that they can participate on an equitable basis in the progress of our country" (Fiji Government 2000: 1). The document set out ways in which indigenous Fijians could "fully exercise their rights of self-determination within the unitary state of the Republic of the Fiji Islands" and "safeguard the paramountcy of their interests in our multi-ethnic and multi-cultural society" (ibid). So, essentially, the thrust of the Blueprint revolved around the notions of advancement, equity and self-determination – terms which were not new at all; but in the circumstances they provided hope for many indigenous Fijians caught up in the political melee. The major proposals of the Blueprint are summarized in Table 6. 2.

The Blueprint consisted of a total of 42 programs, comprising 12 legislative initiatives (Table 6.3), 15 policy directives (Table 6.4), and 15 budgetary provisions (Table 6.5). These tables show a common dilemma of affirmative action in Fiji – that is, in order to carry out a project which is fundamentally for the indigenous community, the entire state machinery had to be mobilised to enact the relevant legislation, formulate policies and fund the initiatives. The question of whether this is fair in a multicultural society is often contentious. Given the circumstances in Fiji after the 2000 coup, the case in support of conflict resolution was a powerful and convincing one which had ramifications not just for indigenous Fijians, but also for the entire nation.

Table 6.2 Summary of the Blueprint proposals

Concepts	Description
Constitution	Promulgation of a pro-indigenous constitution (such as the 1990 Constitution)
Land	Transfer of some state land to indigenous landowners
Land lease	Revocation of the Agricultural Landlord and Tenant Act (ALTA) which formed the basis of agreement between indigenous land owners and Indo-Fijian farmers to be replaced by the Native Land Trust Act (NLTA)
Fishing rights	Transfer of ownership of offshore areas (i qoliqoli) from the state to landowners
Land compensation	Land compensation for landowners whose land is used for commercial and other purposes
Fijian administration	Strengthening the Fijian administration and Great Council of Chiefs as independent institutions
Fijian trust	Establishment of a Fijian trust fund to facilitate saving and investment for the indigenous community
Fijian foundation	Establish a Fijian foundation to carry out research into Fijian culture, language, ethno-history and ethno-geography and make these compulsory subjects in schools
National saving	Establish a compulsory national savings scheme to finance indigenous business and education
Affirmative action law	Enactment of an affirmative action enabling law
Mineral royalty	Review of underground mineral and water legislation to increase royalty for indigenous Fijians
Tax exemption	Enact enabling legislation for tax exemption for indigenous Fijian companies
Land administration	Improvement of service by NLTB and Native Lands and Fisheries Commission
Government assistance	Government financial assistance for NLTB and Fijian Holdings Ltd

Source: Fiji Government 2001.

Table 6.3 Legislative initiatives under the Blueprint

Legislative initiatives	Ministry responsible
Preparation and promulgation of a new Constitution	Prime Minister's Office
Affirmative Action Legislation	Prime Minister's Office
Return of Schedule A & B Lands to NLTB	Lands and Mineral Resources
Removal of native land from the ambit of ALTA to NLTA	MALR/NLTB/SLO
Ownership rights of traditional qoliqoli to land owners	Fijian Affairs and SLO
Establishment of Land Claims Tribunal	Fijian Affairs, SLO and PM
Review of Fijian Affairs & GCC Regulations	Fijian Affairs
Establishment of the Fijian Development Trust Fund	PM
National Savings Scheme for Fijians and Rotumans	PM and Finance
Review of Mining Laws	Lands and Mineral Resources and SLO
Review of Company Tax Act	Finance
Review of NLTA & ALTA	Native Land Trust Board and SLO

Source: Fiji Government 2002.

As Table 6.3 shows, relevant pieces of legislation were meant to be passed by parliament to legalize and safeguard the Blueprint. Of the proposed legislative initiatives at least three were eventually carried out. These included the Social Justice Act of 2001; return of some state land to indigenous landowners; and the switch from the Agricultural Landlord and Tenant Act (ALTA) to the Native Land Trust Act (NLTA). By and large, ALTA was seen as more favourable to Indo-Fijian tenants because of the lower rent paid under its provisions and NLTA was seen as more favourable to indigenous Fijians landowners because of the higher rent. The attempt to enact the law on fishing rights (Qoliqoli Bill) later fuelled tension between Qarase's government and the military, as we will see later.

Table 6.4 Policy directives under the Blueprint

Policy directives	Ministry responsible
Review of the Fijian Administration	Fijian Affairs
Reservation of 50% of Government shares in companies for Fijians and Rotumans as they become available	Public Enterprise
Reservation of 50% of major licences or permits for Fijians & Rotumans	Business Development and Investment
Reservation of 50% of Government contracts for Fijians & Rotumans	PM/Finance
Continuation of FDB Interest Scheme for Fijians & Rotumans	Finance
Establishment of Small Business Equity Scheme for Fijians and other races	Finance
Establishment of a National Centre for Small and Micro Enterprise Development	Business Development and Investment
Dealings relating to mahogany	PM/Fisheries and Forestry
Discontinuation of Land Use Commission	NLTB/Land and Mineral Resources
Establishment of assistance scheme for Fijian landowners taking up cane farming on their reverted lands	Land Reform
Determining of % of mining royalties to be paid to landowners	Land and Mineral Resources
Royalty regime for artesian or ground water	Land and Mineral Resources
Resumption of Government Tenancy in provincial & tikina owned commercial office buildings	Public Service Commission
Granting tax exemption to Fijian & Rotuman owned companies	Finance
Preparation of a Twenty Year-Development Plan for Fijian and Rotuman development	Finance

Source: Fiji Government 2002.

Policy directives provided more specific details of how the Blueprint was to be implemented, as Table 6.4 shows. Perhaps the most significant policy was the preparation of the 20YP. Most of the other policy initiatives were contained and elaborated on in the 20YP. This will be discussed in more detail later.

Table 6.5 Budgetary provisions under the Blueprint

Budgetary provisions	Ministry responsible
Government subvention to fund entire operation of Fijian Administration	Fijian Affairs
Government annual grant to NLTB	Fijian Affairs
Budget Provision of $1.5m payment to NLTB of arrears in rent for leases on State Schedule A Land	Lands and Mineral Resources
Grant to endow the proposed Fijian Development Trust Fund	PM
Government provision for Fijian Education Fund	Education
Assistance to Fijian schools and research into Fijian education	Education
Conversion of $20m interest-free loan to FAB to a Government grant	Fijian Affairs
Government provision of interest free loan to FAB for purchase of shares in Yasana Holdings Limited (YHL)	Fijian Affairs
Reinstatement of Government budget provision to assist Fijians in buying back ancestral land alienated as freehold land	Lands and Mineral Resources
Reinstatement of annual allocation from Government to Provincial Councils	MFA - Fijian Affairs
Land development for settlement of tenants whose ALTA leases have expired	ALTA and Land Resettlement
Land development for low cost housing	Housing
Land development for resettlement of squatters	Housing
Assist commercial development of native land through NLTB	Fijian Affairs
Village Improvement Scheme	PM

Source: Fiji Government 2002.

The budgetary provisions relied heavily on state funding (Table 6.5) and some initiatives, such as the provision for Fijian education, were old ones; some, like the village improvement scheme, were relatively new ones.

The ethnic-based initiatives of the Blueprint were seen by critics such as the Fiji Human Rights Commission to be at odds with the spirit of the social justice provisions of the 1997 Constitution (Fiji Human Rights Commission 2001). However, given the tense political situation at the time, it was considered a possible remedy for communal tension. Even the military, which was opposed to indigenous ethno-nationalism, endorsed it on the ground that it would provide a good platform for peaceful transition away from the 2000 turmoil by appeasing the nationalists who were seen to pose a serious threat to security and stability.

The proposed new constitution in the Blueprint was meant to replace the suspended 1997 Constitution. The suspension of the 1997 Constitution by the military was welcomed by many indigenous Fijians who were, ironically, opposed to the general position the military had taken during the coup. A constitutional review process was put in motion and the review commission was headed by Professor Asesela Ravuvu of the University of the South Pacific, an avid indigenous development advocate. The interim government envisaged that given the events of 2000 a constitution which would guarantee indigenous political supremacy similar to the 1990 one was the most appropriate. However, the constitutional process was later discontinued after the 1997 Constitution was reinstated by the Supreme Court on 15 November 2000.

There were other pro-indigenous proposals which were seen to have direct consequences on the economic wellbeing of other ethnic groups and thus provoked protests. They included the transfer of state land to native land, revocation of ALTA in favour of NLTA and transfer of ownership of offshore areas from the state to indigenous landowners. Indo-Fijians saw the land transfer and revocation of ALTA as a direct assault on their community interest while tourism industry business owners, many of whom were foreign nationals, saw the transfer of ownership of offshore areas as a threat to their business.

The compulsory savings proposal was seen by some as another form of taxation on top of contributions to church, provincial levies, land rates and other forms of traditional obligations. It was a form of communal capitalism but on a much larger scale. There was no suggestion as to how the money collected was going to be used and what the potential benefits were, except for the fact that they were to be used for "Fijian business." A proposal to set up a Fijian trust was based on the relatively successful Malaysian Bumiputera trust fund model; but after the Fijian Holdings fiasco almost a decade earlier, there were doubts as to how it was going to operate, let alone benefit ordinary indigenous Fijians, especially those in the rural areas and those involved in the informal economy.

The tax exemption proposal for indigenous Fijian companies was an interesting one because for some time indigenous entrepreneurs had been making demands for special preferences to protect their businesses in an entrepreneurial environment dominated by Indo-Fijian business. The failure of previous governments to heed this call contributed to political agitation which led to the formation of the Fijian Nationalist Party in the 1970s. By 2000 these familiar demands were still echoing loudly. Tax exemption would have benefitted individual indigenous Fijian entrepreneurs as well as community-based companies. However, it would have provoked widespread protest from other communities.

The establishment of a Fijian foundation had been suggested in the past; the problem was that, given the climate of ethno-political brinkmanship, any suggestion that dealt with researching and studying indigenous Fijian culture was often interpreted by Indo-Fijian leaders as nationalistic or even in some cases as "racist." Proposals for communal projects had to be seen to be balanced and supportive of multiculturalism. Since independence, the fine line between what was "cultural" and what was "political" was always contentious and it has not been easy to make that distinction.

Other suggestions in the Blueprint, such as land compensation, strengthening of the Fijian administration and the Fijian trust, compulsory savings, an increase in mineral royalties, improvement in native land administration, affirmative action law and government assistance for NLTB and Fijian Holdings, were not new at all. In fact some of these have been part of on-going discussions since independence. The issue of land compensation and mining royalties, for instance, had been a major cause for grievance amongst landowners for years and was taken up by Bavadra during his reign as FLP leader in the 1980s.

The Blueprint, like past affirmative action initiatives, naturally attracted criticism from other ethnic groups. The favourite charge was that it was a "racist" document. The ensuing political debate was a replay of the same old tunes of ethnic condemnation and counter-condemnation. Despite the criticisms, Qarase was determined to use his position as head of the interim government to implement a comprehensive program of affirmative action to transform the lives of indigenous Fijians. The military had chosen him as interim prime minister because of his acclaimed commercial and public service background and as development adviser for various indigenous Fijian groups, including the GCC. Qarase quickly grabbed this opportunity to implement and institutionalize on a much larger national scale his ambitious plans for indigenous advancement.

The main principles of the Blueprint were similar to those of the post-1987 affirmative action programs. However, the major difference between affirmative action in 1987 and that of 2000 was that in the case of the former, the programs were driven by ad hoc policies compared to the latter, which attempted to be more coherent in the form of a state-sponsored formal framework. Nevertheless there were two major problems with the Blueprint. Firstly, there was no attempt to examine how similar programs failed in the post-1987 period. It would have been prudent to identify the causes of the failure and put in place remedies to ensure that the same mistakes were not repeated. Unfortunately the same players involved in the 1987 fiasco were also involved in creating the Blueprint. Secondly, the provisions of the Blueprint focused primarily on strengthening communal institutions rather than developing independent entrepreneurial skills. The assumption was that indigenous Fijians could survive only in a communally protected environment, a view which had its origins in Gordon's orthodoxy, as we saw in Chapter 2, and which was perpetuated in the communal capitalism framework, as we saw in Chapter 5. A symbolic gesture to reinforce this belief was when the Blueprint was presented to the GCC for its blessing on 13 July 2000. Instead of re-thinking new strategies (such as generating indigenous Fijian innovation and entrepreneurial training) which were more relevant to the contemporary economic climate, it was much more politically and culturally convenient to simply use old bottles to brew new wine. The lessons of history were ignored and this turned out to be costly later.

Implementing the Blueprint: The 20YP

While the Blueprint provided the broad framework for affirmative action, the 20YP was much more comprehensive and detailed and was meant to be the implementation manual for the Blueprint. Nevertheless, there were a number of major differences between the Blueprint and the 20YP.

While the Blueprint conceptualized affirmative action as a natural right for indigenous Fijians by virtue of their status as indigenes, the 20YP attempted to position affirmative action in terms of Fiji's multi-cultural context and in terms of how it could contribute to the creation of an equitable solution, fostering multiculturalism and lessening ethno-political tension. The mission statement of the 20YP talked about the need to socially engineer Fiji to become "a multi-ethnic and multi-cultural society"; a society where "the special place of indigenous Fijians and Rotumans as the host communities are recognized and accepted, and where their rights and interests are fully safeguarded and protected, alongside those of other communities, in the overall national development and in the interests of maintaining peace, stability, unity and progress in Fiji" (Fiji Government 2001: 1). Affirmative action was no longer seen as a given but as a historical necessity to help foster a multicultural society.

Furthermore, the Blueprint was more a political declaration inspired by the political sentiments of the time, where the 20YP was a much better-researched document with detailed statistics about the socio-economic performance of the different ethnic groups, the areas of inequity and how to target and address these over a twenty-year period.

Another important difference was that while notions of human rights and social justice did not feature in the Blueprint (this was one of the criticisms of it), the 20YP addressed them directly as a way of building up legitimacy and winning cross-communal and international support. For instance it argued that affirmative action was permissible under international legal instruments such as the UN Declaration of Human Rights and the ILO Convention on Indigenous Rights if it was geared towards addressing inequality and empowered a disadvantaged group. Instead of asserting the rights of indigenous Fijians to preferential development, as was the case in 1987, there was a new shift in tone in the 20YP, signifying the diminishing influence of ethno-nationalists in the drafting of the document.

One of the most significant features of the 20YP was the formulation of the Equity Index (EI), which was meant to assess the levels of inequities between the different ethnic groups. It was based on a simple formula which took into account the different levels of achievement of the different ethnic groups (Current Distribution Ratio (CDR)) in relation to the national population, expressed as the Target Equity Ratio (TER) of 1:1. The TER depended on the population distribution and the ratio of the group designated as recipients of affirmative action to the rest of the population. Different countries would have different TER. The TER for Fiji was based on the premise that under the 1996 census the designated groups (indigenous Fijians and Rotumans) made up about 52% of the population and other ethnic groups made up about 48%. This approximated a 50-50 distribution or 1:1 ratio, thus the TER of 1:1. Achieving the 1:1 (50-50) equity scale became the 20-year affirmative action target. Thus the EI represented the number of times indigenous Fijian output must be increased to achieve the 1:1 TER within 20 years. Table 6.6 shows the relationship between the TER (what is to be achieved), CDR (the situation at the moment) and EI (the number of times the indigenous output should be increased to reach TE). TE represents the equity threshold that needs to be targeted. According to this formula, real equity can only be achieved after CDR reaches the threshold of 1:1.

Table 6.6 Equity Index for selected occupational categories between Indigenous Fijians and other ethnic groups, showing Target Equity Ratio (TER), Current Distribution Ratio (CDR) and Equity Index (EI)

Occupational category	TER	CDR	EI
Corporate Manager	1:1	1:6	6
Physical, Mathematics, Engineering Sciences	1:1	1:3	3
Business and Legal Professionals	1:1	1:3	3
Physical and Engineering Science Technicians	1:1	1:2	2
Finance and Sales/ Business Service	1:1	1:3	3
Extraction and Building Trade	1:1	1:3	3
Plant and Machine Operators/Elementary	1:1	1:3	3

Source: Calculated from Fiji Government 2000: 49-54.

Table 6.6 shows that indigenous Fijians were substantially disadvantaged compared to other ethnic groups in various occupational categories such as corporate manager; physical, mathematics, engineering sciences; business and legal professionals; physical and engineering science technicians; finance and sales/ business service; extraction and building trade (1:3); and plant and machine operators/elementary. In occupational categories such as education, tourism and in the primary industries, indigenous Fijians had performed well; but in some areas where technical skills were needed there was still a wide gap. The optimistic belief was that by 2020 every sector in Fiji where indigenous Fijians were lagging behind should have achieved a 1:1 ratio with other ethnic groups. To ensure this was achieved, a monitoring system was to be designed and, in addition, there were to be a major mid-term review and minor quarterly reviews.

There were problems with the 20YP from the beginning. Perhaps the major weakness was the lack of a coherent link and coordination between the document framework and the various government ministries and their respective sectors. The sectors identified for reform were education, population, human resources development and utilisation, commerce and finance, public enterprise reforms, health, resource-based industries, tourism, culture and heritage and rural development. The idea was that relevant ministries in charge of these sectors were to carry out the affirmative action strategies in accordance with the prescribed processes in the plan. But often the ministries would do things through the initiatives of the departmental personnel. Because the 20YP provisions were mainstreamed into the respective line ministries, there was confusion as to the distinction between affirmative action initiatives and normal ministerial programs. It appeared that ministry officials were not well trained in the matter.

Furthermore, while there was a monitoring system in place, it was not strictly adhered to. It was quite difficult in the beginning to ensure accountability, transparency and the tracking of financial flows, partly because there was no professional training carried out of those involved in the implementation of the programs and disbursement of funds. The agriculture scam which we will discuss in detail later was due in part to this lack of capacity.

Another major problem was the politicization of the 20YP. The draft of the 20YP document was completed before the September 2001 election and the Affirmative Action Unit (AU) responsible for its implementation was transferred from the Central Planning Office within the Ministry of Finance to the Prime Minister's Office. The SDL used the 20YP and Blueprint quite extensively for its election campaign by presenting it to indigenous Fijians as the "solution" to their socio-economic problems. This may have contributed to the SDL's election victory in 2001. Meanwhile, there were allegations of vote buying in rural areas in various parts of the country. Voters were offered farming implements, amongst other things, for their vote. This led to the infamous 'agriculture scam'. The scam was identified before the 2001 election and the investigation continued for a number of years after the election.

Post 2001 election: Unearthing the scam

The results of the 2001 election (see Table 6.7) show that the two major ethnic parties, the SDL and FLP, won most seats. The SDL won 32 seats and the FLP won 27 seats. The Matanitu Vanua (MV), a party linked to George Speight, the leader of the 2000 coup, won six seats. The SDL and MV formed a coalition, thus establishing indigenous Fijian dominance in parliament and control of government.

Due to fundamental political differences, the SDL refused to include the FLP in the cabinet as required by the constitution's multi-party provision and this led to a court battle which was eventually won by the FLP in 2005. In response to the court ruling the SDL allocated some junior cabinet positions to the FLP, but did not include Chaudhry. One of the SDL's concerns was that, given its antagonism to affirmative action since the 2000 coup, the FLP's presence in cabinet would compromise the SDL's affirmative action project.

Table 6.7 Results of the 2001 election by political parties

Party	Communal		Open		Total	
FAP	-	-8	-	-	-	-9
FLP	19	+1	8	-10	27	-9
MV	5	+5	1	+1	6	+6
NFP	-	-1	1	+1	1	-
NLUP	1	+1	1	+1	2	+2
NVTLP	-	-1	-	-1	-	-2
PANU	-	-4	-	-	-	-4
SDL	19	+19	13	+13	32	+32
SVT	-	-6	-	-3	-	-9
UGP	1	-1	-	-	1	-1
Others	1	-6	1	-1	2	-7

Source: Fiji Election Office 2002.

With overwhelming indigenous Fijian support, the SDL victory was seen as an endorsement of its pro-indigenous policies and provided the political confidence needed to carry through the SDL's affirmative action policies with greater vigour. However, from its first day in office, the SDL had to deal with the irregularities and scandals which had plagued the affirmative programs since 2000 and which continued to 2006. Even before the 20YP was eventually endorsed by cabinet in August 2001, abuse had already started.

The most high-profile scandal was in the Ministry of Agriculture (MOA), where more than FJ$18 million was used without proper authorization. As we saw earlier, agricultural development was a common target of affirmative action in the immediate post-independence period; but after the 1987 coups there was a shift towards developing an indigenous entrepreneurial class. One of the reasons for this change was the prominent support by the rural poor for the 2000 coup. Rural villagers turned up to parliament in their hundreds to publicly express their grievances and support the coup. There was a realization amongst those who drafted the 20YP that addressing rural poverty was critical in the long run for both national development and political stability.

The scam came to light after an audit by the auditor general and published in his report for the tear 2000. The report revealed that out of a total of FJ$18,344,696 used on affirmative action, FJ$2,093,599 was incurred in 2000 and FJ$11,059,129 in 2001; and there were outstanding payments totalling FJ$5,191,968. Of the outstanding payments, a total of FJ$1,421,141 of unpaid vouchers were held back due to lack of funds; FJ$676,072 worth of Local Purchase Orders (LPOs) had been issued but not paid; and there was a total FJ$3,094,755 of orders made without LPOs (Fiji Office of Auditor General 2002).

Most of the money was spent on farming implements and *dalo* (*taro*) suckers for planting. A total of FJ$3,094,754.75 worth of farming implements were purchased from Suncourt Hardware, a company owned by a prominent Indo-Fijian company, at inflated prices. As Table 6.8 shows, the prices of farming implements from Government Supplies, where implements for government use were normally sourced, were considerably cheaper than the Suncourt Hardware prices. This became a central issue in later police investigations and subsequent court cases which led to the conviction and imprisonment of some government officials and the Suncourt managing director.

Table 6.8 Comparisons between Suncourt Hardware and Government Supplies Prices

Item	Suncourt Hardware price	Govt Supplies Dept price	Difference ($)	Difference (%)
Digging fork	125	71	54	76
Digging shovel	30	18	12	66
Digging spade	75	31	44	142
Post hole spade	95	50	45	90
Cane knife	14	7	7	100

Source: Fiji Office of Auditor General 2002: 10.

A total of 5,587,327 *dalo* suckers worth $838,099 were bought from eight suppliers and sold to farmers in the rural areas. Ironically, of the eight suppliers, only four were indigenous Fijians and the other four were either Indo-Fijians or Chinese. Most of the *dalo* suckers were supplied to the following clients: Naitasiri Provincial Farm-Navuso (120,000); various other Naitasiri districts at a rate of 1,000 a month; district of Vuna in Naitasiri (15,000); Vanuakula Catholic Mission in Naitasiri (15,000); Wailevu Rural Development Co-operative Society (Tailevu), consisting of 210 farms in five villages (240,000); Sabeto Village Community Development Project; and Nadroga-Navosa province (454,400) distributed to 660 farmers. Of the *dalo* suckers distributed in Nadroga, 17% or 75,000 were distributed to coastal and cane land areas from Namatakula to Malomalo and Raviravi towards Nadi. Interestingly, an Indo-Fijian farmer in Ba was also supplied with 20,000 dalo suckers. As part of the MOA diversification program, there was an attempt to encourage *dalo* farming amongst indigenous Fijians in certain parts of the Nadi and Nadroga as an alternative to cane farming on land returned from Indo-Fijian farmers after the expiration of land leases.

The major beneficiaries of the *dalo* project were from the three provinces of Naitasiri, Nadi and Ba, out of a total of 14 provinces in Fiji. A possible explanation was that most *dalo* suckers were sourced in Viti Levu and it was easier to deliver them to these places. However, this does not explain why no *dalo* suckers were supplied to farmers in Rewa, Ra, Namosi and Serua, which were also located in Viti Levu. Widely circulated rumours in Fiji pointed to the role of ministers in the interim government and SDL candidates actively involved in the distribution of *dalo* suckers and farming implements as part of their 2001 election campaign. The reason provided by the interim Minister for Agriculture, Apisai Tora (whose own village of Sabeto was one of the beneficiaries) for the preferential distribution of *dalo* suckers was that "these areas had largely made up the crowd of agitators in Parliament" during the 2000 coup so "We thought we should give the initial concentration there" (Manueli 2001).

The way the purchasing of goods was carried out became one of the major concerns of the auditor general, who described the irregular processes used as tantamount to "risks of fraud and corruption" (Fiji Office of Auditor General 2002: 14). The MOA officials broke the normal rules for purchasing and created their own system on a scale which was unprecedented in Fiji's history. Table 6.9 shows a comparison between the normal purchasing process and the irregular process used by MOA officials.

Table 6.9 Comparison between the normal process for Government Local Purchase Order and the irregular

Normal LPO process	Irregular process used by MOA
Original and duplicate issued to suppliers of goods and services;	Certified applicants' letter is taken to the supplier;
Supplier keeps original and returns duplicate to Ministry with its invoice, and supplies good or service. From invoice, a liability is entered into the commitment ledger to record the expected amount owed by Ministry to the suppliers;	Supplier processes the Order; Goods are supplied to the applicants; Invoices are sent by the supplier to the Ministry; Orders are raised & Commitment ledger is updated; Payment is then made to the suppliers
Ministry on receiving the goods, checks the goods against triplicate copy of the LPO, certifies that goods have been received in good condition, and processes the order for payment;	
Fourth copy retained in the book.	

Source: Summarized from Fiji Office of Auditor General 2002: 12-13.

Over time, the link between the MOA officials and Suncourt became very personal and trusting, to the extent that even without an LPO Suncourt would deliver the goods on the strength of the customer's application. About half of the approvals for the Naitasiri applicants were done this way. It was also found that some LPOs issued to suppliers were open and the items to be supplied and their prices were left entirely to the discretion of the supplier and farmers.

Another company involved in the supply of goods was Morris Hedstrom (MH). However, one of the MH employees, Pita Koney Alifereti, wrote and authorised all quotations from MH, Coral Island Traders (a subsidiary of MH) and Repina Wholesalers, Alifereti's own company. The Repina price was often accepted because it was lower than the other two. It was later revealed during Alifereti's trial that he also gave money to a number of senior officials of the MOA to ensure that his company, Repina Wholesalers, continued to be awarded the MOA contract (Fijilive, 11 September 2008). A total of FJ$336,246.52 was given to Repina between 8 September 2000 and 15 January 2001. It was a case of insider information, deception and bribery, for which Alifereti was later jailed.

The five MOA officials responsible for the approval process signed LPOs above their limits. The rules specified that the permanent secretary could approve an LPO up to $10,000 and those below him had lower ceilings. However, a total of FJ$2,083,787.34 worth of approvals was signed beyond the authorized limits of the senior officers, as shown in Table 6.10. The actions of these officers were deemed to be in breach of the Public Service Code of Conduct (Fiji Government. 1999b).

Table 6.10 Amount signed by senior officers of the MOA beyond the authorized limits

Designation	Name	No. of orders	Total value (FJ$)
Permanent Secretary	Peniasi Kunatuba	43	636,451.13
Deputy Secretary (Services)	Samisoni Ulitu	67	545,983.66
Deputy Secretary (Operations)	Ken Cokanasiga	36	340,834.44
Director, Administration and Finance	Sereani Bainimarama	2	18,120.00
Principal Accounts Officer	Suliasi Sorovakatini	78	542,398.11
Total		**226**	**2,083,787.34**

Source: Fiji Office of Auditor General 2002: 14.

Kunatuba, the permanent secretary, was the first to be jailed for abuse of office in 2006 and was handed a four-year term. In her ruling, High Court judge Justice Nazhat Shameem described the case as the most serious abuse of office to be brought before the Fiji courts so far (*The Fiji Times*, 16 November 2006).

On 17 September 2008, Alifereti was jailed together with Peli Kete Doviyaroi, a MOA officer who was given FJ$8,000 by Alifereti. Suncourt Hardware director Dhansukh Lal Bhika, the managing director for Suncourt, and Suliasi Sorovakatini, the principal accounts officer, were sentenced to five years and four-and-a-half years respectively by the High Court in March 2011 for official corruption. Bhika was accused of providing Sorovakatini with airline tickets to Australia and FJ$51,921.12 credit facilities in his company – all to ensure that Sorovakatini continued to approve the purchase of farming implements from Suncourt. Needless to say, the agricultural scam further tarnished the already negative image of affirmative action.

I have discussed these developments in detail in order to address two issues which have plagued other affirmative action policies in the past. The first is that without proper monitoring, affirmative action as a politically driven project can be subject to arbitrary manipulation and abuse by those concerned. Secondly, mainstreaming affirmative action programs into line ministries can cause confusion over which programs are routine and which ones are affirmative action initiatives.

A further issue here is the question of responsibility. Who was ultimately responsible for the debacle? Cabinet did not formally endorse the 20YP until 14 August 2001, just 11 days before the election, although the program had been in place since 2000 (Fiji Parliament 2001b). There were conflicting messages from the MOA. Kunatuba, the permanent secretary, stated that the interim minister, Apisai Tora, had approved of the program in writing; but the letter was not found during the police investigation. Interestingly, the MOA's official statement defended the minister and contradicted the permanent secretary's position. Kunatuba maintained his innocence during the court case and appealed. Kunatuba was later sacked by the minister before being imprisoned.

During Kunatuba's trial, the prime minster, Qarase, and 11 other cabinet ministers and senior civil servants were named in court documents in relation to their role in the scam as part of the election campaign. The court affidavit said that the interim government had "known and had given its approval to the use of the farming assistance scheme to fund its policy on the development of indigenous Fijians and Rotumans" (AAP, 22 June 2002: 1). It was also claimed that Finance Minister Jone Kubuabola was fully aware of the abuse because the ministry had to make approvals of FJ$28,000 daily; and that by the end of 2000 the government had approved FJ$2 million under the scheme. Mr Kunatuba claimed that he had become a scapegoat in a systematic scam involving the entire affirmative action program.

In hindsight, it is inconceivable that Tora, Qarase, Kubuabola and other ministers of the interim government were not aware of what was happening. For instance Tora's village had been a beneficiary of affirmative action in the form of dalo suckers and farming implements, while Qarase had accompanied the Assistant Minister for Agriculture, Marieta Rigamoto, in a trip to Rotuma, Rigamoto's island, to distribute FJ$100,000 worth of farming implements in July 2001, a month before the election (*The Fiji Times*, 10 July 2001). Kubuabola was responsible for overseeing the use of funds. Rigamoto stood as an independent in the Rotuman communal seat during the 2001 election and won. Rigamoto was not new to scandals. In a separate case, she was ordered by the Fiji Court of Appeal to pay back more than US$850,000 to the National Bank of Fiji (later to become Colonial Bank and lately Bank South Pacific) in September 2011 for her loan in the 1990s.

Tora defended himself during the trial by blaming the military for the scandal, arguing that they were the ones responsible for introducing affirmative action after the 1987 coup and for endorsing the post-2000 coup affirmative action to "diffuse the tension caused by the political crisis" (*Radio NZ*, 13 Oct 2006). The witch hunt was on and there were questions raised about the ethical practices of public servants, the reliability of the state in implementing affirmative action and more importantly the appropriateness of affirmative action itself. Despite the noble political intent the scam had further eroded the integrity of affirmative action and was a major slur on the indigenous Fijians' reputation in the utilization of communal resources, although only a minority was involved. As a precaution against political backlash on the eve of the election, the interim government, which had by now formed the SDL Party, suspended the affirmative action program in August 2001.

Nevertheless, it appeared that the scam did not deter indigenous Fijian voters from voting overwhelmingly for the SDL, perhaps because the publicity value of the affirmative action programs may have overshadowed an understanding of the actual outcomes. With the embarrassing scam in mind, parliament enacted the Social Justice Act on 21 December 2001 as required under Section 44 of the Constitution to provide the legal framework for future affirmative action initiatives.

Attempts at reconciliation and tension: Towards another military coup

Affirmative action programs after the 2001 election and before the 2006 coup faced numerous challenges. The agriculture scam had shaken people's confidence in the government to administer affirmative action. As investigations, court cases and recriminations continued for the next few years, ministries became more cautious and civil servants and ministers became more aware of the need to practice good governance. But this did not stop other scams (as we shall see later) from taking place. The Social Justice Act of 2001 provided affirmative action with more legitimacy and this gave the SDL new confidence in its desire to push forward pro-indigenous reforms.

The Social Justice Act was timely because it created an environment in which the 20YP could be more inclusive; and it also gave credibility to the SDL's national dialogue and reconciliation policy, which was implemented in the form of the *talanoa* sessions, facilitated by Dr Sitiveni Halapua of the East-West Center in Hawaii. The government decided to expand the affirmative action provisions to include other ethnic groups, as required under the Social Justice Act and as a gesture of national unity.[1] In addition, the SDL initiated a national reconciliation process which, unfortunately, was later overshadowed by the unpopular Reconciliation, Tolerance and Unity Bill (RTUB). However, thirdly, affirmative action and national reconciliation were challenged by growing protest and tension and, perhaps most seriously was the growth of protests and tension and, perhaps the most seriously, by pressure from the military on Qarase's government to remove the RTUB and Qoliqoli Bill. These will be discussed in detail later.

In a report to Parliament on 4 October 2004, Qarase stated that since 2001 a total of 27 affirmative action projects had been implemented for indigenous Fijians

---

1   Affirmative action for Indo-Fijians and other ethnic minorities was administered under the Ministry of Multi-ethnic Affairs (MMA). While scholarships for indigenous Fijians under the FAB were based on ethnicity and academic performance, scholarships under the MMA were based on ethnicity and parents' income, set at $10,000 or less.

and Rotumans and 19 for Indo-Fijians and minority communities (Qarase 2004). There were problems in implementing some of the provisions because of a lack of indigenous Fijians in critical areas such as contracting. For instance, of the FJ$33.6 million worth of contracts awarded from July to December 2003, only $5.6 million (17%) went to indigenous Fijian-owned companies compared to $12.6 million (38%) to Indo-Fijian companies and $15.4 million (45%) to other minority groups. This was still a long way from the 50% target for indigenous Fijian participation envisaged under the 20YP.

The SDL put a lot of emphasis on indigenous education. It was realized that education was the most successful of the affirmative action initiatives since affirmative action started in the 1970s. In fact a large number of current politicians, civil servants, military officers, professionals and corporate sector employees were products of educational affirmative action in the 1970s and 1980s; thus there was significant interest in this area. It is estimated that by 2011, of those who had graduated, almost 7,000 were serving in Fiji. The success rate for indigenous students improved considerably over the years from below 50% in the 1970s to 90.42% in 2011 (Fiji Ministry of Information 2011).

There were other initiatives, such as village banks, for grassroots people as part of the 20YP savings scheme. By 2004 total savings of $71,000 from 659 clients had been deposited. Perhaps the most significant increase in the participation of indigenous Fijians in business was in the taxi business, where the number of licences given to indigenous Fijians increased from 85 in 2001 to 123 in 2003; whilst for Indo-Fijians there was an increase from 2 in 2001 to 310 in 2003. As at 30 September 2004 the total number of taxi permit holders was 5,456, of which indigenous Fijians held 2,275 (42%), Indo-Fijians 2940 (54%) and for other minorities held 4%.

Despite these achievements, criticisms of affirmative action continued unabated. In its 2003 report on Fiji, the UN Committee on the Elimination of Discrimination noted that affirmative action did very little to address the issue of poverty. The Committee strongly recommended that affirmative action policies be devised to ensure that "poverty alleviation programs benefit all poor Fijian citizens, irrespective of their ethnic origin, to avoid undue stress on already strained ethnic relations" and that "the adoption of any affirmative action program be preceded by consultations involving all ethnic communities" (United Nations Committee on the Elimination of Discrimination 2003). It has been argued along the same lines that affirmative action led to economic distortion, stifling of competition and corruption while sustaining, rather than alleviating, poverty (Chand 2007). In its review of affirmative action in Fiji the Fiji Human Rights Commission [FHRC] (2006) concluded that there was no coherent approach to addressing the problems of disadvantaged groups and added that the situation of other disadvantaged groups such as ethnic minorities and women were not catered for. The FHRC recommended that the Social Justice programs should be reviewed and the affirmative action policies be removed because they discriminated against other groups and thus breached the human rights provisions of Section 38 (2) of the Constitution.

In another major shock reminiscent of the agriculture scam, the Auditor General identified irregularities in a $2 million project to promote educational centres of excellence as a way of upgrading indigenous education. A number of schools were identified as centres of excellence and the intention was that the facilities of those schools would be upgraded and the quality of education would be improved through increased resources in order to attract the best students and promote educational achievement and innovation in the region. However, the auditor general's report in 2005 showed unauthorised advance payments for building materials, purchase of rugby jerseys for a team, unaudited accounts, unauthorised payments and excessive payments for casual labour (Fiji Office of Auditor General 2005).

The auditor general recommended that the principal of the Naitasiri Provincial High School be investigated for wrongfully authorising LPOs and payments in relation to the following: $215,000 paid in advance to HP Kasabia, an Indo-Fijian retail company; $26,870 used to buy school uniforms that were not approved under the scheme; and $12,180 used to buy jerseys for a rugby team. These were expenses illegally diverted from the following approved allocations: upgrading of staff quarters ($135,000); upgrading of classroom blocks and a science laboratory ($65,000); a vocational centre ($20,000); building of toilets ($30,000); improvement of water supply ($10,000) and electrical wiring and a switchboard ($15,000). About half of the $2 million grant for the project was subject to misuse (Fiji Office of Auditor General 2005).

It was alleged by the Fiji Labour Party Deputy Leader, Poseci Bune, on 23 November 2005 that the company, Safeway Marine and Rabitech was contracted by the Ministry of Fisheries to build 90 fibreglass boats which were distributed before the August 2006 election (*The Fiji Times,* 24 November 2005). He also made revelations of villagers receiving grass cutters, outboard motors, digging forks, cane knives and other farming implements in various provinces. Allegations were also made of people being freely given airfares, refrigerators, dinner packs and accommodation.

It was the agriculture scam all over again, although on a much smaller scale. The auditor general's report questioned why Naitasiri High School was chosen ahead of the dozens of indigenous schools. The SDL party was formed by the Naitasiri chiefs and there was an unwritten understanding that Naitasiri, which had been neglected in the area of development and education since independence, was to be a priority beneficiary of affirmative action. The workers employed in the building projects were all from the tribe of the local chief, one of the founders of the SDL Party. The contract for the building works was awarded to Baba Forests, a company owned by SDL national secretary, Jale Baba. The report noted that the building work was not properly completed. It was obvious that the SDL had a direct hand in the implementation of the scheme and in the irregularities.

The hallmark of the client-patronage relationship, a common feature of past affirmative action, was clearly visible. The SDL had projected the image of being the saviour of the indigenous Fijians and was desperate to fulfil the heightened expectations in whatever way possible. Because of its political malleability, affirmative action was the perfect tool that could be utilized at will to achieve this purpose. Again like the agricultural projects, Naitasiri, a major SDL stronghold, was a major beneficiary. The unfair distribution of affirmative action projects amongst indigenous Fijians remained an unresolved issue.

Noble intentions turned sour: The RTUB and Qoliqoli Bill

With a comfortable parliamentary majority and overwhelming support amongst the indigenous Fijian people and indigenous institutions such as the powerful Methodist Church and the 14 provincial councils, the Qarase government initiated two bills which it hoped would transform indigenous political and economic life for the better. Although the intentions of the RTUB and Qoliqoli Bill may have been noble, they nonetheless invoked widespread resistance.

The RTUB was a form of political affirmative action first introduced into parliament on 4 May 2005, almost five years after the May 2000 coup. The RTUB proposed a Reconciliation and Unity Commission to grant amnesty to perpetrators of the 2000 coup and compensation to those who suffered as a result of the coup during the period from 19 May 2000 to 15 March 2001. The president was to have a veto power over the granting of amnesty. On the advice of the prime minister and in consultation with the leader of the opposition, the members of the commission were to be appointed by the president.

A Joint Parliamentary Select Committee on Justice, Law and Order, chaired by the Deputy Speaker of the House, Manasa Tugia, was set up to conduct public consultations around the country and altogether the committee received 272 written and oral submissions. However, the Fiji Labour Party boycotted the committee and refused to provide a representative for it. The RTUB was presented as "a genuine attempt at political stability and unity in Fiji" after various nation-building approaches such as "multiparty Cabinet, the *talanoa* session, Parliamentary Standing Committee, Ministry of Reconciliation, prosecution and jailing of offenders etc. have failed" (RTUB 2005). It proposed that the way forward for Fiji was through national reconciliation, forgiveness and tolerance. Since the 2000 coup had fractured and scarred Fiji deeply, the most appropriate way forward to nurture and consolidate inter-ethnic trust and unity was through restorative justice (*Fiji Sun*, 2 December 2005). The idea was to shift the conflict resolution approach from retributive justice, which was based on punishment, to restorative justice, which was based on reconciliation between the victims and perpetrators of the 2000 coup. The RTUB emphasized the importance of giving victims of the May 2000 events a chance to be heard as well as to apply for compensation and reparation. It also gave a chance for the perpetrators to ask for forgiveness and apply for amnesty. Earlier, a number of coup activists had been released under the Compulsory Supervision Order (CSO) and this had provoked criticism and opposition from the military and human rights groups.

The RTUB was the result of months of nation-wide consultations by the Ministry of National Reconciliation (MNR) as a build-up towards a national reconciliation week from 4 to 11 October 2004. The program for the week included public meetings and lectures on peace-building and multiculturalism around the country as a build-up to a public reconciliation ceremony at Albert Park in Suva on 10 October. The reconciliation ceremony was based on the indigenous Fijian model of peace-building known as *veisorosorovi* (forgiveness and reconciliation). The national ceremony, which was broadcast live around the country, consisted of inter-group forgiveness and acceptance of forgiveness between the various ethnic groups and religious groups. It was a solemn and moving occasion and the first of its kind in Fiji. A peace-building model which had been used for hundreds of years within the indigenous Fijian community was being used in the national context across ethnic, cultural and religious divides.

However, while the reconciliation program was hailed by participants as a success, it failed to achieve total reconciliation because two major players in the 2000 coup boycotted the ceremony – the military and the FLP. They both preferred "justice" through the retributive method (arrest, trial and imprisonment) to deal with the coup perpetrators. This exacerbated the already simmering tension between the military and the Qarase government and this antagonistic relationship spilled over into the RTUB debate.

The controversy over the RTUB was worsened by the existing climate of political animosity and suspicion. People's reactions showed a clear ethnic demarcation. A public opinion poll by Tebbutt, published on 21 June 2005, indicated that 55% of indigenous Fijians supported the RTUB compared to only 19% of Indo-Fijians; also 29% of indigenous Fijians and 60% of Indo-Fijians opposed it. About 10% of indigenous Fijians and 14% of Indo-Fijians said they did not care one way or the other (*Fiji Times*, 21 June 2005). A public opinion poll on 2 July 2005 suggested that only 4% of the population had read the RTUB fully and 16% had read it partially only (*Fiji Times*, 2 July 2005).

Critics argued that the RTUB would help legitimize the 2000 coup and promote a coup culture in the process. The military saw it as a direct affront to their role as the last bastion of state security during the 2000 upheaval. Some saw it as an attempt to undermine the rule of law and the constitution, especially the constitutional and statutory powers of the judiciary, DPP, police, military and other constitutional offices. The amnesty provision of the RTUB in particular was objectionable since it was seen as an insult to the rights of the victims of the coup to have their situation addressed.

The RTUB was in itself a form of political affirmative action to supplement the economic affirmative action programs of the 20YP. It was hoped that a reconciliatory political climate created by the RTUB would make the Blueprint and 20YP more acceptable to other ethnic groups and critics. The RTUB did not get off the ground, as the protests intensified and stern demands for withdrawal by the military commander, Commodore Frank Bainimarama, worsened the tension between the government and the military.

The Qoliqoli Bill (QB), first proposed in the Blueprint, was one of the SDL's major indigenous projects. The QB proposed that ownership of offshore indigenous fishing rights (*qoliqoli*), which hitherto had been under state jurisdiction, should be transferred to indigenous landowners. Part 2 of the Bill stated that "the State shall cease to be, and the Board shall be, bound by the terms and conditions subject to which such legal interests and rights were originally granted"… and "all *qoliqoli* areas are deemed to be native reserve unless the Minister upon application by the *qoliqoli* owners, declares by order in the Gazette such areas as outside native reserve within the meaning of the Native Land Trust Act" (Soqosoqo Duavata ni Lewe ni Vanua Party. 2006: 4-5).

By law, the state had legal jurisdiction over minerals found below the surface of the soil as well as in the sea area up to the high water mark. While the state had legal jurisdiction over the offshore areas, there was also recognition of landowners' traditional fishing rights or *qoliqoli*. While the two modes of jurisdiction existed harmoniously, there had also been cases of conflict between them, especially when issues of foreshore development and access to hotel beaches, private property and development projects were involved. In the case of the hotels, because of the often close ties between hotel owners and landowners through employment of local landowners in hotels or even shareholding, these problems had often been solved amicably. During the 2000 coup a few resorts and hotels were forcefully taken by landowners to show their grievances.

The country was divided as a result of the QB. The SDL government and its supporters, including the Methodist Church and a number of chiefs, argued that the QB was an important lever to enhance indigenous economic progress. It was argued that indigenous Fijians rarely benefitted from their *qoliqoli* in terms of compensation, rent and royalty and that ownership of the offshore area meant control of sea travel, resource exploitation and trade. It was seen not only as a potential source of economic wealth for the landowners, it was also a source of social and political empowerment and a basis for the self-determination prescribed in the Blueprint. For the SDL this could guarantee its continued political support amongst the indigenous population. The passage of the QB was timed to coincide with the election campaign for the 2006 general elections.

Opposition to the QB was widespread. Opponents included hotel operators, business people, NGOs, the military and a host of indigenous Fijian individuals and groups. There were a number of reasons for the opposition. First, tourist operators feared that the QB would put restrictions on tourism activities such as snorkelling, surfing, swimming and fishing and also create potential conflict with landowners over use of the *qoliqoli* for these activities. This would seriously impact on Fiji's largest industry. In addition to this they would have to pay extra fees for use of the *qoliqoli* on top of the lease and royalty they paid landowners. Second, many of those in the real estate, development and business industry feared that the QB was going to impact on their capacity to invest and generate income. Third, the military was more concerned about the security implications of the QB, particularly as it could potentially lead to more intra-communal conflict between landowners. Tension over fishing rights, some ending in physical assault, has been a cause of concern in many parts of Fiji over the years. Unlike the land area, there were no reliable boundaries for the *qoliqoli* and it was assumed that the land boundaries somehow would extend in an imaginary perpendicular line into the sea. The boundaries were supposed to be determined by a commission to be set up by the QB.

Another complication was that indigenous Fijians held a very flexible concept of traditional fishing rights and people from various localities could fish in other *qoliqoli* through mutual agreement with the local landowners. In some parts of Fiji, it was assumed that the *qoliqoli* was owned by everyone and everyone had rights of access to it. In some places such as Cakaudrove and Lau, the *qoliqoli* was said to be "owned' by the paramount chief and thus it was open for fishing access by everyone as long as they used it for purely subsistence purposes. Commercial fishermen needed a government licence for fishing within designated *qoliqoli,* which were policed by fishing wardens, who were usually from the local landowning unit. The fear was that the QB could lead to disputes over sea boundaries and that such disputes might escalate and lead to instability within the indigenous community and beyond.

The Fiji Law Society was opposed to the bill because it felt that it was unconstitutional, since it interfered with the Native Lands Act, which protected Fijian landownership; and also because it would weaken the sovereignty of the state as well as undermine the rights of other ethnic groups (*Radio NZ*, 2 November 2006). The same view was echoed by the Fiji Human Rights Commission.

What was meant to be a major affirmative action program for indigenous Fijians became the final straw which contributed to the intensification of tension between the military and the government, culminating in another military takeover on 6 December 2006.

Conclusion

The seven years between 1999 and 2006 were among the most turbulent in Fiji's history, with two coups and three elections. As this chapter has shown, there were different trends in affirmative action programs within this period and, beneath the veneer of indigenous advancement, affirmative action was utilized to serve various political interests such as appeasement, conflict resolution, mobilization for electoral support and the strengthening of political patronage.

The scams associated with affirmative action were indicative of how economic prudence became subservient to political expediency. There was no attempt to learn from the lessons of the post-1987 scandals, which cost the country more than FJ$200 million. Instead, political ambition and optimism overshadowed rational judgement in a negative way. Just as with the Alliance and SVT in the past, the desire of both the FLP and SDL to influence and transform the immediate political conditions in their favour through affirmative action became a primary consideration which outweighed the importance of indigenous advancement. The political rather than the transformational value of affirmative action became a priority consideration.

This was one of the reasons why affirmative action programs had very little creativity and innovation in relation to the self-empowerment and positive social transformation of the indigenous Fijian community.

As an example of this, there was a lot of emphasis on helping existing rural communal farming through provision of implements and *dalo* suckers, rather than reorganizing rural production using new knowhow and innovation to develop entrepreneurial skills, and to boost value-added productivity and large-scale marketing. Many of those who were supplied with *dalo* suckers and implements were community groups which produced agricultural produce for community projects. This was a form of communal capitalism which, as we saw in previous affirmative action projects, would have promoted community solidarity but undermined entrepreneurial innovation. No doubt a significant amount of *dalo* produced by the village farmers would have been "lost" through communal obligation and subsistence consumption. There was no proper monitoring system to determine the contribution of these rural plantations to transforming and advancing the economic status of individual indigenous Fijian families

Worse still, there was no vision for an ideal future society which rural indigenous Fijians must work towards. For instance, there was no plan for improving rural housing, education, health and infrastructure through *dalo* farming. It was assumed that an increase in *dalo* production would automatically have multiplier effects in other areas of the community. Furthermore, overproduction of *dalo* would have flooded the market and the impact of increased *dalo* production in real terms might have been negligible. There were no supporting innovative projects such as using *dalo* for large-scale industrial processing such as chips and other secondary food products to sustain large-scale *dalo* production in the long run.

The shift from urban-based projects after 1987 to rural-based projects after 2000 may have made political sense given the circumstances, but despite this, little changed in terms of the capacity of the state to carry out affirmative action programs effectively. This was a major shortcoming which had unfortunate consequences. The interests of the political masters rated higher than those of the group designated as recipients of affirmative action, the ordinary indigenous population. The distribution of affirmative action resources was skewed in favour of politically favoured provinces such as Naitasiri. Although affirmative action policies might have failed to achieve their objective of boosting economic advancement for indigenous Fijians and creating a more harmonious multicultural society, they nonetheless served more immediate political objectives in helping boost the SDL's chances of winning the 2001 and 2006 elections.

The period between 1999 and 2006 was one of lost opportunity. Both Chaudhry and Qarase squandered a great opportunity to use their potential to work together to address the grievances of indigenous Fijians as well as address the broader issues of national prosperity and peace. Failure to do this unfortunately helped to create the environment for yet another coup.

7. Post-2006 coup affirmative action: Development at gunpoint

Bainimarama's desire to forcibly remove Qarase's government started not long after Qarase won the 2001 election and in the five years before the December 2006 coup Bainamarama had made it clear a number of times that Qarase had to go (Tuatoko 2004; Fraenkel, Firth and Lal 2009). Two theories have been put forward to explain Bainimarama's persistent eagerness to usurp power. The first and more widely accepted 'official' version was that Bainimarama came to the realisation that Qarase was strongly sympathetic to the ethno-nationalist ideology used to justify the 2000 coup. This was manifested in Qarase's pro-indigenous policies including the release of coup perpetrators from prison and the proposal for the Qoliqoli and RTU Bills. Added to this was the argument that corruption and racial politics were endemic in the system and a "clean-up" campaign was imperative (Fraenkel, Firth and Lal 2009).

The second theory claims that Bainimarama had more sinister motives and used the clean-up excuse as an escape mechanism. Because of the investigation relating to his possible involvement in the 2000 coup, the death of a number of soldiers during the November 2000 mutiny and possible treason charges relating to his threats to usurp state power, Bainimarama staged the coup as a way of avoiding dismissal and prosecution which would result in possible long-term imprisonment. Those who take this line of argument have quoted 'inside sources' within the military, such as Lt Col Tevita Mara, a close associate of Bainimarama who defected to Tonga, as well as the Republic of Fiji Military Forces (RFMF) Board of Inquiry's report on the involvement of the military during the 2000 coup (Republic of Fiji Military Forces 2000).

Whatever the truth is, the coup on 6 December was very much a slow and public process, with Bainimarama warning of an impending takeover if Qarase could not fulfil certain conditions such as withdrawal of the Qoliqoli and RTU Bills, and treason charges against Bainimarama, amongst others. Although these conditions were later fulfilled, Bainimarama was uncompromising and was still determined to stage the coup. Amongst the targets for his 'clean up' campaign were indigenous-based institutions and policies, including affirmative action (Ratuva 2011). This was a clear reversal of the military's initial support for the Blueprint when it was launched in 2000, as we saw in Chapter 6. In the light of this policy reversal, it can be argued that Bainimarama's opposition to affirmative action was only temporary because, as this chapter shows, pro-indigenous policies were implemented in earnest as part of the post-coup economic development policies of the regime.

Affirmative action after the 2006 coup was characterized by four major developments. The first was the attempt by the military to abolish affirmative action, at least in terms of public rhetoric; and simultaneously to weaken the indigenous Fijian middle class and those institutions which were suspected of providing support and legitimacy to the Qarase government and its affirmative action policies.

The second feature was the militarization of development, as military officers were substituted for displaced senior civilian officials in key positions in cabinet, the civil service and state corporations. Of particular significance was the deployment of military officers as regional commissioners to directly supervise rural development programs outside the cumbersome government bureaucracy and also to act as political links between the rural indigenous population and the military-led state. The term 'affirmative action', which was heavily demonized by the military, was removed from the development vocabulary and replaced with *vakatorocaletaki ni taukei* (Fijian development), the same term used to describe pro-indigenous affirmative action immediately after independence. It was a case of using a different vocabulary for the same thing.

The third feature was the creation of a consolidated national development and rebuilding framework in the form of the People's Charter (hereafter referred to as "charter"). The charter was a major framework for rebuilding a new order which was considered suited to Fiji's multi-ethnic community. However, there were contradictions within the charter which undermined its credibility.

The fourth feature related to the paradoxical shift in the regime's ideological position from opposition to ethno-nationalism to reinvention of its own brand of ethno-nationalism by proactively mobilizing indigenous Fijian support and loyalty at the grassroots level through implementation of pro-indigenous development initiatives for rural indigenous Fijians.

These four features are discussed here not necessarily in any chronological sequence' since they were taking place simultaneously and were part of the same 'clean up' process, which involved unpacking the old order and rebuilding a new one. Where possible, parallels will be drawn with the Malaysian and South African situations – however, it must be noted from the outset that one of the major points of contrast with these two countries is that, unlike Fiji, both these countries have not had coups and direct military rule, although they have experienced degrees of repression by their security forces. Thus this chapter examines the distinctive affirmative action programs under a military regime.

Paralysing the opposition and demonization of affirmative action

Upon taking over power, the military put in place a number of draconian measures to consolidate its control, thwart opposition and give credence to its rhetoric of an 'anti-racist' and 'pro-multiethnic' coup. These mostly involved weakening indigenous Fijian institutions deemed to pose a threat to the post-coup transformation process.

The first target for political control and repression was the SDL, the biggest indigenous Fijian political party. Formed in 2000 to contest the election in the same year, the SDL was no different in terms of political ideology from the SVT, which it replaced as the main indigenous Fijian party. Some leaders of the SDL were harassed, arrested and detained and the headquarters of the party was raided several times. Disabling the SDL, which had supporters all around the country both in the rural and urban areas, was critical if the military was to uproot its political influence and avoid potential grassroots mobilization against the coup. The complex military intelligence network planted within the community seriously handicapped the work of the party.

Meanwhile a systematic witch-hunt for suspected coup opponents within the state hierarchy commenced as early as one month after the coup. After the ministers were removed on the day of the coup, a number of CEOs of government ministries and government corporations, diplomats and senior civil servants also met the same fate. Within a few months, about 200 senior executives and civil servants were removed and replaced by military officers, expatriates, known civilian coup supporters or those seen to be 'neutral' and politically trustworthy. This was a highly significant process because a large number of those removed were products of educational and employment affirmative action over the years and were the cream of the indigenous educational and professional achievement. Although, the attempt to build up an indigenous business middle class did not fully succeed, as we saw in Chapter 5, it was a different story for the establishment and expansion of an educated professional middle class. Educational affirmative action created a dynamic indigenous professional class mostly in the public and semi-public sector. This group had been a major pillar of Fiji's economic and social development and also acted as a strong stabilizing force. Most of those removed were charged with 'corruption', which was to be investigated by the all-powerful Fiji Independent Commission Against Corruption (FICAC) which was set up to perform multiple roles including investigation, arrest and prosecution (Fiji Government 2007). Successful prosecution by FICAC has been very low because of insufficient evidence and a lack of professional competence among the legal staff.

The systematic 'dismantling' of the indigenous Fijian professional class has seriously damaged and even reversed the concerted efforts over the years since independence to provide high-level training for indigenous Fijians as part of the localization process. Because Australia and New Zealand banned members of cabinet, heads of government departments and members of government boards and their families from travelling to those countries, many professionally qualified locals refused to take up government appointments. Many qualified locals also left the country and many Pacific island states have benefitted from Fiji's loss as many professionals took up senior advisory posts in those countries.

While it was easy for the regime to remove individuals from their positions, it was not easy to dismantle existing corporations and institutions which came into being through affirmative action. For instance, Fijian Holdings Limited (FHL), with 30,464,650 communal and individual shares, still remains as the flagship of indigenous Fijian business under the patronage of the military regime (Fijian Holdings Limited 2011: 3). The original CEO, Sitiveni Weleilakeba, a close associate of Qarase, was removed and replaced by Sereana Qoro, an accountant, who was also later removed and replaced by Nouzab Fareed, an accountant. Since the 2006 coup the members of the board have all been replaced.

The breaking up of the indigenous middle class in Fiji is in stark contrast to events in Malaysia and South Africa, where there has been concerted effort to consolidate rather than dismantle the gains of past affirmative action policies. It seems that Fiji has somehow ditched the Malaysian lesson which it so meticulously and zealously followed in the 1980s.

The Great Council of Chiefs (GCC) was also targeted because a number of senior members were opposed to the coup and, also, it represented the apex of indigenous socio-cultural power both in terms of symbolism and applied power politics. The GCC has always been the major political driving force behind affirmative action. FHL, for instance, was first conceived by the GCC; and scholarships for indigenous Fijian students funded by the Fijian Affairs Board were ultimately sanctioned by the GCC. Although the GCC operated on the basis of consensus, that consensus concealed the deeper power dynamics within the institution.

Amongst the competing chiefly blocs were the Mara and Ganilau faction on the one hand and the Cakobau family and its allies on the other. Prior to the coup, Ratu Epeli Ganilau was removed as chair of the GCC; however, later, as Minister for Fijian Affairs (which had responsibility for GCC) he used the opportunity to get back at his adversaries in the GCC by carrying out Bainimarama's order to suspend the institution. Subsequently, two committees were set up to oversee the reform of the indigenous Fijian governance system – one was to review the GCC and another to review the Fijian administration system generally, including the role of the Fijian Affairs Board and the provincial councils.

The recommendations of both committees were accepted by the regime. One of the recommendations of the GCC review was that only formally installed chiefs were to be members of the august body (GCC Review Committee Report 2007). This meant that a large number of high chiefs, including those of the Cakobau family, supposedly Fiji's most paramount chiefly family, were ruled out. Because of the long-running dispute within the Cakobau clan over the Vunivalu titleholder, this provision may see their removal from the GCC and thus weaken their national significance considerably. Ironically, Ganilau later resigned from cabinet as Minister for Home Affairs due to differences with Bainimarama over the deportation of a Fiji Water company executive. The GCC was eventually de-established by the I-Taukei Affairs Revocation Decree on 16 March 2012. While some indigenous Fijians may see this as an act of cultural sacrilege, Bainimarama justified his decision saying:

> The Great Council of the Chiefs (sic) is a product of our colonial past and Fiji must now focus on a future in which all Fijians are represented on the same basis. If all Fijians are to have their say during the consultations for Fiji's new constitution, we must ensure every voice is equally heard and equally represented (Fiji Ministry of Information 14 March 2012).

Instead of nipping ethno-nationalism in the bud, as it were, the abolition of the GCC simply spawned a new wave of protest and nationalist agitation through the media and blogs. Now that the public emergency decree was being relaxed, the stage was set for more public debate on the issue. One of Fiji's leading paramount chiefs, Ro Temumu Kepa wrote to Bainimarama complaining that the abolition of the GCC was based on a "serious error of judgement," as the GCC "lives forever in the hearts of the people." The letter asserted that the GCC was a "stabilizing factor for Fiji and they have helped to control the ethno-nationalism and helped facilitate ethnic conciliation in Fiji" (Ro Temumu Kepa 2012). The regime had underestimated people's loyalty to the GCC and the potential destabilizing effect it could create and this could be a critical factor in determining Bainimarama's fate in the 2014 general election.

The GCC controversy coincided with the announcement on 9 March 2012 of the appointment of a five-member constitutional review committee chaired by Prof Yash Ghai, an internationally renowned constitutional expert with a long association with Fiji. Other key components of the constitutional reform process included a national civic education process to take place from May to July; consultation between the constitutional commission and citizens (2 July to 30 September); collation of public submissions (October to December); convening of the a constituent assembly to receive, discuss and endorse the draft (January 2013) and promulgation by the president in February 2013 (Fiji Ministry of Information, 9 March 2012). This process was to produce a new constitution after the old one was overturned in 2009. The draft constitution duly emerged in late 2012, only to be rejected by the government and replaced in early 2013 with a draft of its own.

The suspension of the constitution on 10 April 2009 was one of the most dramatic acts by the military regime to eliminate opposition and entrench once and for all the military regime's hegemony. This was in response to the decision on Thursday 9 April by the Fiji Court of Appeal, regarding the litigation brought by Qarase and the SDL, that the Bainimarama regime's December 2006 takeover of executive power was unlawful. In response to this the president declared the Fiji Constitution abrogated and put forward a number of proposals for a "new legal order." The declaration by the president also terminated all judicial and other constitutional appointments and nullified provisions relating to the role of the GCC and affirmative action. To the regime, the removal of the constitution was a blessing because it basically formalized its intentions to "wipe the legal slate clean and start again" (Iloilo, J. 2009). The newly proposed constitution is expected to have some "non-negotiable" provisions in the form of non-ethnic representation and the reduction of the voting age to 18 years. The electoral system is also expected to be based on the proportional representation model and there is expected to be a multi-party cabinet as a way of sustaining an institutionalized multi-ethnic order.

Another powerful indigenous institution, the Methodist Church, also became a target of military censure because of its close links with the SDL and its long association with indigenous ethno-nationalism since the 1987 coup. The military's strategy was to dent the Methodist Church's nationalist political base by demanding the removal of the leaders, who were well known ethno-nationalist sympathisers, and also to undermine the influence of the Methodist Church (to which 53% of the total indigenous population adhere) on the community by disallowing it from holding its annual conference as well as restricting its public activities under the Public Emergency Decree in 2009 (Fiji Government 2009b 2009). This had a crippling effect on the institutional operation of the church, which relied on the money raised from the fundraising during the annual conference to pay for its administration and outreach activities. Even after the lifting of the Public Emergency Decree on 7 January 2012 and its replacement by the equally draconian Public Order Act 2012, the church was still refused permission for an executive meeting. It might be relevant at this stage to note that Malaysia had similar draconian legislation in the form of the Emergency Public Order and Prevention of Crime Ordinance 1969, which was repealed on 24 November 2011, and the Internal Security Act of 1957. Both were used to suppress opposition and also to push affirmative action legislations forward unilaterally.

The weakening of indigenous Fijian institutions was further reinforced by media restrictions under the Emergency Decree and later reinforced by the Media Decree 2010. Force or its threat was widely used to silence opposition and a large number of people were arrested, detained and some were physically abused. Within this general atmosphere of repression, opposition took the form of blogging and other "underground" forms of resistance (Walsh 2009).

In the beginning the crippling of the indigenous Fijian institutions was often represented as a necessary 'clean up' measure to rid Fiji of ethno-nationalism and race-based politics. The next step was to abolish policies, such as affirmative action, which were considered contrary to multicultural values. Affirmative action was seen to be associated with ethno-nationalism, Qarase's government, the GCC and the indigenous professional middle class, the very institutions which had been targeted for reform. Chaudhry, who was a strong critic of affirmative action as leader of the opposition prior to the 2006 coup, took the opportunity as Minister of Finance to help phase out affirmative action and shift the policy focus towards poverty alleviation. For example, in a highly publicized case, under the pretext of an "ownership issue," Chaudhry personally intervened to stop the government from renting Kadavu House, an office block owned by an indigenous development company linked to the province of Kadavu and acquired through an affirmative action loan from the Fiji Development Bank (*Fiji Times*, 9 February 2008).

Initially, many Indo-Fijian supporters of the coup saw Bainimarama's attack on indigenous institutions as politically justified "vengeance" against nationalists who staged the 1987 and 2000 coups, in which Indo-Fijian-led governments were overthrown and Indo-Fijians victimized. The Methodist Church and GCC were two of the prime players in the wave of anti-Indian politics after the two coups. The view that the coup was "pro-Indian" and "anti-Fijian" slowly changed as Chaudhry himself was removed as Minister of Finance because of allegations of money laundering and tax evasion and also because of the increasingly trans-ethnic nature of those supporting or opposed to the coup. The support for Bainimarama amongst some groups was due largely to the regime's pro-indigenous rural development initiatives.

Militarizing indigenous development

With affirmative action officially declared moribund and with the loss of significant Indo-Fijian support for the coup due to Chaudhry's dismissal, one of the regime's urgent tasks was to put in place development initiatives which would serve two important political purposes. The first was to appease the indigenous Fijian people and chiefs who felt betrayed and insulted by

Bainimarama's attack on the GCC, Methodist Church and other indigenous Fijian institutions. Bainimarama needed indigenous support to make up for the loss of Indo-Fijian support, however small it may have been, and also to dispel the general belief that the coup was anti-indigenous. Secondly, the regime needed to provide something concrete or at least needed to be seen to be doing something substantive to give credence to the 'clean up' rhetoric.

Rural development was a major strategy to achieve both of these purposes; and the most convenient way to go about this was for Bainimarama to be directly in charge of all government matters relating to indigenous Fijians, rural development and information. To further speed up and ease the process, military officers were appointed heads of department, chairs of boards and regional commissioners to carry out Bainimarama's direct orders.

Chaudhry's removal made things easier for Bainimarama as he was now directly in charge of funds as Minister of Finance. In addition he was also responsible for the Ministries for i-Taukei Affairs, of Provincial Development and of Information, three key ministries which would ensure his direct access to and influence amongst indigenous Fijians. As Minister for i-Taukei Affairs, Bainimarama was in charge of the entire indigenous governance structure at the state, provincial, district and village levels and as Minister for Provincial Development he was directly responsible for the infrastructural developments and delivery of services to indigenous Fijians in the rural areas. Bainimarama's control of the Ministry of Information allowed him to directly influence the contents and method of delivery of information to the people.

The officers appointed as commissioners at one stage were Commander (Navy) Joeli Cawaki for the western division, Colonel Inia Seruiratu for the northern division, Colonel Mosese Tikoitoga for the central division and Colonel Ifereimi Vasu for the eastern division. There have been changes in these posts over time as colonels have been moved from position to position. The commissioners assumed multiple roles as regional administrators, development advisors, public relations experts and political commissars of the regime. In many respects they were powers unto themselves over and above the normal state bureaucracy and were directly and dually accountable only to Bainimarama, who was both their ministerial head and their military commander.

Despite breaking almost every normal civil service regulation and procedure, this militarized structure ensured that delay in the implementation of development projects – a common feature of the previous system – was reduced considerably and services were directly delivered to targeted groups. The system also minimized corruption by civil servants, some of whom had amassed fortunes by milking the previous system, which often lacked proper accountability and transparency. Because of this, many rural people who were often cynical about the efficiency of the government bureaucracy became converts to the new militarized system. Another reason for popular support was that the new authoritarian structure allowed for greater accessibility of the ordinary people to Bainimarama himself, who continually received personal requests for infrastructure and accolades for his "man of the people" generosity during his rural tours.

Bainimarama's rural tours became frequent and were seen as important in terms of public relations for the regime. It was an opportunity to personalize and sell the human face of the coup with the hope of mobilizing political support at the village level. In an atmosphere of media censorship, these trips were widely publicized not so much for their news value but for their political and strategic purposes. The strategy seemed to work as chief after chief from different provinces declared public support for Bainimarama and asked for forgiveness for their initial opposition to the coup. This has given Bainimarama confidence that he would "win" the 2014 election if he stands (*Sky TV Australia,* 3 March 2012). Qarase responded saying that he still commanded support and would "win" (*Radio Australia*, 13 March 2012). However, Qarase's political future is in doubt after he was imprisoned for abuse of office in 2012.

While Bainimarama's tactical manoeuvre appeared to be working favourably for him, one should not dismiss the rural people as merely an ignorant and passive audience. In the context of traditional indigenous politics, the rural villagers would no doubt be playing their own *politiki gata* (sharp politics). This consists of the dual approaches of *veivakabekabei* (public glorification) often followed by the stealth strategy of *liumuri* (backstabbing). This well-rehearsed, age-old political tactic involves publicly elevating someone's ego through noble words at the manifest level and later pulling the rug from under their feet at the latent level – a tactical ploy indigenous Fijians routinely play on each other in either humorous or serious situations. For some, singing praises to Bainimarama was a way of attracting more development, while for others it was a genuine expression of gratitude for direct and quick provision of services that past elected governments failed to deliver.

Another effective means of changing the perception of villagers was the use of the large number of retired soldiers in villages as links between the commissioners and villagers. The link between the military regime and the local communities were strengthened by the fact that almost every indigenous Fijian had a relative in the military. In fact many indigenous Fijians believe that soldiering is a natural profession for them.

No doubt both the indigenous rural communities and the military regime have benefitted from the development initiatives. However, the militarization of the development process (that is the use of military officers as well as military-style decision making and norms) would have broader consequences in the long run.

First, overdependence on authoritarian decision making outside the normal bureaucracy could breed collective sympathy and preference for military and authoritarian governance over democracy and thus has the potential to nurture pro-coup sentiments in the future. In fact, a number of chiefs had openly stated that Bainimarama should be in power for as long as he wanted since, based on past experience, an elected government would not have the will and honesty to fulfil its promises to the people.

Second, the militarized development process and circumvention of normal government structure has undermined the systems of accountability and institutionalized decision making which were once the hallmarks of constitutional state governance. After the 2014 election the civil service governance process will need to be re-established and reformed for greater efficiency and public servants need to be re-trained and re-programmed to fit back into the normal civil service procedures and culture.

Third, by responding so readily and generously to direct requests by the community, the regime is in danger of creating a "cargo cult" mentality predicated on the belief that requests will always be honoured by the regime. Ironically, while the regime has been generous with disbursement of development resources, Bainimarama has also been advising people in no uncertain terms not to rely on handouts but to work hard to achieve things for themselves.

Fourth, rural development projects, like the SDL's affirmative action policies, are unevenly distributed amongst the provinces. The most favoured provinces tend to be those on the island of Viti Levu, especially Tailevu and Naitasiri. The regime is determined to appease these two provinces through rural development because of their well-known opposition to the 2006 coup.

Fifth, one of the consequences of military-based development has been that projects tend to be too ad hoc, rather than being part of a coherent development design with a systematic sequence of implementation. This is because of the tendency to speed up the project implementation process to mobilize people's support and loyalty through making visible changes before the 2014 election, in which Bainimarama is expected to stand.

Sixth, many civil servants have withdrawn into themselves or silently rebelled by refusing to commit themselves fully to their work because of the new authoritarian military work culture. Many continue to work in an environment of fear and suspicion after many were sacked and detained for making statements deemed by the military to be provocative and undesirable. Bainimarama has denounced the lack of commitment by civil servants as one of the biggest obstacles the regime is facing in its desire to move Fiji forward.

The direct involvement of the military in the conceptualization, framing and implementation of the rural development projects for indigenous Fijians has redefined the structure and modus operandi of the state's engagement with the community. While it has distorted the regular procedures, it has also sped up the implementation process. However, because the colonels do not have any economic and social development qualifications or experience, the effectiveness and sustainability of these projects need closer scrutiny. The desire to deliver is incompatible with the available skills and qualifications of the military decision-makers. This has been a major dilemma faced by the coup-makers since 1987 and one of the solutions adopted by the military has been to hire willing civilian collaborators and even reluctant followers to carry out skill-based jobs. This is not to downplay the high level of training and the expertise of senior military officers. Many of them hold Masters-level degrees, but most of their skills revolve around military-related areas such as strategic studies, political analysis, security studies and, for some, engineering.

After the 2014 election, the military officers will have to make a choice either to remain in civilian service and maintain links with the military or return to the barracks with significant skills learned in the field that could be used to transform the military into a more development-friendly institution. Either way, these factors would have significant implications on the civil-military relations in Fiji in the long run.

From affirmative action to national development: The People's Charter

One of the dilemmas Bainimarama faced after systematically demolishing opposition and neutralizing the power of state and indigenous institutions of governance was to provide an alternative system to move Fiji forward towards the non-racial utopia he had promised. Part of the initiative to fulfil this promise was the setting up in January 2008 of the National Council for Building a Better Fiji (NCBBF) an organization consisting of cabinet ministers and "moderate" community leaders from different ethnic and religious groups (see Table 7.1), which was charged with putting in place a framework for change and reconstruction, popularly referred to as the People's Charter. The assumption was that for any credible change to take place there should be visible broad participation by representatives of the different communities.

Table 7.1 Composition of the National Council for Building a Better Fiji

Name	Designation
Commodore Voreqe Bainimarama	Co-Chair, Interim Government
Archbishop Petero Mataca	Co-Chair, Civil Society
Mr Mick M. Beddoes	President, United People's Party
Mr Daniel Urai	President, Fiji Trades Union Congress
Mr Patrick Wong	Fiji Islands Hotel and Tourism Association
Mr Desmond Whiteside	President, Fiji Manufacturers Association
Mr Dijendra Singh	Chairman, Fiji Girmit Council
Mrs Lorine Tevi	President, Fiji Council of Social Services
Mr Dewan Chand Maharaj	President, Shree Sanatan Dharm Pratinidhi Sabha
Mr Kamlesh Arya	President, Arya Pratindhi Sabha of Fiji
Rev. Akuila Yabaki	Executive Director, Citizens' Constitutional Forum Ltd
Mr Tarterani Rigamoto	Chairman, Council of Rotuma
Mr Teatu Rewi	The Chairman, Rabi Council of Leaders
Mr Rajeshwar Kumar	The President, Fiji Local Government Association
Mr Daryl Tarte	President, Media Council (Fiji) Ltd
Mrs Penelope Moore	President, Womens' Action for Change
Ratu Jolame Lewanavanua	Chairman, Lomaiviti Provincial Council
Ratu Filimoni Ralogaivau	Chairman, Bua Provincial Council
Ratu Wiliame Katonivere	Macuata Provincial Council
Ratu Meli Bolobolo	Chairman, Ra Provincial Council
Ratu Josateki Nawalowalo	Chairman, Kadavu Provincial Council
Atunaisa Lacakabuka	Chairman, Serua Provincial Council
Josefa Serulagilagi	Chairman, Tailevu Provincial Council
Mr Rupeni Silimaibau	Provincial Youth Forum of the Fiji Islands
Mrs Selina Lee Wah	Female social worker, Labasa
Mr Filipe Bole	Minister for Education, National Heritage, Culture & Arts, Youth and Sports
Mr Mahendra Chaudhry	Minister for Finance, National Planning, Sugar Industry and Public Utilities (Water & Energy)
Mr Joketani Cokanasiga	Minister for Primary Industries
Ratu Epeli Ganilau	Minister for Defence, National Security and Immigration
Dr Jiko Luveni	Minister for Health, Women and Social Welfare
Ratu Epeli Nailatikau	Minister for Foreign Affairs, International Co-operation and Civil Aviation
Mr Tom Ricketts	Minister for Industry, Tourism, Trade and Communications
Mr Aiyaz Saiyed-Khaiyum	Attorney General and Minister for Justice, Electoral Reform, Public Enterprises and Anti-Corruption
Mr Netani Sukanaivalu	Minister for Lands, Mineral Resources and Environment

Source: National Council for Building a Better Fiji 2008.

However, despite attempts to create an ethnically balanced council, the membership was heavily slanted towards indigenous Fijians and "other" minority groups. Out of the 34 members, 18 were indigenous Fijians, 5 were Indo-Fijians and 10 were ethnic minorities. As Table 7.2 shows, the minority groups were over-represented and Indo-Fijians were extremely under-represented. The gross disparity may have been due to difficulties in recruiting people to join the NCBBF, but in terms of public symbolism it undermined the very principle of equal participation and representation which the NCBBF claimed to represent.

Table 7.2 Proportion of membership of NCBBF

Ethnic group	Number	% Membership	% Population
i-Taukei	18	54%	57%
Indo-Fijians	5	16%	37%
Other minorities	10	30%	6%
Total	34	100%	100%

Source: National Council for Building a Better Fiji 2008.

Nevertheless, the main task of the NCBBF was to put together the charter, a summary document derived from a collection of commissioned papers that were earlier published under the *State of the Nation Report*. Over 250,000 copies of the charter were published in English, Fijian and Hindi and distributed throughout Fiji. The NCBBF claimed that 65% of the population supported the charter but critics argued that people were literally coerced into endorsing it. It should be noted here that the charter was similar to the Malaysian New Economic Policies (NEP) in the sense that it was meant to be a "bible" for "structural" transformation. However, the differences were that the charter addressed both political and socio-economic transformation while the NEP dealt only with socio-economic transformation. Furthermore, while the NEP was driven by ethnic-based affirmative action, the charter attempted to remove ethnic preferences in favour of class-based preferences.

The overarching objective of the charter was to "rebuild Fiji into a non-racial, culturally vibrant and united, well-governed, truly democratic nation; a nation that seeks progress and prosperity through merit-based equality of opportunity and peace" (National Council for Building a Better Fiji 2008: i). These objectives were guided by the following principles: "a just and fair society; achieve unity and national identity; merit-based; equality of opportunity for all Fiji citizens; transparent and accountable government; uplifting of the disadvantaged in all communities; mainstreaming of the indigenous Fijian in a modern, progressive Fiji; and sharing spiritualities and interfaith dialogue" (Peoples Charter 2008: ii).

The provisions which perhaps related directly to affirmative action were: firstly, "uplifting of the disadvantaged in all communities" and secondly, "mainstreaming of the indigenous Fijian in a modern, progressive Fiji." These two policy statements were meant to displace preferential indigenous development in favour of a national development framework.

The first statement no longer identified indigenous Fijians as a disadvantaged ethnic group as the Blueprint had, and instead the term 'disadvantaged' was defined in trans-ethnic socio-economic terms. The intention was to take ethnicity out of development. Indeed the economists who drafted the economic development papers were hostile to affirmative action as a form of ethnic preference. This position was a major shift from the 1997 designation of affirmative action target groups, namely indigenous Fijians and "other disadvantaged groups."

While the first statement may be commendable, the second one, which suggested "mainstreaming" indigenous Fijians, may have been ideologically contentious. It was tantamount to the colonial social-Darwinian stereotype that indigenous Fijians were backward *jungali* (bush people) who needed to be "modernized" and "civilized" to reach a higher stage of human progress. Sadly, it may have reflected some of the latent ethnic prejudices still prevalent in Fiji. This perception failed to recognize the fact that indigenous Fijians were already politically, economically and culturally mainstreamed into the global community. However, their local and international success stories and achievements in the fields of education, commerce, technology and other areas have not been highlighted sufficiently to show that they had potential to be just as competitive as any other ethnic group in the world. The problem was not about mainstreaming indigenous Fijians into modernity but identifying the right development model, right leadership style, right environment and appropriate skills' level to further enhance their achievements.

The charter's shift from preferential development to national development was a reversal of the Blueprint but, ironically, it might even be beneficial to the poor and disadvantaged indigenous Fijians. As we have seen in previous chapters, the corruption and scandals associated with affirmative action under Rabuka and Qarase (see Chapters 5 and 6) were often linked to well-placed individuals and groups using affirmative action resources not on the basis of need, but to satisfy their own economic and political interests. Amongst the major beneficiaries were middle-class indigenous Fijians who did not need affirmative action at all.

Another major dilemma of the charter was that its claim to "Affirm that our Constitution represents the supreme law of our country" became void after the removal of the constitution by the President Iloilo, acting on behalf of the military, in April 2009. This was after the Supreme Court declared the 2006 coup, the action of the president in appointing a new government and post-coup decrees, including amnesty for the military coup leaders, illegal. The removal of the constitution effectively meant that the affirmative action provisions under the constitution were no longer lawful. It was replaced by the development strategy under the charter.

Moreover, although the affirmative action proposals of the Blueprint and 20 Year Plan had been replaced by the charter, affirmative action had not been completely removed. Perhaps one of the last elements of affirmative action to continue is the provision of scholarships for indigenous Fijians and for economically disadvantaged minorities. There has been talk of disbanding ethnic scholarships in the future. If this happens indigenous Fijians will have to work extra-hard to get their children through university. Because higher education scholarship is the most successful affirmative action policy and the most important means of social mobility, poverty eradication and socio-economic progress for indigenous Fijians (despite the failure of business and development affirmative action), the termination of Fijian Affairs Board scholarships might have a profound impact and could be a recipe for instability in the future.

While there has been loud public rhetoric since 2006 to phase out affirmative action policies in the name of multiculturalism, ironically, the regime has for pragmatic political reasons made a policy commitment towards indigenous Fijian development, but without using the term "affirmative action."

Reinventing affirmative action for indigenous Fijians

In his speech to the UN General Assembly in September 2011, Bainimarama said:

> Communal philosophy has not served our people well. Affirmative action policies which were not based on acceptable definitions of disadvantage, but on racial origin alone, created a more divided society, and one in which many depended on handouts rather than on personal enterprise. Politicians represented particular ethnic groups, and drove policies which were intended to further divide the people of our nation. As in all parts of the world, ethnic origin and religious divisions simply became a tool to maintain power. I am determined that our society will remove the narrow walls of ethnicity and communalism to create unity and strength as a nation (Bainimarama, Speech to UN General Assembly, 22 Sept 2011).

Most of the contents of the speech were highly commendable in principle, except that, on closer examination, by the time of his address to the world leaders, Bainimarama had initiated a development process which was pro-indigenous for all intents and purposes. A detailed reading of the various policy documents relating to national development (see Table 7.3) shows that while the term 'affirmative action' has been eliminated and ethno-nationalism cast as a political scourge, the actual implementation process of the development initiative reveals a different story.

Table 7.3 Levels of development policy making

Policy-making level	Focus
People's Charter	Broad philosophy for change
Strategic Framework for Change	Key milestones to be realized with specific timelines to be achieved leading up to the elections in 2014.
Government Roadmap for Democracy and Sustainable Economic Development (2009-2014)	Sets out a framework to achieve sustainable democracy, good and just governance, socio-economic development and national unity.
Strategic Plan (3 years)	Sets out specific strategies and objectives to be developed within 3 years (e.g. 2009-2011).
Ministry Corporate Plan (Yearly)	Individual Ministry internal priorities based on Strategic Plan.

Source: National Council for Building a Better Fiji 2008. 2008; Fiji Government 2009c; Fiji Government 2009d.

The five hierarchies of development policies summarized in the table above were based on the trickledown effect from the charter to the ministry's corporate plan. However, behind the technical language were latent political interests. For the regime, two important political considerations were at stake. The first was how to "sell" the coup and its "achievements" to the indigenous Fijian audience, many of whom opposed the takeover on the grounds that it appeared to be anti-indigenous and pro-Indo-Fijian. Bainimarama no doubt wanted to leave behind a legacy as a "man of the people," a term often used to describe him (*Radio New Zealand*, 18 January 2012) and the only way he could do that was to make exceptions to the non-discriminatory spirit of the charter and directly implement pro-indigenous development policies. The second issue was that Bainimarama, who is likely to contest the 2014 election, needed something substantive to attract voters during the coming election campaign.

To fulfil these two aims, the regime has made it a priority to focus on very visible infrastructural rural and outer island development programs. Table 7.4 provides a summary of the rural and island budgetary allocation for 2007, 2008 and 2009. It shows that the allocation increased in 2008 and decreased in 2009 as the financial squeeze forced the government to cut down on expenditure. Except for the multi-ethnic affairs allocation, most of these budgetary rural allocations were directed primarily at indigenous Fijians.

Table 7.4 Allocations towards rural and outer island development programs: 2009 Budget (FJ$ million)

Sector	2007 (FJ$m)	2008 (FJ$m)	2009 (FJ$m)
Fijian Affairs	0.92	0.90	0.90
PM's Office (for village improvement)	1.12	0.80	-
Agriculture	10.55	16.15	21.40
Fisheries & Forestry	1.8	2.4	1.15
Provincial Development	10.5	8	5.5
Multi-Ethnic Affairs	1.6	1.6	1.60
Lands & Mineral Development	0.23	0.23	0.40
Youth Development	-	-	0.20
Health	3.8	5.2	2.50
Infrastructure & Works	80.1	80.15	38.30
Total	**110.62**	**115.43**	**71.95**

Source: Fiji Government 2009a.

Rural infrastructure developments covered a wide range of sectors and geographical areas including electricity developments such as the Nadarivatu hydro dam, Buca and Taveuni hydro scheme, and electrification works in Tailevu, the interior of Naitasiri and Macuata. Roads were built in Wainibuka, Sigatoka, Kadavu, Naqali and Serea and will soon be built in the interior of Nadroga and Ba. A number of schools were also built and health centres were improved in places like Navua, Kadavu and Cuvu. A new development was the building of a bio-fuel plant on Koro Island to convert coconut oil into engine fuel. Many of these projects were funded through Chinese aid. China has already pledged more than $500 million worth of aid to Fiji (Fiji Government 2012).

About $200 million worth of road projects have been planned for 2012, including the 10-kilometre Buca Bay Road in Vanua Levu, the 19-kilometre Sawani-Serea Road in Naitasiri, the 15km Sigatoka Valley Road in Nadroga and the sealing of 5km of the Moto Road in Ba (*Fiji Sun*, 8 March 2012). These roads are very crucial for agricultural production and would benefit indigenous Fijians greatly. In addition, government has announced financial assistance for three hundred home owners around the country through a $2 million grant from government and, in addition, 92 families had their home loan accounts completely written off in 2011 (*Fiji Times*, 14 January 2012). Most of these are indigenous Fijians.

One of the most explicitly pro-indigenous policies of the regime was in the form of concessions first outlined in the 2009 Budget, without, of course, the use of the contentious words "affirmative action". Bainimarama stated that the state would transfer ownership of thousands of hectares of mature mahogany forest to indigenous landowners. In addition, tax holidays were to be offered to investors who established partnerships with indigenous Fijians in the areas of tourism, agriculture, forestry and fisheries (Fiji Government 2009a).

Other areas of potential indigenous development include resource-based projects such as the Bua bauxite mine, which opened in 2011, the planned huge Waisoi copper and gold mine in Namosi province, the proposed iron ore sand mining near the Ba River and a few other mining projects. These are major projects worth billions of dollars, in which Bainimarama has directly been involved either to intervene in compensation disputes between a company and landowners, as in Namosi, or to help facilitate the process to make it easier for the company to invest and maximize economic benefits for landowners, as in Bua.

Another issue which the current regime has been very sensitive about is land. Previous governments since independence had seen indigenous land both as a blessing and a curse. However, none of them succeeded in devising a system which could advance the socio-economic development of indigenous Fijians. Even the current regime, despite the introduction of new concepts such as the land bank, continues to perpetuate commercial land arrangements which led to the neo-colonial servitude of indigenous Fijians in the past. The exploitative division of labour during the colonial and post-colonial period was characterized by provision of land for mining and dumping waste as well as the provision of cheap, unskilled, manual labour by landowners, while the mining companies provided capital and expertise and were allowed to accumulate and repatriate massive profits.

Perhaps one of the most progressive policy initiatives by the regime was the suggestion for shareholding in and joint-ownership arrangement of the mining operations. One way of making this possible is to use land as an equity share for landowners but legislation (or a decree) has to be in place to make this happen. To enhance and facilitate shareholding and joint-ownership, the mining company should provide scholarships for locals to study relevant aspects of mining at the degree level (for example mining engineering, environmental science, mining economics, resources development, social and economic policy analysis) as a way of empowering locals to progressively assume a greater share and control of the mining operations. This is a way of consolidating the partnership between the landowners, company and government in the future. A full partnership cannot be realized when there is a large skills, knowledge and power differential.

One of the most contentious development policies of the regime is land reform. The regime hopes that reform will speed up agricultural production and help indigenous landowners:

Land reform in particular in relation to resource-based sectors is paramount. Issues pertaining to the ailing sugar sector, the need to diversify into other crops and the imperative to have commercial farming can only be addressed in a meaningful way if more land is available for productive use on long and secure tenure basis (Fiji Ministry of Information 2010).

Land reform is part of the broader development framework encapsulated in the Ten Point Economic Plan (TPEP), which sets out specific targets to be achieved by 2020. These are: (a) GDP to be increased two-fold; (b) balance of payments current account deficit to be eliminated; (c) poverty to be reduced from current levels to less than 5% of population; (d) visitor arrivals to increase to 6 million; (e) financial sector to be liberalized with a view to eliminating exchange controls; (f) Fiji to grow its communication services sector business by 100%; (g) Fiji to achieve self- sufficiency in rice, meat and liquid milk; (h) Fiji to convert up to 90% of all electricity generation from fossil to renewable sources; (i) Fiji to convert up to 80% of all arable land area into productive use; and (j) Fiji to reduce unemployment rate to less than 3% (Fiji Ministry of Information 2010).

While these targets are impressive, they are not clear in terms of the role of the landowners. Of particular interest here is the land bank, which has been used as an example of breakthrough in inter-ethnic cooperation in land development. While the idea of "depositing" land in the "bank" is novel, the underlying principle has not changed from the colonial and neo-colonial arrangement where landowners gave up their land for lease and the tenant farmers worked on the land. This arrangement contributed to the retardation of commercial participation of indigenous Fijians because, as landlords and recipients of lease money, they were not encouraged to develop their commercial farming skills and expand their business acumen. Since independence, government after government under a succession of prime ministers – Mara, Bavadra, Rabuka, Chaudhry, Qarase and now Bainimarama – perpetuated this landlord and tenant agreement, first under the Agricultural Land Tenancy Ordinance or ALTO (1966), then ALTA (1976) and now under NLTA, all of which locked indigenous Fijians into the role of passive providers of land rather than active entrepreneurs.

More innovative options for land use have not been explored. One suggestion would be to form business partnership arrangements between Indo-Fijian farmers and indigenous landowners in the form of cooperatives or other forms of commercial enterprises, which would entail development and sharing of skills, knowledge and resources by both sides. The same partnership model should be encouraged in urban-based industries where Indo-Fijian and indigenous Fijian entrepreneurs can engage in commercial collaboration to ensure sharing of skills, expertise, resources and wealth as well as contributing to multiculturalism and inter-ethnic goodwill. The government can encourage this by granting tax concessions for companies which are based on inter-ethnic cooperation. Accepting and reinforcing the stereotype through policies that assume that only Indo-Fijians are business-minded and indigenous Fijians are not will continue to be divisive and potentially destructive.

However, while there is political aspiration for indigenous Fijian development, there is an absence of conceptual skills to define a new development paradigm that is forward-looking, relevant and sustainable. This deficit is partly due to the current and previous governments' flirting with neoliberal development thinking, inspired by the IMF's constant prodding for neoliberal reform. Part of the liberalization approach is the freeing up of indigenous land for international investors through the regime's land bank policy. One of the latent results of the land bank policy is that it redefines the role of the state as a land agent to facilitate international investment.

The last issue is the most worrying, especially when large international companies gain control of local land and use it for intensive farming to send food back to their countries in a process that is known globally as "land grab". Instead of benefiting indigenous Fijians, the land bank concept can potentially undermine their development aspirations in the future as good land is taken up by foreign investors.

Fiji's land reform is in direct contrast with land reform in Malaysia and South Africa. While land reform in Malaysia was inspired by raising the level of entrepreneurial engagement and the skills of Malay farmers to alleviate poverty, in South Africa it was based on how to redistribute 87% of commercial farmland owned by 13% of the population (whites) to the other 87% of the population (blacks, coloureds and Asians). In both cases, the idea was to enhance commercial agriculture for the indigenous population – the land bank in Fiji does not have this in mind.

A way forward for Fiji would be the formation of business partnerships between foreign business and landowners for agricultural development, using land as equity. Again, as suggested in the case of mining, laws should be changed to enable this to happen. Another way forward is to begin to move away from the notion of land protection and rights towards land innovation. It has been established by law that native land cannot be removed from native ownership. With this in mind, the next step is to cultivate a culture of innovation by sponsoring students for high-level post-graduate training in land utilization, agricultural engineering, crop science, food technology and legal patents to raise land development to a higher level of entrepreneurial innovation. Some of the innovative initiatives such local experts might produce are in the areas of crop engineering for patenting, crop and vegetable preservation techniques for export and value-added food processing. These will take care of four major concerns: effective use of land, development of innovative skills, empowerment of landowners and increased agricultural production, all of which would be good for the national economy.

For those reasons the NLTB should move away from its protectionist and bureaucratic role to one based on innovation and productivity. Increasing the land rent, as the Qarase and Bainimarama governments have advocated, is a minimalist and very short-term solution and does not solve the problem. Effective reform must not be driven solely by the neoliberal notion of liberalizing landownership; rather, it should be driven by considerations centred on innovation, empowerment and sustainability.

While the Bainimarama regime has spent significant resources, effort and time on indigenous development, as we have seen, it must be asked how much that expenditure has lifted the indigenous Fijian population out of poverty. Poverty eradication and social protection was a priority for the regime. The question can be partly answered by Table 7.5, which shows that there was a decrease in the level of poverty between 2002-2003 and 2008-2009. The level of poverty amongst indigenous Fijians decreased by 10% and amongst Indo-Fijians by 11% during that period. The decrease may have been due to a number of factors, including an improved method of data collection or a change in the definition of 'poverty'. If neither of these changed during the period under review, then it may be concluded that the reduction in the incidence of poverty can be associated with government policies. However, based on the figures presented, such a judgement is inconclusive.

Table 7.5 Percentage of population in poverty

	2002-2003	**2008-2009**	**% Change**
Fiji	35%	31%	-10%
Urban	28%	19%	-34%
Rural	40%	43%	8%
I-Taukei	35%	31%	-10%
Indo-Fijian	36%	32%	-11%
Others	24%	25%	4%

Source: Fiji Bureau of Statistics 2011.

The Bainimarama regime may take credit for the decrease in the incidence of poverty; however, the 31% poverty rate amongst indigenous Fijians is still very high and needs to be reduced even further.

Conclusion

Despite public denial, Bainimarama's pro-indigenous development initiatives are tantamount to affirmative action and tend to be very similar to the Qarase government's approach. The only difference was that Qarase was more explicit about his pro-indigenous policies while Bainimarama is less so. While Bainimarama has been careful not to contradict his purported multicultural ideology, he is under immense pressure to put in place pro-indigenous policies as a way of mobilizing indigenous support and loyalty. However, his pro-indigenous development initiatives perhaps betrayed the ethno-nationalist side of him, which he has often concealed and even denied. The major difference between Bainimarama's and Qarase's versions of pro-indigenous policy is that Qarase tries to appeal to the indigenous sense of culture and identity through use of the mainstream institutions such as the GCC, the Methodist Church and provincial councils. On the other hand Bainimarama tries to appeal to people's sense of socio-economic need by directly engaging and influencing the indigenous people himself through personal appeal and rural projects while weakening indigenous institutions which he thinks are in the way. With the 2014 election looming, Bainimarama and other potential indigenous Fijian leaders will be in competition to win indigenous Fijian seats, and one has to play the ethno-nationalist game strategically. This is despite the new proportional open-list electoral system, which is meant to nullify ethnic mobilization and promote trans-ethnic voting. Bainimarama has been doing his own indigenous mobilization through rural development initiatives, despite the well-rehearsed rhetoric of multiculturalism and opposition to ethno-nationalism.

Despite the crippling of the old order and the attempt to re-create a new one, very little has changed in terms of the development paradigm for indigenous Fijians. No innovation in land development and indigenous entrepreneurship has occurred. The same rural division of labour based on leasing indigenous land, which kept indigenous Fijians economically marginalized, persists, and it could even be deepened by the land bank project. Indigenous Fijians continue to be tools of political manipulation by their own elites to serve their economic or ethno-political interests. As this book has demonstrated, all the coups since the first one in 1987 have made insignificant changes to the lives of indigenous Fijians generally, although some individuals were direct beneficiaries.

Like Rabuka, Qarase and Chaudhry, Bainimarama has missed another important opportunity to raise indigenous development to another level of innovation. His major problem was not his lack of commitment to reform or enhancement of indigenous interests, but rather his contradictory approach: preaching against ethno-nationalism and affirmative action but practising them at the same time under different guises. Affirmative action under Qarase, as we have seen, was subject to abuse. However, because of heavy censorship of the media, possible abuse under Bainimarama cannot be fully ascertained and things may surface later after the eagerly awaited 2014 election.

8. Ethnicity, reform and affirmative action in Malaysia

This chapter examines some of the salient features of Malaysian affirmative action and some of the important challenges associated with it. As discussed earlier, Fiji and Malaysia enjoyed a special relationship over the years based on assumptions about shared ethnic problems and other historical links. Some aspects of British colonial policies in the two countries were similar, especially in relation to the co-option of traditional elites into the colonial governance structure, the importation of foreign labour and provision for protective cultural political mechanisms commonly referred to as "paramountcy of Fijian interest" and Malay "special privileges."

Affirmative action in Malaysia faced considerable dilemmas in relation to the authoritarian role of the state in determining resource redistribution, the interplay between state bureaucrats and business interests, the creation of an indigenous middle class through ethnic preferences and the issue of inequality within the Malay community itself. Nevertheless, despite their problems, Malaysian affirmative programs have been hailed as a model to be emulated by countries such as Fiji and South Africa.

This chapter first discusses the relationship between ethnicity, socio-economic development and politics during the colonial period. It will then look at how economic disparity led to ethnic tension, culminating in the 1969 ethnic riots which accelerated the implementation of the New Economic Policy (NEP), the major development and affirmative action plan meant to address the issue of poverty and ethnic inequality. The chapter then examines attempts to eradicate poverty and how this transformed the rural sector. This is followed by a discussion of the growth of the Malay middle class as a result of the NEP. It also examines the processes of industrialization and privatization and their contribution in building up a Malay entrepreneurial class and the role of the state in actively encouraging and facilitating the process through preferential policies. As examples of Malay investment, the chapter discusses the operation of two of the biggest Malay trust companies, the Permodalan Berhad (PNB) and Amannah Sahm Nasioanale (ASN). The chapter then discusses some of the results of the affirmative action programs and implications on ethnic relations and national development.

Independence and Malay preferential policies

The ethnic division of labour in Malaysia had its origins in colonial capitalism. Tin mining was one of the major factors which attracted the British into the interior of Malaysia's peninsula and Chinese miners began arriving in large numbers from China, lured by the new-found wealth. They formed loose mining confederations with local *sultans* in the states of Perak. Other Chinese made their fortune in retail trade.

Chinese immigration was followed by an influx of Indian immigrants, who mostly worked in government service and in rubber plantations. Some, like the Chinese, became merchants and retailers. Throughout the colonial period the Chinese and Indians dominated the mining, rubber plantation, manufacturing, service and retail trade sectors of the economy while the Malays were largely agricultural peasants and a few worked in government positions. Significantly, the relative class positions of various ethnic groups were tied to their occupational status (see Jomo 1986). This was a common tendency, where the colonial economy engendered the emergence of 'racial-class' groups which reflected identifiable parallels between economic division of labour and division by ethnicity. We have seen how this type of socio-economic differentiation also characterized the Fiji colonial economy, in which Indo-Fijians were largely engaged in sugar plantation work and indigenous Fijians remained locked into the communal semi-subsistence sector. The socio-economic disparity in Malaysia led to simmering ethnic tensions which needed to be addressed urgently upon independence.

To address potential conflict, the Malaysian independence constitution of 1957, like the 1970 Fiji independence constitution, was essentially a consociationalist compromise by political parties representing the major ethnic groups – the United Malays National Organization (UMNO), Malaysian Chinese Association (MCA) and Malaysian Indian Congress (MIC) for national consensus and unity under the umbrella Malaysian Alliance Party. Equally significant was the provision on the "Special Rights Programme" in Article 153 for preferential policies on economic development priority, obtaining business and professional licenses, civil service appointment and educational scholarships in respect of Malays (Lee 2005; Lee, Gomez & Yakob 2010).

By and large Malays interpreted the constitution as a mandate for their political ascendancy and this nationalistic interpretation became the 'official' version after it was adopted by the *Bumiputera* leadership of the UMNO. To cement this position, Malay traditional rulers who were co-opted into the British colonial system were made constitutional and religious heads of their respective states

(Lee 1990). Support amongst Chinese and Indians was canvassed through the MCA and MIC communal patrons by delivering economic and social development to the grassroots.

Meanwhile, class differentiation within the economy continued to widen and this had serious political consequences for the Alliance. For instance, between 1957 and 1970, intra-ethnic income disparity (in terms of Gini Coefficient ratio) grew by 36.2% for Malays and 21.6% for Chinese (Osman-Rani 1990: 8). This generated the feeling that the Alliance had failed to deliver on its promises and, as a result, the poorer classes of various communities withdrew support from the Alliance and support fell from 79.6% of the vote in 1955, to 51.5% in 1959, increasing to 58.5% in 1964 before plunging to 48.5% in 1969. Most of the poor Malays who deserted the UMNO supported the extremist nationalist Parti Islam Se Malaysia (PAS), which believed in total Malay supremacy and the declaration of Islam as the state religion. This shift in loyalty indicated the failure of the Alliance patronage system and the desire to "search for alternative and more effective communal patrons on the part of the racially clustered subordinate class fractions" (Brown 1994: 234). Fearing that PAS would hijack the *Bumiputera* agenda and break up its support base, UMNO began pursuing *Bumiputera* economic interests in earnest. With the threat from the PAS on one side and the non-Malay parties on the other, the UMNO had to achieve a delicate ethnic balancing act. The big test came during the 1959 election, when non-Malay parties, especially Chinese parties, made some gains on the basis of their opposition to *Bumiputera* special preferences. The UMNO lost some of its Chinese votes and had to rely largely on *Bumiputera* support (Hua 1983).

Nevertheless, the lack of substantive improvement in Malay socio-economic life increased the tempo of opposition the Alliance rule. The number of public enterprises increased from 22 in 1960 to 109 in 1970 and this was hardly satisfactory in a situation of dire inequality (Gomez and Jomo 1999). By 1970 only 2.4% of the total equity was owned by the Bumiputera while the non-Bumiputera Malaysians held 28.3% and foreigners 63.4%. From 1957 to 1970, the income share of the top 5% of households increased considerably. The average income for Chinese was 1.89 times higher in 1957 and increased to 2.47 in 1967, while Indian average income increased from 1.51 to 1.95 times higher in the same period (Anand 1981). The increasing disparity naturally heightened tension.

The 1969 violence and the New Economic Policy

During the 1969 election the Alliance captured the majority of seats in Parliament but its majority shares of the vote actually declined from 58.4% in 1964 to 48.8%. A "victory march" by supporters of the opposition on 13 May triggered off a spate of violent attacks by Malays who felt threatened by the march. Four days of bloody violence led to the suspension of the constitution and the declaration of an emergency. The riots manifested the way in which longstanding socio-economic grievances were readily and spontaneously translated into ethnic violence when the circumstances were ripe.

One of the most significant lessons of the 1969 riots was the realization by the younger generation of UMNO leaders who assumed leadership after the demise of the old order that more aggressive socio-economic transformation was needed to avoid further crisis. This hastened the implementation of the New Economic Policy (NEP), which had been planned for some time. The NEP contained both a broad development framework for the nation and specific affirmative action provisions for the *Bumiputera* to address ethnic-based economic inequality.

First launched in association with the *Second Malaysian Plan for 1971-75*, the NEP consisted of two prongs: (a) the reduction and eventual eradication of poverty, by raising income levels and increasing employment opportunities for all Malaysians, irrespective of race and (b) the acceleration of the process of restructuring Malaysian society to correct economic imbalance, so as to reduce and eventually eliminate the identification of race with economic function (Malaysia 1973).

The NEP allocations for poverty eradication and restructuring society from 1971 to 1985 are shown in Table 8.1. The pattern shows that there was a gradual shift in emphasis from poverty eradication to restructuring. The ratio of allocation for restructuring compared to poverty eradication rose from 21.6% during 1971–75 to 37.3% during 1976–80. Under the *Fourth Malaysian Plan*, 1981–85, the ratio rose to 47.2%. During the *Second Malaysian Plan*, the poverty eradication allocation was 4.7 times that of allocation for restructuring but this ratio declined to 2.7 for the *Third Malaysian Plan* period (1976–80).

Table 8.1 Malaysian Development Plan allocation for poverty eradication and restructuring society, 1971-1985 (M$ million)

	Second Plan (NEP),1970	Third Plan 1976-80	Fourth Plan (Original) 1981-85	Expenditure 1981-3	Fourth Plan (Revised)
Poverty Eradication	2,350.0	6,373.4	9,319.2	6,699.1	10,497.0
Restructuring	508.3	2,376.0	4,397.6	5,406.8	6,576.8
Overlapping	3.4	149.0	300.5	184.7	464.5
Total	2,861	8,898.4	14,017.3	12,290.6	17,538.3

Source: Jomo 1986: 267.

The disparity between poverty eradication and redistribution showed a clear bias towards middle-class Malays, summed up by Jomo thus:

> Since over half the Malay population were considered poor, theoretically, Malays would comprise the majority of the beneficiaries of poverty eradication measures such as race. On the other hand, the most well to-do, probably comprising no more than 3%, of the Bumiputera community, benefit directly and substantially from efforts to restructure society. Hence, shifting emphasis from poverty eradication to restructuring society would tend to increase inequality within the Malay community (Jomo 1986: 268).

The Politics of Poverty Eradication

Poverty was seen by the ruling UMNO elite as a potentially destabilising aspect in its attempt to unite the Malay community. Concern for poverty was in response to the 1969 riots which was seen as a consequence of the mass migration of rural poor into the urban areas; therefore the aim was to develop the rural areas to increase living standards and so to arrest this drift.

Rural development strategies did not include land reform because it would alienate landowners who were still influential within the UMNO. Thus there was emphasis only on infrastructural development, subsidising resettlement projects and provision of agricultural resources, such as irrigation schemes as a means of increasing productivity (Emsley 1996).

The main NEP targets of poverty alleviation in the rural areas were rubber, palm oil and rice cultivation. About 95% of the rice farmers were Malays. In 1970, the incidence of poverty in the rice sector was reported at 88.1% and at just below 91.8% for the mixed agricultural sector. In 1990, of the 10,500,000 acres of land under cultivation, 1,148,000 acres were for paddy and 7,907,000 for rubber and palm oil. However, because most of the rural farmers were Malays, it was important for political reasons to target them in the NEP poverty alleviation strategies (Ishida and Azizan 1998). As shown in Table 8.2, the incidence of poverty in 1970 for all ethnic groups was 49.3% of households. The target for 1990 was 16.7%, while the achieved figure was 15.0%. The highest incidence of poverty in 1970 was amongst *Bumiputera* with 65.0%, compared to 26.0% for Chinese and 39.0% for Indians. Within twenty years of the NEP, the incidence of poverty was dramatically reduced to 20.8% for *Bumiputera*, 5.7% for Chinese and 8.0% for Indians.

Table 8.2 Poverty eradication targets and achievements, 1976 and 1990 (% of households)

	1970	1976	Target 1990	Achieved 1990
Peninsular Malaysia				
Poverty incidence	49.3		16.7	15.0
By location				
Rural	58.7	23.0	19.3	
Urban	21.3	9.1	7.3	
By ethnicity				
Bumiputera	65.0			20.8
Chinese	26.0			5.7
Indian	39.0			8.0
Others	44.8			18.0
Malaysia				
Poverty incidence		42.4		17.1
By location				
Rural		50.9		21.8
Urban		18.7		7.5
By ethnicity				
Bumiputera		56.4		23.8
Chinese		19.2		5.5
Indian		28.5		8.0
Others		44.6		12.9

Source: Rasiah 1998: 127.

However, the success of the poverty eradication scheme is misleading for two reasons. First, part of the increase in production figures was achieved through heavy government subsidy. For instance, in 1984 about 69% of the estimated net annual income from rice cultivation was from subsidy. Second, the decline in aggregate poverty levels amongst rice farmers camouflaged the widening gap between rich and poor farmers. There was decline in poverty but at the same time there was increased relative poverty.

The NEP ensured direct intervention of the state in rural development. Consequently, the interaction between the state actors and rural peasants increased, creating conditions for potential antagonism when circumstances dictated:

> The state was once largely a bystander or mediator...It is now a direct participant, decision maker, allocator and antagonist in nearly all vital aspects of paddy growing. Most of the buffers between the state and rice farmers have fallen away, thereby vastly increasing both the role of politics and the possibilities for direct confrontation between the ruling party and its peasantry (Scott 1985: 53).

For instance, dissatisfied poor farmers withdrew support from the UMNO and supported PAS. Class frustrations were mobilised along ethnic-religious and cultural lines. Peasant resistance through religious mobilisation (especially the PAS fundamentalist variant) became a political irritant to UMNO hegemony in the rural areas.

Consolidating the *Bumiputera* middle class

The second prong of the NEP was in effect an attempt to build up a Malay middle class through restructuring employment, ownership of share capital in the corporate sector and the creation of a *Bumiputera* Commercial and Industrial Community (BCIC). The focus of redistribution of share capital was most pronounced in the primary and service sectors, while export-oriented manufacturing was largely spared (Rasiah 1998). As Table 8.3 shows, in 1970 *Bumiputera* employment in the agricultural, secondary and service sectors was 66.2%, 12.1% and 21.7% respectively. The NEP aimed at decreasing reliance on the agricultural sector for *Bumiputera* by reducing it to 37.4% in 1990 and increasing employment in the secondary and services sectors by 26.8% and 35.8% respectively. In 1990 employment in the agricultural sector had decreased to 29.0% and secondary and service sectors had increased to 30.5% and 40.5% respectively.

Table 8.3 Restructuring targets and achievements, 1970 and 1990

Sectoral Employment	1970		Target 1990		Achieved 1990		Malaysia 1990	
	Total (000)	%	Total (000)	%	Total (000)	%	Total (000)	%
Bumiputera								
Agriculture	951.1	66.2	1091.4	37.4	875.2	29.0	1404.6	36.7
(%)	67.6		61.4		71.2		76.4	
Secondary	173.1	12.1	782.7	26.8	918.5	30.5	1038.9	27.2
(%)	30.8		51.9		48.0		49.8	
Services	312.4	21.7	1046.8	35.8	1219.8	40.5	1381.9	36.1
(%)	37.9		48.9		51.0		50.9	
Non-Bumis								
Agriculture	454.9	33.5	686.2	27.1	354.0	14.0	433.0	15.5
(%)	32.4		38.6		28.8		23.6	
Secondary	389.7	28.7	725.4	28.7	996.1	39.5	1048.6	37.5
(%)	69.2		48.1		52.0		50.2	
Services	312.4	37.8	1116.6	44.2	1170.5	46.5	1314.0	47.0
(%)	37.9		51.6		49.0		49.1	
% Corporate Ownership								
Bumiputera		2.4		30.0				20.3
Others		32.3		40.0				46.2
Foreigners		63.3		30.0				25.1
Nominee Co.		2.0						8.4

Source: Rasiah 1998: 28.

The NEP led to a dramatic expansion in the size of state employment and employment in quasi-public corporations. The newly created jobs were reserved overwhelmingly for Malays. As a result, between 1970 and 1977 Malays were provided with 68% of the newly created jobs and by 1980 they made up 93% of the total number of new employees. Figures also show that the Malay proportion in the armed forces and police went up from 70% in 1970 to 86% in 1980 (Lin 1984).

Apart from providing public sector employment, the NEP also provided incentives and assistance for Malay entry into industrial and commercial endeavours through provision of equity, capital, loan financing, education and training. It aimed to increase *Bumiputera* corporate wealth from 2.4% in 1970 to 30% in 1990, to create a BCIC under the NEP's *Outline Perspective Plan* (1971-1990) and increase the *Bumiputera* trust agencies share of *Bumiputera* share capital to 83% in 1990 (Jomo 1995: 43). But as Table 8.3 shows, *Bumiputera* corporate wealth in 1990 fell short of the 30% target by about 10%. Nevertheless, there was a growth of state trusts, sheltering the interests of *Bumiputera*, in the mining and service sectors, while the number of public agencies swelled from 109 in 1970 to 656 in 1980 (Jomo 1994a: 8). Amongst these were the well-known and leading trust agencies, Perbadanan Nasional (PERNAS) and Permodalan Nasional Berhad (PNB). Public institutions such as the Majlis Amanah Rakyat (MARA) also extended their role in economic participation by providing generous loans and other assistance to Malays. The Fijian Holdings model was based on the Malay trust concept, and both the *Nine Points Plan* and the *Ten Year Plan* drew inspiration from the NEP's provision for increased indigenous control of the corporate sector.

To facilitate rapid entry of Malays into the civil service and commerce, privileged access to education and scholarships was readily provided. Quotas were introduced in 1971 to counter Chinese dominance in higher education. As a result, the proportion of Malays enrolled for local degree courses increased from 35.6% to 66.7% between 1969 and 1980; and by 1995 Malay students took up about 64% of all university places (Emsley 1996: 40). Preferential entry into university became problematic because Chinese and Indian students had to work extra hard to obtain university places. The use of *Bahasa Malaysia* as the official language of instruction entrenched cultural and communal dominance of Malay students and marginalized non-Malay students, who were required to use the language. Malay students who benefited from the educational quota system and who had a "perception of inferiority" as a result of preferences also resorted to radical Islam to provide moral support and political direction while rejecting new ideas and competition from non-Muslims (Muzaffar 1989: 15).

Industrialization and Malay embourgeoisment

While the quantitative targets of the NEP were set out clearly (as shown in Tables 8.2 and 8.3), there was also an emphasis on achieving qualitative targets in the form of creating a *Bumiputera* business class "so that the NEP's equity participation could be backed by managerial control" (Rasiah 1998: 128). This could be achieved only through a concerted drive towards industrialisation in order to speed up the consolidation of the middle class. At the same time, industrialisation was important for UMNO's mass support by the working class through the creation of employment. Thus growth became a political imperative to gain the loyalty of UMNO's diverse political support base (Jesudason 1996).

Industrialization was really the major economic engine for affirmative action. In the late 1960s import substitution industrialisation (ISI) gave way to labour intensive export-oriented industrialisation (EOI), accompanied by new labour policies, tax concessions and other incentives to facilitate EOI. This policy shift coincided with the introduction of the NEP. Increasingly, the NEP involved greater state intervention by way of public sector expansion and regulation of manufacturing sector investments. The export-oriented industrialisation came to be dominated by Free Trade Zones (FTZ) under the Free Trade Zones Act of 1971. The FTZs, especially the processing of primary products (rubber, tin, palm oil and timber and manufacture of electrical and electronic components), grew at a rapid rate and led to expansion of employment opportunities and rapid rural-urban migration.

In the 1980s, in an attempt to refocus industrialisation, Mahathir, the new Prime Minister, promoted heavy industries to balance the industrialisation process through private investment incentives. The heavy industries were spearheaded by companies relocated from East Asian economies such as Japan, South Korea and Taiwan — South Korea in particular was seen as a model economy by Malaysia. This "Big Push" industrialisation was to involve state corporations acting on behalf of the *Bumiputera* (Jomo 1994b).

However, the international recession of 1985 adversely affected Malaysia's export earnings from palm oil, rubber, tin and electronics, leading to negative growth for the first time since independence. A year later the situation worsened with the collapse of the oil price and Malaysia's option was to restructure along the lines of the Washington Consensus. This meant that the heavily state-subsidised and state-controlled NEP had to be quietly "suspended" in favour of accelerating liberalisation measures under the *Guidelines for Privatisation*, which spelt out the rationale and broad framework of Malaysia's privatisation plans (Jomo 1994a). These were: first, to reduce the financial and administrative burden on the government of maintaining services and infrastructure; second, to promote competition and efficiency; third, to stimulate private entrepreneurship; fourth, to reduce the dominance of the public sector; and fifth, to help achieve the objectives of the NEP, given that *Bumiputera* entrepreneurship had progressed well and *Bumiputera* were ready to take up opportunities in the privatised services. Moreover, the political consequences of this low growth were significant, to say the least. Low growth intensified ethnic tension and factionalism within UMNO (Means 1991: 193-219). There was bitter rivalry for power between Mahathir and fellow cabinet member, Tengku Razaleigh, during the 1987 UMNO leadership elections. The economic recession made it difficult for the top leaders to unify disparate groups.

The privatisation program was closely controlled by the state and was channelled towards politically favoured corporations, thus impacting on ownership and employment patterns, income distribution and the control of vital economic sectors (Jones 1991). As a result there was rapid growth in the manufacturing sector, with eight-fold growth in employment in this sector by 1989. Employment in manufacturing in this period accounted for more than 17% of the labour force. This employment trend was noticeable amongst Malays, whose share of the labour force grew from 20% in 1957 to 29% in 1970 and to 54% in 1980.

The NEP was succeeded in 1991 by the *New Development Policy* (NDP), which put more emphasis on human resource development as a means of achieving the 30% *Bumiputera* ownership target, set down by the NEP (Jomo 1993). While keeping the *Bumiputera* agenda intact, the NDP formed the basis of Mahathir's ambitious "Vision 2020", referring to the date when Malaysia would achieve developed country status. Fundamental to "Vision 2020" industrialisation would be the leading function of the private sector, which was the aim of the accelerated privatisation since 1991 (Chowdhry 1997).

Thus, despite the economic crisis of the early to mid-1980s, affirmative action in Malaysia took place in large measure under conditions of a rapidly growing economy. The NEP coincided with the OPEC oil price rise in the critical years of the new plan, enabling a state-led redistribution from incremental (oil-based) revenues throughout the 1970s rather than a reallocation of existing tight resources. This was in contrast to Fiji's post-1987 affirmative action programs, which tried to create an indigenous capitalist class in a very inhibiting environment of low growth. Industrialisation in Fiji was never associated with affirmative action in any way. The shift from ISI to EOI in the 1970s was part of the general economic policy for growth rather than an attempt to restructure society in a way that favoured indigenous Fijians.

A critical aspect of the process of *Bumiputera* embourgeoisment was state supervision and control of the process of industrialization and privatization to ensure selective targeting. Mahathir himself suggested "The best way to keep the shares in the *Bumiputera* hands is to hand them over to the *Bumiputera* most capable of retaining them, which means the well-to-do" (FEER 13 April 1979). The state was directly involved in *Bumiputera* capitalism through State-Owned Corporations (SOEs) or "state capitalism" (which operated directly on behalf of *Bumiputera* interest), trust corporations and direct preferential deals with *Bumiputera* businesses (Gomez 1994).

The SOEs came to symbolise two fundamental but related aspects of the Malaysian state: first, because SOEs were to secure *Bumiputera* economic interest, they also came to represent an aspect of the state's ethnocratic designs; and second, through state ownership, SOEs confirmed the state's commitment to direct capital accumulation. The assumption was that through direct state accumulation the communal interest of the *Bumiputera* would be protected. Encouraged by this and in the absence of proper regulation, there was a dramatic increase in the number of SOEs, with an increase of about 100 per year by the mid-1970s. This resulted in the creation of companies with *de facto* management acting independently of any shareholder control. Importantly, however, it showed the government's "ignorance of the extent of its assets and liabilities" (Adams and Cavendish 1995: 17).

In the late 1980s, about 25% of the total GDP was from the SOE sector account output (World Bank 1989). In 1990 there were 1,158 SOEs, 78 of which were operational with a total paid-up capital of M$23.9 billion. Of the 1,158, 396 (34%) were fully state-owned, 429 (37%) were majority state-owned and in 333 (30%) the state had a minority equity stake. Table 8.4 shows the three different categories of SOEs (federal, state and regional) by paid-up capital. In all three cases the government had majority equity (with a total of 70% in all cases) in a total of 1,158 companies.

Table 8.4 State Owned Enterprises (SOE) by paid-up capital (in M$) in 1994

	Number of Companies	Total Capital (M$)	Govt. Equity (M$)	Govt. Equity % Capital	Average Capital (M$)
Federal	556	18,521	12,738	68.78	33.3
State	553	5,048	3,829	75.85	9.1
Regional	49	241	170	70.54	4.9
TOTAL	**1,158**	**23,810**	**16,737**	**70.29**	**20.6**

Source: Adams and Cavendish 1995: 20.

Over the years, the SOE sector was dominated by Petroleum Nasional Sdn Berhad (PETRONAS) and its subsidiaries because of its monopoly status, provided for in the 1974 Petroleum Development Act, and also because of its close links to the external markets.[1] Petrochemicals, together with manufacturing and finance, constituted the most important components of the SOE sector. Most of the crude oil (80%) was exported to Japan, Singapore and South Korea and 95% of the liquefied natural gas was exported to Japan. In 1984, 27% of total Malaysian exports was made up of petroleum products, falling to 22% in 1989. In 1988 PETRONAS had a turnover of M$6.7 billion and a profit of M$3.8 billion (Jomo 1994b). However, SOE manufacturing generally underperformed compared to manufacturing by SOEs' private counterparts (World Bank 1989). This led to a major privatisation drive announced in 1983 to increase efficiency and to "curb the subsidy mentality" of the *Bumiputera* (Gomez 1994: 15).

---

1 An attempt to set up a similar state-owned petroleum corporation in Fiji, to be modelled on the PETRONAS concept, failed due to political struggles within the post-1987 coup government and strong pressure from oil companies. The company, to be called Fiji National Petroleum Company (FINAPECO), was to set up a distillery in Fiji to supply the South Pacific. The move was spear-headed by the post-coup interim Prime Minister (and current President), Ratu Sir Kamisese Mara, but after the coup leader, Gen. Rabuka, became PM after the 1992 election, he cancelled the project.

Privatization and Bumiputera preferences

By the time privatisation started, a substantial portion of the corporate stock had already been secured by a small UMNO elite (either through "personal achievement" or proxies) who have been able to exploit their political influence to weave a web of cronyism and patronage within the corporate community. It was really after 1984 that privatisation gathered momentum. By the end of 1990 37 government projects had been privatised, 27 of which had been public enterprises. Another 93 projects were privatised during 1991 and 1992, including about 40 government-owned enterprises which were transferred to *Bumiputera* trust agencies such as the Permodalan Nasional Berhad (PNB) and Amanah Saham Nasional (ASN). About 120 SOEs were sold to the private sector (Gomez 1994).

Privatisation ended the state's monopoly in areas like broadcasting, shipping, airlines, telecommunications and power generation. The listing of shares of these privatised companies on the Kuala Lumpur Stock Exchange (KLSE) expanded Malaysia's capital market considerably, making it the fourth largest in Asia. Since the NDP was implemented, a number of major privatisations took place. By May 1994, the government had privatised 103 entities and over 15 previously government-owned companies. This included the national energy company, Tenaga Nasional, Heavy Industries Corporation of Malaysia (HICOM) and Telecom. Each was listed on the KLSE. A total of 78 projects were identified for privatisation under the *Rolling Action Privatisation Plan* 1994/95, followed by 77 projects in 1995. Privatisation under the 1994 program included the development of seaports in Penang, Johor and Kelang, commissioning of independent power producers and development of a new television station. The 1995 privatisation projects included aspects of the new Kuala Lumpur International Airport, the ports of Kuantan and Kemaman, the National Savings Bank and the housing loan division of the Ministry of Finance (Chowdhry 1997). Operations of financial institutions and equities under the privatization rubric were strictly controlled by the state to ensure conformity to the NEP requirements of 30% *Bumiputera* ownership by 1990. The bumiputerasation of the economy was a huge undertaking, given that in 1971 the *Bumiputera* owned only 4% of quoted equity. To achieve this, quotas were imposed on most types of government procurement. This ranged from 1% for sophisticated defence equipment to 100% for road haulage services for the Federal government. It was usual for *Bumiputera* tenders to be 10% in excess of those from non-*Bumiputera*. Quotas also determined the issuing of licences for a large number of services such as taxis (Emsley 1996).

The equity acquisition process was formalised in the form of the Industrial Co-ordination Act (ICA), which targeted a 30:40:30 (30% *Bumiputera*, 40%

non-*Bumiputera* and 30% foreign) ownership formula by 1990. All companies involved in manufacturing were required to have a licence, the provision of which required that submitted plans must include 30% *Bumiputera* shares by 1990. Mechanisms were in place to ensure that the promise of the 30% equity was achieved. It was assumed that an annual growth of 9% was required to achieve the ICA goals. In fact Malaysia's growth rate was 11.4% annually between 1970 and 1990 (Jomo 1994a).

There were exemptions from the ICA regulations. For instance, equity of less than M$0.10 million was excluded, but this was increased to M$0.25 million in 1977. There was also a limit on the value of fixed assets, set at M$0.5 million in 1977 but raised to M$1 million in 1985 and M$2.5 million in 1986. ICA was also strict on import-substitution foreign investment, while export-oriented establishments were allowed very high numbers of foreign equity shares. These restrictions were relaxed in the late 1980s. The ICA rules encouraged the growth of "Ali Baba" companies, where Chinese businesses were being fronted by *Bumiputera* (Lee, Gomez and Yakob 2010).

Because the privatization process was done in line with the NEP pro-*Bumiputera* objectives, political consideration was an important factor in determining equity. This led to allegations of extensive political nepotism and corruption. In the absence of a formal tender system, political leaders and politically aligned businessmen took advantage of the opportunity to secure stock (Gomez 2009). The privatisation process often meant the prearranged transfer of a state monopoly to private monopoly. The complex web of political patronage and cronyism formed part of the process whereby corporate interest was co-opted into the state system of patronage.

Despite privatisation, government still controlled a substantial share of various aspects of the economy. In 1994 more than 1,100 SOEs made up vital utilities such as transport, communications, water supply, energy, and finance; and SOEs were heavily involved in non-traditional sectors such as services, construction and manufacturing (Adams and Cavendish 1995: 15). By 1992 about 42% of Malaysian Airline System (MAS), 29% of Malaysian International Shipping Corporation (MISC), 75% of Syarikat Telecom (STM) and 77% of Tenaga Nasional (all of which are monopolies) were still under government control (Gomez 1994). But even state-controlled shares were still perceived as *Bumiputera* shares held in state trust.

Apart from the issuing of equity by large financial institutions, the government also provided subsidies for business premises, training, provision of credit and quotas in the issuing of licences and government procurement. In 1985 for instance, 63% of the works contracts by the three largest public sector bodies (Public Works Department, FELDA and telecommunications), worth M$887 million, and 42% of the supplies contracts, worth M$751 million, were awarded to *Bumiputera*.[2] As a result of state preferential policies such as these, there was a significant increase in the number of *Bumiputera* professional and other salaried workers. Between 1973 and 1987, the *Bumiputera* share of the employers' category relative to other ethnic categories increased from 14.2% in 1973 to 32.7 in 1987. For instance within the "commercial" sector there was an increase in the Malay share from 8.6% in 1973 to 36.8% in 1987, while there was an increase in the "finance" sector from 0.0% in 1973 to 27.5% in 1987 (Malaysian Government 1973; 1987).

These figures do not tell the full story. In fact the shortcomings of heavily protected ventures were common – complacency, inability to take risks and lack of business innovation. The Malaysian Central Bank (Bank Negara) required the banking fraternity to reserve 20% of its loan portfolio to *Bumiputera* entrepreneurs, but this target was "overachieved" by 12.7%. The MARA, formed to help *Bumiputera* entrepreneurship, subsidised interest rates on its loans, but despite this only 6,000 of the 55,000 loans granted have been repaid. We have seen that a high arrears rate was also a feature of the Fiji Development Bank's Commercial Loans to Fijian Scheme (CLFS). But, again, the differences were in terms of sheer scale. The banking system in Malaysia lent itself to massive wastage and corruption (Emsley 1996) but, despite the failures, one cannot deny the extent to which state patronage has strengthened the position of the Malay middle class. The middle class manifested "syncretic" characteristics through what Brown referred to as a "balancing act", to provide a favourable climate that best served their interests:

> The picture that emerges is of the state bureaucrats attempting a "balancing act"; employing the state machinery so as to promote their own interests and their emergence as the dominant class, but also willing to compromise their own interests in order to promote international capital, and to mediate between the other dominant and sub-ordinate classes. It is not suggested here that such a "balancing act" is unproblematic. Indeed it is the dynamics inherent in the politics of this venture, which provide the major explanatory focus for the analysis of political change (Brown 1994: 211).

The dynamic interplay between economic aspirations and political power bred widespread corruption. The prevalence of corruption and financial scandals involving senior politicians in the 1980s led to widespread dissatisfaction and the government had to face a broad front of dissenters, including opposition MPs, party dissidents, state land scheme settlers and a broad spectrum of government critics consisting of environmentalists, union leaders and Islamic fundamentalists.

---

2 These figures do not include joint ventures with non-*Bumputera* and foreigners or government procurement.

The government's reaction was, firstly, to deploy the Internal Security Act (ISA) in 1987, which was invoked to detain without trial about 130 people from a diverse range of dissident groups. Secondly, the government co-opted a number of important groups in a strategic approach towards national reconciliation. Most important of all was the attempt by the Prime Minister to move towards a "more consultative style" of government. This involved the setting up of the National Consultative Council in 1988, with 150 members from various interest groups, to formulate national economic policy after 1990, the year the NEP was scheduled to stop. These moves were necessary to appease non-*Bumiputera* demands for ending *Bumiputera* privilege and also because of pressure from the business sector for reduced government intervention in the economy.

The growth of the wealth of the *Bumiputera* elite was facilitated by the dominant UMNO political power and the attempt to keep excessive Chinese and foreign corporate interests in check. Between 1970 and 1990 there was a ten-fold increase in the proportion of share capital in the corporate sector held by *Bumiputera*. This represented an increase of 2.4% in 1970 to 20.3% in 1990, 10% or so short of the 30% target of the NEP. The details are shown in Table 8.5. Of the 20.3% of shares held by *Bumiputera*, which totalled $M22.3 billion, 14% were held by individuals and the rest by trust agencies. At the same time, the number of shares held by Chinese also showed a remarkable increase, from 27.2% in 1970 to 44.9% in 1990. The number of shares held by Indians showed a slight decrease, from 1.1% in 1970 to 1.0% of the total in 1990. The biggest decrease was for foreign investors: the number of shares held by foreigners plunged from 63.4% of the total in 1970 to 25.1% in 1990. However, one of the significant points of comparison with Fiji here is with regard to the difference in shares between individuals and trust agencies. Table 8.5 shows that the number of shares held by individual *Bumiputera* was much higher than of the number held by trust agencies (14.0% in 1990 for individuals, compared to 6.3% for trust agencies), signifying an emphasis on individual equity, as opposed to an emphasis on communal equity in the case of Fiji.

Table 8.5 Ownership of share capital, 1970-90 (in percentages)

Ownership Category	1970	1990
Bumiputera individuals	1.6	14.0
Bumiputera trust agencies	0.8	6.3
Chinese	27.2	44.9
Indians	1.1	1.0
Other non-Bumiputera Malay residents	-	0.3
Foreign residents	63.4	25.1
Nominee companies	6.0	8.4

Source: Gomez 1994: 23.

Nevertheless, the figures for shares held by *Bumiputera* may be misleading, because many *Bumiputera* politicians were involved in "nominee companies" and foreign-domiciled companies. It has also been shown that expatriate Chinese Malaysians invested from abroad (see Jomo 1991). The *Bumiputera* figures could also be exaggerated because over the years a number of *Bumiputera* businesses were subcontracted to non-*Bumiputera* and foreign companies in what has been referred to earlier as an Ali Baba arrangement. This involved *Bumiputera* business licence holders fronting corporations run by Chinese. While it is true that *Bumiputera* investment has dramatically expanded, part of this has been due to the "Ali Baba" phenomenon:

> Statistics in the various industries seem to indicate considerable success in Malay participation; but the reality is less comforting. It is revealed time and time again, in almost every Malay economic conference, that most Malays resell their licenses or corporate control to non-Malays for a lucrative fee and allow their names to be used as fronts for non-Malays who run the enterprise and pay a tribute to the Malays. This problem of sleeping partnership, termed Ali Baba...is as intractable as it is ubiquitous...(Lin 1984: 259).

But this still does not detract from the fact that there has been a dramatic growth in the *Bumiputera* middle class, despite the fact that Chinese still predominated in the economy. Even contracting and sub-contracting licenses between *Bumiputera* and non-*Bumiputera* businessmen constituted a "business" deal in itself, however politically undesirable it might be. Within the cosy and paternalistic climate of UMNO hegemony, the *Bumiputera* who had been granted licences or who had corporate ownership found it easier to sublease or relinquish corporate control in return for a lucrative fee rather than having to operate the business themselves.

Chinese business, with a much longer history of development, had mostly been built up over years of "self-made" accumulation, while *Bumiputera* business had mostly been achieved through heavy state subsidy and political patronage. It has been argued that a significant part of the new *Bumiputera* and non-*Bumiputera* business class were not real entrepreneurs but rentier capitalists, contracting and sub-contracting business licences to each other. *Bumiputera* and Chinese business did not exist exclusive of each other, but intersected through UMNO political links. Many of these involved mergers, take-overs, management buyouts and share swapping, leading to conglomerisation through concentration of stock ownership and monopolies. The conglomerisation of the economy, facilitated by the centralised power of UMNO, has been a dominant trend of the NEP.

Apart from its mediating role as a business broker, UMNO itself (like the MCA and MIC) has been directly involved in "party capitalism" by virtue of its easy access to funds through its undisputed political power, described thus:

> ...a range of practices whereby the beneficiaries of State economic sponsorship and protection are channelled to individuals, groups and private companies associated with ruling political parties, in particular UMNO...the rise of Money Politics has resulted in the blurring of State and UMNO business interests and the increasing dominance of UMNO and UMNO associated enterprises in the economy (Kahn 1992: 2).

Party capitalism had grown into a complex web of political and economic interests which constituted a powerful force in Malaysian political economy. This provided benefit for Malay business at all levels through special access to contracts; and also benefit for the UMNO itself through a steady flow of funds into party coffers (Kahn 1996: 61).

The NEP no doubt led to a rapid pace of political and economic transformation and accelerated growth, but these changes were basically horizontal in nature because instead of bridging the 'vertical' poverty gap it created a much more differentiated middle class and expanded and centralised state power in an increasingly authoritarian way. Thus policies that were meant to advance the political and economic dominance of an ethnic group ended up creating a strong fraction of middle class rentier profiteers.

An area of *Bumiputera* business which deserves special attention and which we examine next is *Bumiputera* trusts, because this area has been emulated as a framework for "communal investment" in Fiji, as we saw earlier. For instance, the Chief Executive of Fijian Holdings visited Malaysia through a Malaysia-Fiji bilateral agreement to study the operation of the PNB and ASN (which now enjoys a dominant position in *Bumiputera* finance) to learn relevant lessons for Fijian Holdings.

The Permodalan Berhad (PNB) and Amannah Sahm Nasioanale (ASN)

As early as the 1960s share reservations for the *Bumiputera* were introduced and implemented informally, but with little success. In 1964 for instance, of the M$15 million allocated to *Bumiputera* investors, only M$3.8 million was taken up, and of this the National Investment Company accounted for M$3.2 million (Jesudason 1990). To boost *Bumiputera* investment, the government-sponsored Yayasan Pelaburan Bumiputera (YPB) set up the PNB in March 1978. YPB was a trust set up in January 1978 to facilitate investment trusts for the *Bumiputera*. PNB acted as a trust corporation to buy equities and hold them in trust until they were resold at a later stage to the *Bumiputera* (Adams and Cavendish 1995: 27). As the executive arm of the YPB, PBN was responsible for the evaluation, selection and purchasing of shares in public and private sector companies and distributed shares to individual *Bumiputera* through the ASN. PNB established the ASN in May 1979 as a subsidiary company to be responsible for administering and marketing a unit trust scheme for equity participation amongst *Bumiputera*.

Equity that was initially allocated for the *Bumiputera* was purchased by the Ministry of Trade and Industry and in 1978 the PNB was created to purchase shares on behalf of the *Bumiputera*. Under the *Third Malaysia Plan* (1976–80) the PNB received a budget of M$500 million, increasing to M$2,923 million under the *Fourth Malaysian Plan* (1981–85). The drive for *Bumiputera* equity was given impetus in 1981 when the Prime Minister, Hussein Onn, launched a two-stage "Scheme Transfer of Shares" to *Bumiputera* individuals through the PNB. The first stage saw the transfer of SOE shares to PNB at par value. By October 1986 shares for 37 companies with a par value of M$1,300 had been transferred to PNB and this increased to 93 companies in 1990. The next stage of the equity transfer involved transfer of the shares to ASN, which then issued par value units against the ASN share portfolio generally (Jomo 1994a).

PNB investments have been mostly of a secondary nature (redistribution mainly), rather than creating new assets. By March 1984 PNB had investments in 139 companies and 91 of these were listed on the KLSE. PNB held majority shares in 17 and 20% to 50% in another 17 companies, some of which were amongst Malaysia's largest companies. PNB's sector portfolio consisted of 51% plantations, 28% finance and 18% industrial. However, in 1981 a total of 660 million shares worth M$1.5 billion were transferred to ASN (552 million) and to subsidiaries of another *Bumiputera* trust company, Perbadan Nasional Berhad (PERNAS) (108 million) for sale to employees. As Table 8.6 shows, since 1981, PNB/ASN had a high rate of return compared to other investment institutions. From 1981 to 1987, due to heavy state subsidy, the nominal rate of return almost doubled those of other major investment institutions. It was really this diverse and high return investment which Fijian Holdings based its investment strategy on. The idea was to invest in blue chip companies which would generate a high return.

Table 8.6 Nominal rates of return by institution, 1981-1987 (%)

	1981	1982	1983	1984	1985	1986	1987
PNB/ASN	20.0	18.0	18.1	17.2	17.2	10.1	10.1
Employees Provident Fund	8.0	8.0	8.5	8.5	8.5	8.5	8.5
Commercial Bank Deposits	7.0	6.5	6.0	7.5	6.0	6.0	4.0
20 year Government Securities	-	-	-	8.6	8.6	8.6	7.6
Kuala Lumpur Stock Exchange Equity	13.9	-18.9	40.8	-19.3	-17.3	12.8	0.5
Kuala Lumpur Stock Exchange Equity (ex-dividend)	-4.6	-4.6	-3.0	-5.1	-5.5	-4.7	-4.7

Source: Adams and Cavendish 1995: 39.

ASN's role as an equity distribution mechanism through wide marketing of units provided high and guaranteed returns for investors. From 1980–89 the dividend averaged 9.8%, with a bonus of 6.3%, which meant that the total return was 16.1%. This was about 10% higher than that offered by commercial banks. Credit was usually made readily available by banks for purchase of the units. In 1990 the total holding was M$6.8 million, with an average of M$2,752 per unit holder (Emsley 1996).

While the PNB-ASN operation opened new windows of opportunity for many *Bumiputera*, the distribution of holdings has been largely unequal and in many instances reinforced the existing class structure within the *Bumiputera* community. Wealthy *Bumiputera* investors (who held as much as 25,000 to 50,000 units) constituted only 0.6% of all unit holders, but held as much as approximately M$381 million worth of equity, or one third of the total equity.[3] The government's decision to raise the investment ceiling to M$100,000 and to grant tax exemption for dividend income of up to M$5,000 was to the advantage of the rich. PNB-ASN shares were distributed on the basis of political patronage and cronyism and mostly benefited those who had close UMNO connections (Emsley 1996). A similar pattern of share distribution was seen in the case of Fijian Holdings, where those with close ties with the banking fraternity and state bureaucracy had the first chance to acquire the limited number of private shares. This also determined the extent of inequality of shares between unitholders. The major difference between PNB-ASN and Fijian Holdings was that the latter involved communal shareholders in the form of provinces, districts and village councils, compared to the former, which was based on individual and state unitholding.

The PNB-ASN was directly subsidised by the government at a zero-interest term without any apparent repayment obligation. In 1983 the value of PNB investment was M$3,650 million, making a profit of M$145 million. The ASN

---

3   One unit was worth M$1. Units could be purchased for as small a number as ten. The gini-coefficient put the distribution figure as high as 0.8.

profits were M$84 million out of an investment of M$1,000 million. The return for both investments was only 4.8%. Similarly the Fiji Government heavily subsidised Fijian Holdings operations through the FJ$20 million zero-interest loan for the "B Class" shares.

While the role of these *Bumiputera* financial institutions has been fundamental to the economy, there have also been growing concerns about their state-patronaged privileged positions. Their mode of operation created distortions and anomalies in the capital market, especially in relation to diversion of *Bumiputera* savings away from competitive investment through cross-subsidisation from other public resources. Through political patronage, PNB had been able to secure all new equity issues, which gave it a dominant role as a shareholder (Gomez 1994).

While large amounts of capital have been transferred to *Bumiputera* commerce, the 30% equity ownership target was still not met by 1990. Individual holdings grew substantially as a result of the ASN activities. There was a slowdown in equity growth after 1985, despite the tremendous growth in the early 1980s. Under the *Fifth Malaysian Plan* (1986–1990) the budget of the PNB was reduced and there was relaxation of the equity purchasing rules for foreigners and Chinese companies (Jesudason 1990). This considerably decreased the proportional value of equity for the *Bumiputera*.

Furthermore, a lot of the so-called *Bumiputera* equity was held by nominee companies, whose ethnic origins could not be identified. Nominee companies controlled 11.55% of the manufacturing sector's capital stock in 1974–75, and this rose to 20.4% by 1983. Some of these were proxy companies which were used to hide the extent of the corporate wealth of politicians and political parties. Nominee companies were the majority shareholders in the 15 UMNO-linked companies.

While the NEP, through the PNB-ASN secured *Bumiputera* equity, "the equity shift has been both highly skewed to the benefit of the richer *Bumiputera* and has offered only very indirect control over the corporate sector...it has acted in large part as an income transfer to the wealthy..." (Emsley 1996: 62). So in a way, the PNB-ASN system provided a false sense of ownership for the *Bumiputera*. I had made the same observation as Emsley, with regards to Fijian Holdings, which under the guise of indigenous business has in fact helped to consolidate the wealth of a few indigenous Fijians through state subsidy. The subsidy also extended to foreign and local non-indigenous corporations in which Fijian Holdings invested. But shares for ordinary indigenous Fijians were held by communal institutions such as the FAB, NLTB, provinces, districts and villages in a way that inhibited individual entrepreneurship.

Some results of affirmative action

Affirmative action in the corporate sector helped build up a Malay middle class as envisaged. As shown in Table 8.7, the share capital ownership for *Bumiputera* increased steadily over the years from 1.5% in 1969 when the NEP was launched to 21.9% in 2008. However, Chinese shareholding has been consistent and between 1969 and 2008 still predominated. Indian shareholding, without the benefit of affirmative action, remained below 2% within the same period.

Table 8.7 Share capital ownership (at par value) by ethnic group, 1970-2008 (%)

	1969	1970	1975	1980	1985	1990	1995	1999	2004	2006	2008
Bumiputera individuals & trust agencies	1.5	2.4	9.2	12.5	19.1	19.2	20.6	19.1	18.9	19.4	21.9
Chinese	22.8	27.2	n.a	n.a	33.4	45.5	40.9	37.9	39.0	42.4	34.9
Indians	0.9	1.1	n.a	n.a	1.2	1.0	1.5	1.5	1.2	1.1	1.6
Other	–	–	–	–	–	–	–	0.9	0.4	0.4	0.1
Nominee companies	2.1	6.0	n.a	n.a	1.3	8.5	8.3	7.9	8.0	6.6	3.5
Locally controlled firms	10.1	–	–	–	7.2	0.3	1.0	–	–	–	–
Foreigners	62.1	63.4	53.3	42.9	26.0	25.4	27.7	32.7	32.5	30.1	37.9

n.a. = not available.

Notes: Par value denotes the price at which the share was first issued; Government ownership is omitted.

Source: Gomez 2009.

The Asian financial crisis in 1997 to 1998 greatly undermined the performance of many state-sponsored Malay entrepreneurs and conglomerates and the response was to re-nationalize them. Many large government-linked companies (GLC) re-emerged and continued to form the backbone of the *Bumiputera* corporate sector (Lee et al. 2010). Even after the exit of Mahathir in 2003, the new government still maintained a commitment to supporting the GLCs while nurturing the growth of small and medium-sized enterprises (SMEs) through loans and other facilities. Part of the support was to link SMEs to large transnational corporations (TNCs) as a way of accessing local and foreign markets. Both the 2007 and 2008 national budgets encouraged companies to award contracts to *Bumiputera* vendors to encourage diversity and to develop human resources. Despite this, the role of the SMEs remained stagnant and did not show signs of the economic dynamism once envisaged (Lee et al. 2010).

One of the shortcomings of affirmative action in the corporate sector was the failure to reduce the involvement of the state in *Bumiputera* business. In 2009 not a single *Bumiputera* company was listed in the top 10 firms, although five of these were GLCs, three were Chinese-owned and one Indian-owned. Likewise, no *Bumiputera* company was in the top 20 firms in the industrial sector. One of the concerns is that, left to their own devices, *Bumiputera* would find it difficult to compete in the liberalized market. This has the potential to cause dissatisfaction and has potential political ramifications.

In the area of professional development, the *Bumiputera* have gained enormously compared to other ethnic groups. Table 8.8 shows that the proportion of *Bumiputera* in the various professional categories rose from 4.9% in 1970 to 38.8% in 2005. This contrasts with the decline in the proportion of Chinese and Indians in the same professional categories.

Table 8.8 Registered professionals[a] by race (% of total)

	Bumiputera	Chinese	Indian	Others
1970[b]	4.9	61.0	23.3	10.8
1975[c]	6.7	64.1	22.1	7.1
1980	14.9	63.5	17.4	4.2
1985	22.2	61.2	13.9	2.7
1990	29.0	55.9	13.2	1.9
1995	33.1	52.4	12.9	1.6
2000	35.5	51.2	12.0	1.3
2005	38.8	48.7	10.6	1.9

a. Architects, accountants, dentists, doctors, engineers, lawyers, surveyors, veterinarians.

b. Excludes surveyors and lawyers.

c. Excludes surveyors.

Sources: Gomez 2009; Lee, et al. 2010.

By and large, affirmative action has helped to advance the economic and social situation of many *Bumiputera* and many goals of the NEP had been achieved. For instance, poverty amongst *Bumiputera* had been substantially reduced from 65% in 1970 to 3.6% in 2007 and there was growth in equity ownership from 2.4% in 1969 to 19.4% in 2006. One of the impacts of the 2009 crisis was to loosen affirmative action policies and allow for greater diversity of government subsidy of corporations and the labour market.

Conclusion

Malaysia's attempt to address ethnic and socio-economic inequality has by some accounts been a success. It is no wonder that countries like Fiji and South

Africa saw it as a model to emulate. However, not all Malays benefitted: intra-communal inequality increased and selected individuals became beneficiaries through state patronage.

Malaysia had some advantages in comparison with Fiji. It had a vibrant economy, driven by industrialization and abundant natural resources and an export-oriented economy. Fiji's economy did not have the same capacity and vibrancy. Malaysia's NEP was also much broader in scope and incorporated a framework for national development including poverty alleviation and affirmative action. In comparison, affirmative action programs in Fiji were largely communally driven and were separate from the national development strategy.

The growth and consolidation of the Malay middle class was a major affirmative action project but the process of achieving this was complex and fraught with patronage and corruption. The role of the middle class was significant because it was the powerhouse of national development and investment as well as having a role as a symbol of progress, achievement and status for the Malay people.

Affirmative action in Malaysia was a major social engineering undertaking which involved restructuring the economy and transforming the civil service and class structure with the hope of achieving peace and stability after the 1969 riots, which still remains as the most significant political watershed in the Malay political consciousness. The strategy for social and political harmony involved experimentation with multi-party and multi-ethnic coalitions, but with *Bumiputera* political hegemony as well as affirmative action. As in Fiji, the politically and demographically dominant indigenous group also became the target group for affirmative action.

One of the original intentions of affirmative action was the gradual withdrawal of state support as a precondition for greater self-reliance. This has been difficult to achieve as *Bumiputera* business had to compete on a level playing field with large and seasoned global corporate players. Thus it seems that state preferences for Malays may last some time yet.

9. "Black empowerment" policies: Dilemmas of affirmative action in South Africa

This chapter examines some of the major dilemmas faced by affirmative action policies in South Africa as it attempts to transform itself into a democratic state. The gap between the abstract ideology of equity and the pragmatic world of entrenched human interests has been a major challenge in the post-apartheid reform process.

Apartheid was a form of pro-white affirmative action which was reversed after the change in government in 1994, when pro-black affirmative action became part of the post-apartheid reconstruction in South Africa as a remedial strategy to address the legal and historical exclusion of the black majority (Jeffery 2009; 2010). Affirmative action was a mechanism for "black empowerment," the term used to ensure higher levels of economic, educational, cultural and political attainment for previously oppressed blacks. A wide range of affirmative action policies were put into place to address issues relating to employment, income, poverty, and education and absence of equal opportunity in education.

As in Fiji and Malaysia, affirmative action has attracted considerable debate. Even in the 1990s concern was raised, ironically by supporters of apartheid, about the creation of a new "victim class" of white professionals, who, if ignored in favour of blacks with lesser skills could be disastrous for economic growth. Some, like Madona Mbatha, a black scholar, even argued that affirmative action was "racism in reverse," and suggested that competence was not determined by colour but by individual skills and thus there should be encouragement of competition on a level playing field (Kemp 1992). The level playing field argument, often used by neo-liberals, was countered by the argument that it was a facade for the perpetuation of inequality. It has been suggested that the "truth is far worse: we are not even on the same playing field" (Sachs 1993: 107). The historical exclusion of blacks from ownership or active participation in the economic arena was deliberate and totalising; and affirmative action was seen as an imperative for the creation of equity and justice as provided for in the 1996 Constitution.

For the new generation of leaders affirmative action was a necessity if the injustices of the past were to be addressed in order to build a more stable future. President Mandela himself emphasised that "the whole social programme of the new democratic government which we envisage for South Africa will be one of affirmative action" (quoted in Sadie 1995: 180). Affirmative action was deemed morally justified because it is based on equity creation by way of "levelling the labour market." Despite recent research that shows affirmative action may have led to problems such as inefficiency, patronage and corruption, affirmative action has led to great strides in the black community politically and economically (Jeffery 2009 and 2010).

Affirmative action in South Africa is often associated with the notion of "black empowerment", a term which parallels the notions of Fijian interest and Malay privilege, except that black empowerment has a more revolutionary connotation which alludes to both economic redistribution and transformation of political power. This chapter examines a number of major affirmative action initiatives which were put in place to address the abject inequality and oppression associated with apartheid.

The chapter discusses some of the historical, economic and political aspects of institutionalized racial segregation in South Africa. It then examines some of the reform initiatives designed to support black empowerment and grow the economy. Of particular relevance is the interplay between the contending notions of growth and redistribution and how they shaped ideological and applied policy approaches to affirmative action. The chapter then examines the relationship between state patronage, privatization and the growth of the black middle class, followed by a discussion of successes and challenges, as well as the influence of the Malaysian experience on South Africa's affirmative action program.

The apartheid legacy

The economy of the Cape revolved around slavery for 175 years until abolition in 1834. In that year, with 36,000 slaves, 59,000 colonists and 42,000 Khoikhoi and "bastards", the colony's ethnicity paralleled its socio-economic inequality. Slavery was the basic social relationship of production and accumulation. Even after slavery was abolished, inequality persisted as freed slaves later made up a class of skilled artisans, forming an underclass in the towns; while rural workers were subjected to even worse, brutal, exploitation.

Major geopolitical changes took place in the 1800s as a result of the British wars of conquest, in part instigated by the discovery of minerals. This led to forced transfer of property ownership and the creation of a new mode of production, resulting from the incorporation of once independent communities under British colonial control in the form of the Union of South Africa (Union). This process had profound effects on Africans: in particular, the emergence of a mission-educated African elite and the inexorable process of black proletarianization on the other side of the social spectrum.

Moreover, although mining was the major economic activity in the early years of the Union, over the years diversification dramatically increased and in the process inequality also grew in other sectors. In many respects the ideology and policies of the political party in power contributed to the growth of inequality. For instance, after the National Party came into power in 1948, deliberate policies for Afrikaner hegemony and ethnic exclusion were rigorously encouraged and practised. The real income of whites in relation to blacks in industry in the first five years of National Party rule rose by more than 10%, while income of blacks decreased by 5%. By 1960, real income of whites had increased by 30% while that of blacks consistently decreased annually by 5%. The large corporations dominated the economy and the National Party government "deliberately appointed National Party Afrikaners to the key positions of control in these corporations to ensure the advancement of apartheid" (Sonn 1993: 7). It was no coincidence that policies of the National Party to encourage the growth of state capitalism since 1948 was tantamount to promotion of Afrikaner business and further marginalization of black workers (Collinicos and Rogers 1977).

The inequality was quite apparent in public corporations. In 1952 about 80% of the employees of South African Railways and Harbours and 68% of public sector employees were Afrikaners. This was despite the growth in the size of the public sector by 50% from 1946 to 1976. In 1968 there were proportionately twice as many Afrikaners in the public sector than there had been in 1948. In 1979 about 35% of economically active Afrikaners were in the public service and around the same time, 90% of approximately 150 key positions in the public sector were allocated to Afrikaners. There was undoubtedly a "direct link between the possession of political power and socio-economic upliftment" (Sonn 1993: 7).

As a result of diversification over a few decades, the South African economy had become "one of the most powerful and sophisticated" in the developing world by 1970 (Yudelman 1984: 2-3). However, this wealth was characterized by massive ethnic and class inequality. The period between 1970 and 1990 saw dramatic changes taking place, as the apartheid state slowly but reluctantly reformed. The pattern of income inequality remained constant from 1924 to 1970, but a substantial process of reform took place in the 1980s. Some of these reforms were encouraged by the corporate sector, which was under pressure from international sanctions and was also beginning to realize the potential market represented by an emerging black middle class. This was, no doubt, a precursor to the pro-black affirmative action in later years.

Interestingly, by 1980 the white share in the economy had decreased to 60%, while that of Africans rose to 29% and this pattern continued well into the 1980s. This trend was largely a result of the redistribution of wage income rather than on fixed assets. In the same period, there was a substantial growth in the number of blacks in managerial, executive, professional and entrepreneurial high-income positions, resulting from the changing pattern of corporate culture and a greater access to tertiary education for blacks. While these changes facilitated the growth of a business and technical class, it did not alter the general trend and degree of poverty and unemployment. It is true that the ethnic income gap had narrowed, but class differentiation between whites and blacks remained structurally entrenched, supported by repressive laws and a white supremacist ideology.

One of the most overt ways of institutionalizing inequalities and white privileges was through direct state funding of budgetary expenditure (Maasdorp 1992). In 1982/83 the defence sector was allocated 13.57% of Government General Expenditure (GGE), increasing to 13.88% in 1987/88. Public order and safety expenditure in 1982/83 was 6.29% and increased to 6.89% in 1987/88 (Lundahl 1998). Both of these expenditures were important because they played a direct role in maintaining the coercive apparatus of the apartheid state. Apartheid created inequality of "unequivocal and extreme proportions no matter what indicator is used" (Lundahl 1998: 26).

The stark disparities of the apartheid era in basic indicators of social well-being such as monthly household income, education, infant mortalities and electricity usage continued even after majority rule was achieved in 1994. By the time of liberation, the infant mortality rate for Africans was eight times greater than that for whites, while there was a difference in life expectancy of nearly 10 years. The United Nations Children's Fund (UNICEF) revealed that South Africa's child mortality rate (number of children per 1,000 live births who died before the age of 5) was 72, compared to the world-wide average of 35 (Sadie 1995: 181). In 1994 only 10% of white households were without electricity compared to 60% of African homes. The National Manpower Commission (NMC) calculated that if the former independent homelands were included in the estimates, as many as 66% of the total population would fall into the category of being illiterate at13 years of age and above, instead of 46%. The high level of illiteracy amongst the unemployed made many of them virtually unemployable.

In 1996, two years after the elections, the poorest 20% of all income earners received only 1.5% of the total income, while the top 10% had 50% of the total income. In 1995, the poorest 20% of households received only 3% of all household income, while the richest 20% of households had 65%. These national figures need to be understood in the context of poverty being concentrated amongst the Africans and Coloureds, with 95% of Africans and 33% of Coloureds being classified "poor" (South African Parliament 1998c: 1).

In a major shift, affirmative action since 1994 boosted the proportion of urban Africans in the top 20% income group, from 2% in 1990 to 6% in 1995 (South

African Parliament 1998a: 1-3). An ILO assessment in 1994 showed that public sector differentials in South Africa had a ratio of 25:1 from top to bottom. However, this was reduced to 20:1 in 1995 with the deliberate policy of freezing the top strata and raising the bottom strata with the target for 1999 set at 12:1. Attempts were made to persuade the private sector to carry out the same labour market reforms, although private owners took some convincing. The idea was to transfer highly qualified personnel from the public sector to the private sector, due to the compression of wage scales in the public sector.

Despite the political transformation since the 1994 election, racial capitalism, a legacy of apartheid, is deeply entrenched in South Africa. While there was political euphoria and optimism for a new South Africa, the ANC, five years after taking power, had to come to terms with the challenges of dismantling structural inequality:

> …1994 did not augur the demise of racial capitalism. The stark reality is that many of the social and economic inequalities brought about by racial capitalism are as acute as ever. South Africa's wealth is still overwhelmingly concentrated in white hands, despite black empowerment, and the crisis of black poverty in the new South Africa is the unacceptable legacy of Apartheid (South African Parliament 1998a: 1).

One of the difficulties in the process of transformation was the reconfiguration of the legal and political structures which supported apartheid. This is where South Africa differs from Fiji and Malaysia – neither of those countries had a minority-dominated apartheid state. For South Africa, apartheid, or separate development, was reinforced by draconian legislation. We examine that legislation next.

'Legalizing' apartheid

The apartheid system was sustained through discriminatory policies, repressive state coercion and deliberate segregationist laws. Even before apartheid became official state policy, segregation laws such as The Natives Land Act No 27 1913, which regulated the purchase or lease of land by blacks, and The Natives (Urban Areas) Act No 21 of 1923, which decreed residential segregation in urban areas, were already in place. Upon assuming power in 1948, the National Party formalized apartheid through various pieces of legislation. Social segregation was enforced through laws such as the Prohibition of Mixed Marriages Act, Act No 55 of 1949 which made mixed marriages illegal, the Immorality Amendment Act, Act No 21 of 1950 (amended in 1957), which prohibited extra-marital sex between whites and blacks and the Population Registration Act No 30 of 1950, which officially classified people into distinct racial categories.

Physical and social separation of people was reinforced through the Group Areas Act, Act No 41 of 1950 and in the same year the Suppression of Communism Act No 44 of 1950 was enacted to curb political resistance. A year later four more acts were passed to further institutionalize segregation. These were the Bantu Building Workers Act, No 27 of 1951, aimed at demarcating racially skilled workers; the Separate Representation of Voters Act No 46 of 1951, which led to the removal of coloureds from the common voters electoral roll; Prevention of Illegal Squatting Act, Act No 52 of 1951, which facilitated forced removal of blacks from public or private spaces; and the Bantu Authorities Act No 68 of 1951 which created separate municipalities for blacks.

A number of laws were passed in succession in the next two years. These included the Native Laws Amendment Act of 1952, which redefined and limited the meaning of the black category and the Natives (Abolition of Passes and Co-ordination of Documents) Act No 67 of 1952, which ensured that every black must carry a pass at all times. These were followed by the Native Labour (Settlement of Disputes) Act of 1953, prohibiting strike action by blacks and the Bantu Education Act No 47 of 1953, which segregated education as well as prescribing an education system which largely reinforced the subordinate and domesticated position of blacks in society. In the same year the Reservation of Separate Amenities Act No 49 of 1953 was passed, paving the way for forced segregation in all public amenities, public buildings and public transport.

These laws laid the legal and political foundation for apartheid and the newly created apartheid constitution was revolutionary in that it totally reconfigured the state and legal system. Inequality was deliberately fostered by law as well as the repressive coercive arms of the state in the form of the police and military. While these apartheid laws were later removed and the state structure which sustained them was progressively dismantled as the transition progressed, the rebuilding process required a deeper process of social engineering and structural reconfiguration through affirmative action.

Dilemmas of post-apartheid reconstruction

The collapse of apartheid was a result of a concerted internal and external struggle. For leaders of the African National Congress (ANC) it meant having to adjust to the new political climate and rising expectations. In its opposition days ANC relied fundamentally on the *Freedom Charter* of 1955 to provide the political and ideological paradigm of resistance, but by the early 1990s, as the prospects of democratic elections loomed, there was increasing pressure to devise new methods of governance for an emerging state (Myburgh 2006). This was a mammoth task because the post-apartheid government "has inherited an insidious past of economic mismanagement, racial and social oppression, enormously complicated and costly bureaucratic structures, and extreme poverty and inequality" (Luiz 1994: 230).

One of the problems of reconstruction was how to facilitate the "trade-off between growth and equity" (Terreblanche 1992: 551). In addressing the equity question, two types of inequality needed to be focused on: "firstly, the (structural) inequality in the distribution of property, power, and control; secondly, the unequal opportunities, income, and consumption available to racially defined groups" (ibid: 552). At the same the economy needed to grow to ensure that redistribution was viable. In fact the growth versus equity debate had its origins in the beginning of 1990 and it sharply polarised the left and right of the ideological divide. On one side was the liberation discourse, which advocated growth through redistribution, and on the other was a more conservative stance, which favoured redistribution through growth. After 1994, the ANC, the vanguard of the liberationist paradigm, managed to merge the two arguments together in response to the need to facilitate both the establishment agenda in order to embrace neo-liberalism and integration into the global economy, and redistributive measures such as the Reconstruction and Development Programme (RDP) and the Economic Equity Bill (EEB). In the circumstances, this "mixed economy" seemed to be the most viable, but in the long run, "the problem is how to arrange the mix to satisfy political, social and economic goals" (Maasdorp 1992: 588).

This debate also saw ideological fluidity and contestation within the ANC itself. For instance, at the time of Nelson Mandela's release in 1990, the ANC had only the *Freedom Charter,* a largely ideological statement of inspiration, rather than a concrete program of reconstruction, as a written guiding vision for the future. The realisation that liberation meant serious political and economic responsibility led to the first two workshops by the ANC and COSATU in Harare in 1990 and a *Discussion Document on Economic Policy* resulted from these. The main thrust of the document endorsed the central role of the state as the guardian of economic development. Redistribution was considered "conducive to growth, via a restructuring of demand leading to a creation of mass markets and as a way of satisfying the basic needs of the population" (Lundahl 1998: 28).

However, later the nationalisation agenda was gradually watered down and came to be seen only as a possible alternative in certain given circumstances. In 1991 there was a further shift away from the primacy of redistribution and in 1992 an ANC political guideline, *Ready to Govern: ANC Policy Guidelines for a Democratic South Africa* was produced. This document emphasised for the first time the desirability of a mixed economy and the importance of the private sector. However, at the same time a research document in 1993 by the ANC-aligned academic network called the Macroeconomic Research Group (NERG) raised important questions of equity and redistribution which became the basis of the Reconstruction and Development Programme (RDP) of the ANC.

The Reconstruction and Development Programme

The Reconstruction and Development Programme (RDP) was one of the very first affirmative action and re-distributive policies of the post-apartheid state. It promised to provide ten years of compulsory education for everybody; the building of at least one million low-cost houses in the next five years; provision of electricity for an additional 2.5 million households by the year 2000; clean water and adequate sanitation for everybody; improved and affordable health, particularly preventive and primary health care for all; and land distribution to the landless. Based on the Malaysian NEP principles, these were ambitious provisions which were to rely heavily on spin-offs from economic growth.

However, the RDP was confronted with a series of challenges, which led to the closure of its office in 1996, after just two years of operation, thus "raising serious questions about the future of development and the government's commitment to it" (Caliguire 1996: 5). Although the RDP Office was closed, RDP as a reconstruction program continued and its programmatic and strategic aspects were shifted to the office of then Deputy President Thambo Mbeki, where reassignment of responsibilities to the line departments was to take place. The dismantling of the RDP office itself was politically symbolic in the sense that it "indicates that economic growth, rather than redistribution, has won the day as the national primary tool for change" (Caliguire 1996: 20).

RDP did not have the institutional capacity for management and disbursement of funds. For instance, 2.5 billion rand were budgeted for 1994-95 and this was expected to increase in 1998-99, but 1.7 billion rand was unused and had to be carried over to 1995-96 (Lundahl 1998). From the beginning, there was confusion as to who was in charge of the RDP budget, the RDP office or the Ministry of Finance.

On other fronts, provision of houses, health and education facilities was frustratingly cumbersome and slow. Of 400,000 houses, which were to be built within a two-year period (1994-96), only 15,000 were built (Caliguire 1996). These problems were mostly associated with the budgetary process, resistance and a lack of commitment in the state bureaucracy, lack of support by civil society organizations and lack of support by the private financial sector for government policies such as extending loans to low-income blacks, for example (Michie and Padayachee 1997: 18-19).

RDP projects were to be carried out in co-operation with civil groups and local government. However, despite the democratised implementation process, it was revealed that RDP would be costly to implement, especially when public investment in infrastructure would have to be increased by at least 21 % per annum. Furthermore, RDP operations came into conflict with existing line departments, which argued that their portfolios were taken over or duplicated by RDP. There were also persistent allegations of corruption, which led to the collapse of some RDP social and physical infrastructural projects, the President's R500 million feeding scheme being one of them (*South Scan*, 18 September 1995).

Probably the most successful RDP project in the 1990s related to the supply of electricity. More than 300,000 new household connections per annum were achieved by the state corporation, ESCOM (Fine and Stoneman 1996: 27). Substantial progress was also achieved in the provision of water: towards the end of 1995 some 300 projects taking water to 4 million people were scheduled for completion within 18 months (*Financial Times*, 21 November 1995).

Neo-liberalism and affirmative action

The *Growth, Employment and Redistribution Strategy,* (GEAR) of 2006 largely reflected the incorporation of neo-liberal policies into the South African development strategy (Fitzgerald, McLennan and Munslow 1997: 49). In implementing GEAR South Africa was mindful of its obligations to the World Trade Organisation (WTO), which it joined in 1993, while at the same time it was conscious of its political and moral obligation to redistribution. GEAR aimed to create almost 1.5 million jobs over five years, as well as to promote competitiveness through trade liberalisation and productivity measures, to support direct investment and export orientation, to enhance the social and economic infrastructure through partnership with the private sector and improved flexibility in the labour market (Cargill 1996). GEAR's fiscal policy was aimed at reducing the deficit by half over a period of six years, while no direct intervention in monetary policy was envisaged. The entire budget process for 1996 and 1997 was committed to reducing deficit, with a target of 4% (Gelb 1997: 4).

GEAR did not adequately address the issue of job creation, which relied heavily on infrastructural and public works programs. To create 400,000 jobs, a 6% growth rate was needed; but this could be achieved only if fixed investment increased 19% to 24% of GDP. Investment needed funding from savings by government, and from the private sector and foreign investors. These were not easy to attract.

Meanwhile, frustrations within the ANC hierarchy over GEAR increased, as there was a strong feeling that focus on growth had undermined the principles of equity and redistribution (Cargill 1996). At the same time, there was a belief that GEAR should fund RDR, but due to the low growth rate (minus 2.2% in 1992; 1.3% in 1993; 2.7% in 1994 and 3.3% in 1995) this expectation seemed to ring hollow. This was a huge contrast to events in Malaysia, where a growth rate of almost 10% in the 1980s provided the necessary resources for the NEP. For South Africa, the "growth before redistribution" neo-liberal transformation has been in part stimulated by multilateral intervention by the WTO and IMF.

ANC's shift towards the "Washington consensus" caused fractures within the democratic alliance. For instance, two major pillars of the alliance, the South African Communist Party (SACP) and the Congress of South African Trade Unions (COSATU) criticised the ANC-dominated government for "yielding to World Bank pressure on privatisation and the reduction of trade tariffs" (*Star*, 4 July 1995). The ANC government was in a difficult situation and, given the economic realities, it had to reposition itself to address the looming crisis. One way of doing this was to redefine its strategic alliances to include an enlarged circle of players: the emerging black middle class, certain sections of the white entrepreneurial class (with whom the ANC had a love-hate relationship) and global multilateral capital. To consolidate this partnership, the National Economic Development and Labour Council (NEDLAC) was established as part of the corporatist strategy of the government to engage business, labour and the community in dialogue and to negotiate policy on the economy and social equity. In addition, the National Empowerment Consortium (NEC) and New Africa Investments Ltd (NAIL), which were based on the Malaysian Bumiputera trust companies, were set up to facilitate the black empowerment policy (Kallaway 1997: 38).

The building of this mainstream alliance tested the democratic provisions and resilience of the constitution because it marginalized extreme politics. The excluded political forces included the white right, consisting of the Afrikaner Weerstandsbeweging (AWB) and the Freedom Front (FF) and the black radical groups such as the Pan African Congress (PAC), the Azanian People's Organisation (AZAPO) and the Black Consciousness Movement in general.

Interestingly, the neo-liberal reforms benefited the emerging black business class through a carefully orchestrated mix of liberalisation policies and affirmative action. An example of this was the preferential award of privatised utilities' contracts to black companies. While redistribution and poverty alleviation was foremost in the minds of the political elites, there was also a strong belief that building a strong black middle class was imperative for the country's prosperity.

Transformation in the labour market: The Employment Equity Act (EEA)

The Employment Equity Act (EEA) of 1999 was intended to address the specific question of equal opportunities and preferential employment of blacks in the labour market. Section 5 (1) prohibited discrimination in employment on the grounds of "race, gender, sex, pregnancy, orientation, age, disability, religion, conscience belief, political opinion, culture, language and birth." Apart from targeting employment, the EEA also had implications for black business because it aimed to absorb more blacks into the private sector, where there would be increased chances of directly participating in entrepreneurship. Blacks were fast-tracked to managerial positions so that they could launch their own business careers. The EEA also made businesses more accountable to state regulation, thus ensuring that competition took place within the framework of employment equity. There was an expectation that EEA would generally encourage inter-ethnic integration in the labour force.

The concept of EEA was a revolutionary one in that it linked employment equity to the democratization of the workplace, worker training, recruitment, and promotion and worker empowerment through collective bargaining. The challenge was to transform the racially based and authoritarian nature of the apartheid workplace into a more democratic one which recognized the racial equality of all workers. The EEA also identified blacks, women and the disabled as designated groups who needed to be empowered through a two-pronged approach: firstly, the creation of employment audit or analysis by employers to publish the profile of their entire workforce; and secondly, the creation of an employment plan by employers which, in consultation with the workforce, would outline the targets for employment equity within a one- to five-year period. The plan was to be submitted to government, monitored and reported on regularly and appropriate sanctions were imposed for breach of these provisions. At the state advisory level the EEA established the Commission for Employment Equity (CEE) to provide advice and strategic directions for the Minister.

However, despite these preferential provisions, the EEA made certain concessions and included delicate balancing which proved to be problematic. For instance, there was provision for both state regulation and self-regulation by employers and employees. In addition, there was provision for both rigid targets and negotiated targets. State regulation through the quota system tended to benefit a small group of individuals who were thrust into management positions in what was perceived to be mere tokenism. At the same time, imposing targets from above did not take into account the actual problems of industries and individual enterprises and had the potential to undermine the collective process of workplace transformation and the workplace empowering process of labour generally.

However, on the other hand, abandonment of state intervention in favour of "self-regulation" proved to be counter-productive, as there were no incentives for companies to implement affirmative action nor disincentive to not implement it. Many private enterprises did not have the political commitment to implement what they perceived as something outside their narrow business interests and there was resistance to the EEA by white employers.

There was a fear amongst the labour unions that the EEA had the potential to reinforce employer hegemony by providing that "a designated employer must take reasonable steps to consult and attempt to reach agreement", especially when it has been established that the "burden of proof is placed on the employer … and that the employer has to justify any action that might be considered unfair discrimination" (South African Parliament 1998c). The response to this provision by COSATU was one of reserved suspicion because of the fear that employers were going to drive, and ultimately decide, the employment equity plans and outcomes. This was deemed inconsistent with the principle of a labour market democratized through collective bargaining.

Conservative white critics argued that the EEA would re-racialize South Africa, lower standards, introduce unfair quotas, encourage rigidity in the work place and put an unsound economic burden on business. The Government rejected these criticisms, saying that opponents of the EEA were misled by self-interest and were bent on conspiring to "create fear and insecurity by attacking affirmative action aspects of the EEA" (South African Parliament 1998c).

State patronage, privatization and black empowerment

One of the major lessons which South Africa leant from Malaysia was the complex art of finely balancing the paradoxical interface between state intervention and control on the one hand and liberalization and privatization on the other. The interplay between neo-liberalism and state interventionism helped build a huge and vibrant Malay middle class, which provided the inspiration for South Africa's move towards the dual system of growth and redistribution. A more regulated form of capitalism was needed to build up and expand a black middle class which would not only provide a lucrative market and professional skills, but also act as a visible political symbol of liberation and empowerment.

The 'hows' of privatisation were outlined in the 1995 Discussion Document by the Government of National Unity on the Consultative Implementation Framework for the Restructuring of the State Assets, which attempted to deal with the complex question of privatising government assets worth between R30 billion and R120 billion. Five key areas of concern in the privatisation debate were identified. These related to meeting RDP goals, including black empowerment; addressing trade union concerns related to debt and interest payment relief; preventing big business domination; mobilising local and foreign capital; and improving managerial efficiency. Initially, there was a fear that privatised state assets would end up with white-dominated conglomerates and privatised para-statals. That would not be in the best interest of the rural and urban poor and would undermine the re-distributive and developmental aims of the RDP and the ideological thrust of the ANC.

However, there was a strong argument that privatisation could in fact be an ideal vehicle for affirmative action and black empowerment by ensuring preferential black shareholding of privatised enterprises and by allowing black professionals to fully participate in the privatisation process (Thomas 1995). There was growing pressure from the emerging African middle class for a greater share in privatisation assets and, in response, by 1997 the government had already earmarked 10% of the para-statal telecommunication company TELKOM for black empowerment groups (Adam, van Zyl Slabbert and Moodley 1997: 217).

The group which was most sceptical about privatisation was COSATU, which was angered by the government's privatization of crucial areas of the public service. There was fear that job rationalisation and tougher labour relations would hit the unskilled and poor hardest. The other faction of COSATU, especially those who had benefited from the new alliance with the white corporations, argued that privatisation would be a "golden opportunity to establish participatory management and more enlightened labour relations" (Thomas 1995: 6).

Pressure had been mounting from multilateral institutions, private corporations and groups within the government to speed up the privatisation process because of escalating public debt and the need for growth. Accumulated debt has been blamed on the "irresponsible spending" of the apartheid regime (South African Parliament 1998b: 2). Foreign debt made up 2.2% of GDP in 1996, while domestic debt was 56.0% of GDP. South Africa needed to spend 6.5% of its GDP to pay for interest on these debts. Around R39, 643 billion was spent on servicing the interest alone. Growth in the 1990s was slow but steady. The economy grew by 3.1% in 1996, the fourth consecutive year of growth, but the general picture of the economy was still one of mixed fortunes.

To enhance growth and support black empowerment, reform in strategic areas of the economy was critical. The provisions for reform included an increase in funding for industrial development and research and technology, from R454 million to R604 million; setting up of a new Competitive Fund and sectoral partnership facility to enable firms and organisations to draw on consultant advice in advancing competitiveness; and creating a new short-term Export Finance Guarantee Scheme for small and medium-sized firms.

The impact of neo-liberal policies on affirmative action was quite direct. The African bourgeoisie or "liberation aristocrats", as Adam et al. (1997) called them, were the most direct beneficiaries of the privatised assets. Some of them were independent entrepreneurs while a sizeable number were "black" fronts for white companies (or "Ali Baba" companies as the Malaysians called them). An emerging trend was the consolidation of entrepreneurial links between the white and the black middle class. Often blacks were used as token representatives to enable white-run companies to acquire privatized assets. Recruitment of blacks into the managerial ranks of white corporations was found to be advantageous "both for a progressive public relations image and the utilisation of an additional pool of talent, but above all for the advantages black management bestows in marketing to a fast growing black consumer market and establishing linkages with government for state contracts" (Adam et al. 1997: 210). By 1997, just three years after the ascendancy of the ANC, black conglomerates controlled 10% of market capitalisation in the Johannesburg Stock Exchange (JSE). A powerful and wealthy black middle class, increasingly isolated from its original political base, and progressively identified with the corporate status quo had firmly consolidated itself.

While there was a phenomenal rise in a black middle class which benefitted from privatisation and preferential policies, there was also a growing mass of poverty-stricken citizens, which posed a direct challenge to the new political order. A lot of the poor were recent arrivals from the countryside and did not have any formal employment whatsoever. This underclass was not being addressed adequately by the EEB because of its primary focus on the formal sector. That worsened the socio-economic inequality and led to an escalation of violent crime.

The situation was made more critical by the loss of jobs as a result of privatization. GEAR's aim of creating 1.5 million jobs within five years was mocked by the actual net loss of 80,000 jobs emanating from GEAR's own privatization policies. Although 11,000 posts were reserved for affirmative action candidates in the public service in 1994, the cost-cutting rationalisation process led to a net loss of jobs. This trend continued, even after the government's *White Paper on Transformation of the Public Service* (1996), which identified a number of relevant policy areas such as the introduction of a minimum wage, equal pay for equal work value, reduction in differentials, development of appropriate career paths, occupational transformation and improvement of conditions for women and the disabled.

Meanwhile, privatization continued to help the black middle class to expand into diverse sectors of the economy, classified by Iheduru (1998) into seven categories: (a) holding/listed companies, or what white stockbrokers derogatorily referred to as "black chips;" (b) potential listed companies; (c) portfolio investment trusts; (d) professional women investors; (e) micro and small enterprises (MSE) ranging from registered unlisted companies to "closed corporations" to sole proprietorships and partnerships; (f) the informal sector, where the majority of black entrepreneurs operated; (g) political business entrepreneurs. The majority of black businesses were MSE, which numbered one million, or informal sector businesses, with a total of 2.5 million: but because they were so small and had few resources they had to struggle hard to survive. On the other hand, the companies listed on the Johannesburg Stock Exchange (JSE) were the most prominent in terms of the publicity they received. Although only eight black-owned companies were listed on the JSE in July 1997, this number increased steadily over the years.

It is worth noting that the development of the black entrepreneurial class had its roots in the 1960s, when a number of black business organisations were formed. The first was the Greater Soweto Chamber of Commerce and Industries (GSCCI), from which the National African Chamber of Commerce (NAFCOC) emerged, and others followed. Membership of these business organisations varied from 300,000 to 400,000 in the case of the Foundation for African Business and Consumer Services (FABCOS) to 40, as in the case of the Western Cape Black Builders' Association (WCBA) (Sidiropoulos 1994). FABCOS and NAFCOC were in fact umbrella organisations, to which other small organisations were affiliated. The leaders of these organisations were closely linked to the ANC leadership and were part of the emerging middle class discussed earlier.

NAFCOC's affirmative action plan, accepted during the 1990 annual conference, provided for the following targets for corporate changes by the year 2000: (a) 30% of all board members of companies listed on the Johannesburg Stock Exchange (JSE) should be black; (b) 40% of all shares on the JSE should be black-owned; (c) 50% of the value of all outside purchases by the companies listed on the JSE should come from black suppliers; (d) 60% of top management in JSE-listed companies should be black (Nkuhlu 1993: 16). FABCOS's membership comprised individuals from different political parties such as ANC, Azanian People's

Organisation, Inkatha Freedom Party and Pan-Africanist Congress. It was set up primarily to negotiate with the government for the removal of all discriminatory laws and policies; ensuring the establishment of independent companies and institutions for the purpose of fostering black economic advancement; and raising awareness about the need to extend the free enterprise system to the black community. Both NAFCOC and FABCOS have been criticised for being too undemocratic, "top heavy", and based on "petty hierarchies" dominated by clique loyalties (Sidiropoulus 1994). Despite their own conflicts, their new-found power in the form of their alliance with the ANC and membership of the National Economic Forum (NEF) provided them with the necessary political legitimacy.

The proliferation of black entrepreneurship was encouraged by the lifting of various restrictions which once prohibited black participation in business. An example was the abolition of the Group Areas Act, which had prohibited black businesses from operating in white areas and vice versa. Paradoxically, during the apartheid era, the state poured money into black business, principally for the purpose of building a large black middle class that would become a willing ally of the apartheid state and to overshadow the radicalised urban political and youth leadership (Iheduru 1998). Black business was also boosted after many official restrictions on business ownership by blacks disappeared by the 1980s and by the removal of many of the pillars of apartheid by President F.W. de Klerk, facilitated by the passage of the Abolition of Racially Based Measures Act of 1991.

Many black businesses were voluntarily integrated with white companies and black businessmen quickly developed corporate skills in acquisition, equity purchase and takeovers in respect of dozens of existing white and black businesses in the areas of banking, insurance and other financial services, transportation, construction, print and electronic media, tourism, health care and manufacturing. Some black businessmen also formed close links with African and American diplomats, politicians, sports and entertainment superstars, business people and legal luminaries and broadened their shareholdings in the process.

The potential listed enterprises, which were mostly founded in the 1990s, were the fastest growing black holding companies. Their interests ranged from financial services, tourism and aviation, entertainment and leisure to industrial holdings in catering services, computers, educational publishing, properties, and printing (*SouthScan*, 16 June 1995). A number of the founders and directors of these companies were ex-guerrillas and former anti-apartheid activists who later forged ties with mainstream white business.

Black entrepreneurs consolidated their interests with ease. For instance, in 1991 blacks occupied only 30 (less than 2%) of the 2,550 directorships available in the top 100 companies listed on the JSE. This number increased to 120 in 1993 and by May 1995 black males held 276 directorships. This accelerated growth was accompanied by a debate about "integration" and "parallelism." Should black business integrate with white business or maintain a separate identity? Economic pragmatism and political imperatives dictated that there should be increasing integration to boost the national economy as well as to provide black entrepreneurs with the skills and resources they needed. Integration rather than isolation was critical for black empowerment.

Results and challenges of black empowerment

The optimism of the early years of affirmative action after 1994 could not be matched by the complex realities. Some of the targets were met while some were not. For instance, in 2008, despite attempts to improve the level of education to match the demand for blacks to enter the higher levels of management, only about 379,000 Africans, or 1.8% of the African population, had completed higher education (Jeffery 2010). Despite this shortcoming, a concerted effort to achieve the aims of black empowerment led to accelerated transformation of the labour market. By 2008 blacks, who made up 74% of the economically active population, were well represented in public sector management positions, where they held 76.41% of the total public service positions compared to 11.31% for whites, 3.2% for Asians and 8.74% for coloureds. For senior management positions, blacks made up 57.31%, compared to 26.87% for whites, 7.81% for Asian and 7.59% for coloureds (*Business Day*, 11 February 2008).

The original target for black managers in the public service was 50%, but this was increased to 75% in 2003, to be achieved by March 2005. Of these, 30% were to be women. By 2005 these targets had been more or less achieved, with blacks accounting for 70% of senior management posts, 29% of whom were women (President Thabo Mbeki, *State of the Nation address to Parliament*, February 2006). This provided the platform for ambitiously increasing the target for women to 50%. However, part of the problem was that, while there was intense political will for the empowerment of blacks and women, the level of education and skills in the target population could not match up and this led to a failure to meet targets (Jeffery 2010).

The proportion of blacks in the civil service varied from department to department. For instance, in 2009 more than 80% of the top posts in the Department of Home Affairs, Department of Science and Technology and the Independent Complaints Directorate of the South African Police Service (SAPS) were held by blacks. This was a comparatively high proportion, given the fact that blacks made up 79% of the population and 74% of the economically active population (*Business Report,* 9 April 2010).

The impact of affirmative action in the corporate sector has also been significant. In September 2009 black executives held an estimated 25% of senior management positions, a major increase compared to 5% in 1994. Nevertheless, this was still a long way from the initial target and only a slight increase compared to 22% in 2004. The inability to reach the target was due to a skills' shortage, lack of suitably qualified black executives and "job hopping" by affirmative action appointees who tended to change jobs due to "attraction premiums" paid to affirmative action appointments (P-E Corporate Services (SA) Pty Ltd 2009). Also, in 2009, about 32% of middle management positions were held by blacks compared to 7% in 1994. Once again there was only a modest increase since 2004, when blacks held 28% of middle management positions. This was far below the government targets. At the same time, the proportion of blacks at the lower management level increased from 26% in 1994 to 55% in 2009. This was a rather slow increase given the 49% level in 2004 (P-E Corporate Services Pty Ltd (SA) 2009).

The emphasis on black employment equity targets meant that businesses had to configure their employment structure in a pro-active way. The targets included 60% for senior management within a ten-year period and 80% for junior management, also within 10 years. This is a big ask, given the fact that less than 17% of Africans are of senior managerial level age (40 to 64 years) and only 1.8% of them hold degrees. In 2006 blacks with degrees made up 28% of legislators, senior officials and managers and 41% of professionals. This is an indication that skilled blacks were already established in certain positions (Jeffery 2010).

A survey by the Unilever Institute at the University of Cape Town showed that the black employment equity strategy has helped consolidate a "black diamond" class, which in 2007 was estimated to number about 2.6 million, with a spending power of R180 billion. Within a year the black diamond class had grown to 3 million people, with an increased spending power of R250 billion. This analysis was based on the definition of middle class as those, including civil servants, earning at least R5,000 a month. This definition has been criticized for being too broad. The alternative definition, which puts the required income at R16,700 a month, yields a much lower figure of 322,000 "core" black middle class in 2004 (15% of total core middle class); 454,000 in 2007 (20% of total core middle class) and 788,000 in 2009 (31% of total core middle class) (Jeffery 2010).

It has been argued that affirmative action has been used by the ruling ANC as a tool for hegemony. One such case refers to the "cadre deployment" program, in which ANC supporters were assigned headship positions in local government, government institutions and other areas of political significance as a way of overseeing the operations of those organisations and linking up to the central state apparatus. This has led to cronyism and has undermined efficiency in governance and productivity. It also contradicted Section 197 of the Constitution, which made illegal favouring or prejudicing a person "because that person supports a particular political party or cause," an argument supported by a recent High Court decision in the Eastern Cape (*ConsWatch 2008:* 1–3).

While cadre deployment was categorized as an affirmative action program, it was seen by political opponents of ANC as a political instrument of control. As the leader of the Democratic Alliance, Helen Zille, argued:

> Cadre deployment went undetected for what it was for so long because it was disguised by the fig leaf of affirmative action. Now, more and more South Africans are beginning to see the policy for what it really is: a means to centralise power, accumulate wealth corruptly, and subvert the Constitution (Zille 2009: 1).

ANC's attempt to control the public service and different levels of governance and the drive to create a black middle class has created distortions within the economy and greater society. Many unqualified people are being thrust into senior positions and as a result there has been visible degradation of the standard and quality of service, infrastructure and neglect of the lower end of society. About 19.65 million people are still in poverty and subsist on an average of about R3,000 a month for a household of eight members or more. About half of the youths between the ages of 15 and 24 are unemployed and this has helped to escalate the problem of crime and violence. Crippling poverty, inadequate education, high crime rate and the HIV/AIDS crisis have all given the ANC heightened challenges.

A further problem is the issue of the foreign labourers who have been attracted to South Africa since the early 1900s. Initially most of them were from Mozambique, Malawi, Botswana, Lesotho and Swaziland; over the years workers have come from other countries. In 1971 there were about half a million foreign workers in South Africa, more than double since the first decade of 1900 (Prothero 1974). This grew over time as the South African economy prospered, attracting both skilled and unskilled foreign workers. Some employers gave preference to skilled foreign workers over locals and this caused considerable opposition, which led to racial violence.

The Malaysian connection

South Africa imported the celebrated "Asian Renaissance", to use Malaysian Prime Minister Mahathir Mohammed's term, to provide inspiration for what former president Thambo Mbeki referred to as an "African Renaissance." The new South African leaders saw in Malaysia a vision for what they wanted: economic growth and economic empowerment of the indigenous population (Hyslop 1997). Mbeki's political adviser reinforced this thinking, stating that, "The advent of the East Asian Economic miracle is one of the most important socio-economic developments of the 20th century...This miracle has offered hope to the people of Africa that economic development can be rapid" (*Sunday Independent,* 15 June 1997).

After 1994 Malaysia became the fastest growing source of investment in South Africa within a short time. Malaysian companies initially invested in hotels and in the leisure and tourism fields and later expanded into investment in petrol, telecommunications, baking and stock brokering. The cumulative effect was that South Africa increasingly came under considerable Malaysian influence (Hyslop 1997). During his 1996 visit to Malaysia, Mandela praised Malaysian affirmative action for overcoming the legacy of colonialism and poverty and the economic policies which made economic development possible; and suggested that South Africa had a lot to learn from Malaysia in the areas of training and technology, in creating an investment climate, in privatisation and in affirmative action (Gopher://gopher.anc.or.za, 7 March 1997). The *Bumiputera* middle class inspired the ANC to focus its attention on building a black middle class within the shortest possible time. Stell Sigacau, the Minister responsible for the privatisation of public industries, suggested that South Africa must emulate the Malaysian affirmative action target of 40% of *Bumiputera* ownership of the economy in 20years and suggested that 40% of the South African economy should be in black hands by the year 2000 (*Business Day,* 9 May 1995).

South Africa's incorporation into the "the globalisation of Bumiputeraism" has been described by Hyslop as "almost hegemonic:"

> The Malaysian intervention in South Africa has involved the export of not only economic but also socio-political organization. Some South African business ventures have become incorporated into the structure of Malaysian business empires. Forms of economic indigenisation have not only been copied from Malaysia, but also undertaken in co-operation with Malaysian companies. Malaysian companies have become entangled with South African patronage networks (Hyslop 1997: 16).

A number of so-called "empowerment partnerships" between Malaysian and black entrepreneurs were entered into. The formation of the Black Economic

Empowerment Commission (BEECom) in 1998 as the powerhouse for the creation of a black middle class through direct state intervention was based on the Malaysian NEP. The links between the emerging South African and Malaysian middle classes have been consolidated over the years through joint investments and the formation of business and friendship societies.

A National Empowerment Trust (NET) was also set up to facilitate this partnership. Among its projects was the development of a new bank and a shipping line, in co-operation with Malaysian concerns. Although a number of deals relating to awards of contracts by both sides were based on cronyism, this was seen as important in growing and consolidating transnational alliances between the *Bumiputera* and black middle classes.

Conclusion

Affirmative action in South Africa involves a major social engineering project aimed at reconfiguring the political power structure and the economy and transforming society at different levels to meet high expectations locally as well as internationally. While the political triumph of Mandela and the ANC over white minority rule is an epic moment in world history, the actual process of transformation to ensure black empowerment continues to be a momentous challenge as poverty continues to increase and crime reaches record high levels. Although affirmative action has transformed the political and economic face of the once-apartheid state, it has not been the awaited saviour for many poor and marginalized citizens.

Indeed, there is pressure to withdraw some preferential policies. However, the ruling ANC is not in a position to turn the clock back, because affirmative action has served a very important political function in consolidating ANC power and hegemony. The challenge is to devise ways and means to address the rising poverty, inequality and crime. The ideology of a people's democracy and multiculturalism has been politically unifying but the hard realities of economics means that constant adjustments and negotiations between contending positions need to continue in order to look for a consensus. Consensus is becoming increasingly difficult because of the continuing political differences within the country.

Nevertheless, by and large the strides made for blacks have been momentous, as can be seen in the public service and corporate sector, where the initial targets have been achieved. However, the political imperative to achieve equity is often complicated and at times is undermined by the lack of higher education and expertise amongst blacks. The fact that politically defined objectives and targets have to be achieved means that compromises have to be made and, at times, quota fulfilment takes precedence over quality. This has led to deterioration in the area of services and infrastructure and provoked criticisms of patronage, corruption and inefficiency. However, the push for dramatic transformation of the system is inevitable, given the high expectations driven by the mass euphoria of the post-apartheid era. Nurturing and consolidating a black middle class is a desirable political tactic to assimilate and appease disgruntled and potentially disruptive educated blacks and intelligentsia, thus lessening the prospect of intra-communal tension and instability.

Unlike Fiji and Malaysia, where affirmative action has more or less reached saturation point, in South Africa, despite continuing problems, there is still political demand for more affirmative action. The rise in poverty and crime means that a more substantive focus should be placed on addressing the plight of the poor, rather than just focusing on empowering the black middle class. The dilemma is how to create a balanced affirmative action paradigm which addresses the divergent interests of opposite ends of the social spectrum.

10. Trans-global affirmative action: Some critical lessons

We need to learn broader and deeper implications and critical lessons from the trans-global study of affirmative action in Fiji, Malaysia and South Africa. No doubt it provides an insight into diverse experiences of different countries, which nevertheless may be using the same affirmative action template.

Although countries may be using the same affirmative action framework, justification and philosophy, the local political, economic and socio-cultural conditions do matter in determining the final outcome of preferential programs. The preferential policy templates are often reconfigured to suit local circumstances and interests. This is usually the prerogative of local elites in power. In ethnically divided societies, different political parties can use affirmative action programs as short-term leverage for ethnic and political mobilization as well as using them as a long-term mechanism for institutionalized ethno-nationalist appeal.

The role of the elites needs to be emphasised here because of the dual role they play in being communal elites as well as state elites. As communal elites they are able to use cultural appeal to mobilize support within their community; and as state elites they are able to make use of the powerful state machinery and resources to further consolidate the political power of their respective communities. They are thus placed strategically to act as ethnic entrepreneurs in rallying their own ethnic group against the other or, when the circumstances demand, in assuming the role of trans-ethnic national leaders. Ethnic elites often negotiate these two seemingly opposing roles amidst multiple oppositions from opposing ethnic elites, more 'liberal' members of their own communities, civil society organizations, intelligentsia, and international organizations concerned with human rights, equity and justice.

As the case studies have shown, consolidation of state control and power by ethnic elites is often more complex than it seems. A critical aspect here is the formation of complex patronage systems consisting of co-option of strategically located players such as businessmen (both indigenous and non-indigenous), political party leaders, local community leaders and others considered significant. The patronage system has its own power dynamics and accountability is usually to itself. This may change from time to time as new political parties come to power, as in the case of Fiji. For easy and ready access to the benefits of affirmative action, being associated somehow with the patronage system does help. The patronage system may lead to institutionalized and entrenched hegemony of the ruling elites as well as to abuse of power and corruption. Consequently, the classical notion of the state as an independent arbiter of competing interests is seriously compromised and thus needs to be redefined. The cases of Fiji, Malaysia and South Africa clearly demonstrate these dynamic tendencies.

Another significant issue in relation to the patronage system is how the notion of merit as a means of social mobility is being redefined. The system of meritocracy, which is often associated with fairness and equal opportunity, is subject to reinterpretation based on one's contribution – monetary, political or professional – to the party hierarchy. Disbursement of affirmative action benefits can be used as payoff for political loyalty.

The concentration of resources within an elite group associated with the patronage system contributes directly to intra-communal inequality. This is a serious consequence of politically driven preferential policies. It reflects the skewed allocation of resources in favour of those who least deserve assistance. This raises the moral issue of justice and its paradoxical usage. Affirmative action is used as a means of achieving equality and justice, yet in the process, it leads to inequality and denial of justice for the less fortunate members of the community. This is a fundamental contradiction the three case studies share.

In an era in which neoliberal development policies predominate, affirmative action is often seen as a distortion of economic strategies because it is not based on growth-based outcomes. Perhaps the real picture is more complex and involves a mixture of both preferential access to shares and investment of these shares for growth. However, the environment for growth is carefully nurtured and supervised by the state rather than being dictated solely by the market. This ensures the development and consolidation of the indigenous middle class.

As the three case studies have shown, the development of an indigenous middle class is in itself a major social engineering undertaking. This is not always recognized because of the tendency to focus on the specific policy prescriptions of affirmative action rather than the broader structural dimension. The ensuing structural transformation involves reshaping the relationship between class and ethnicity in a way which reverses the old order in favour of the designated group. While there is usually a time frame for the changes to take place, this is often ignored because of ever-emerging factors which demand the continuation of affirmative programs.

We need to be mindful all the time of the differences between majority-based and minority-based affirmative action models because of the different political dynamics they represent. The affirmative action models used by Fiji, Malaysia and South Africa are majority-based – the designated group is also politically and demographically dominant. This is in contrast to minority-based models as in the United States and New Zealand, where the designated group is also politically and demographically a minority. Affirmative action programs in the United States were put in place as a means to redress its racially turbulent history, characterized by slavery and institutionalized racial discrimination. It is meant to provide equal opportunity in the areas of employment, education and contracts to ensure that public institutions such as universities, hospitals and police forces reflect in such areas proportions in the wider population they serve. Like the United States and unlike Fiji, Malaysia and South Africa, affirmative action in New Zealand is not entrenched in the constitution but is legislated and treated as a normal policy program. Also there are no strict quotas in employment, business licences or contracts unlike in Malaysia and South Africa. However, some New Zealand universities provide enrolment quotas for Maori and Pacific Islanders as part of their equity programs. Critics of affirmative action in New Zealand argue that affirmative action is tantamount to handouts and encourages parasitism on the state, but advocates of affirmative action contend that the state has a moral obligation to compensate Maori for the loss of their land and sovereignty through colonialism.

No other Pacific island state, apart from Fiji, provides ethnic-based affirmative action programs. Although they have minorities such as Chinese, most minority populations are economically well-to-do and are not considered eligible for affirmative action. Although there are no affirmative action policies, even for the majority indigenous population, often those in politics and the state bureaucracy have better chances of access to state services such as scholarships and business deals. Pacific Island migrants in New Zealand become 'disadvantaged' minorities and have access to affirmative action.

The impact of ethnic-based affirmative action on ethnic relations cannot be understated. Preferential treatment for an ethnic group is bound to generate hostility from others who feel deserving but have been left out. Charges of reverse discrimination and worse still ethnic stereotyping which depict designated groups as social parasites are often used. Instead of improving race relations, as the initial justification intends, affirmative action has the potential to widen the ethnic gulf and increase tension.

The last question which needs to be asked is whether affirmative action has led to a fairer, more just and peaceful society or has it simply worsened the existing situation. In other words, have the reasons and ideological justifications behind affirmative action been achieved? It is not easy to answer this question with a blanket "yes" or "no" because of the complex sets of factors which support or negate either side of the debate. The answer very much lies in how one justifies one's discourse and how much that is supported by selected empirical evidence. Whatever one's position is, the undeniable fact is that because affirmative action has served the interests of many people well and it will continue to exist as a major developmental strategy in the foreseeable future.

These lessons, drawn from a trans-global study of Fiji, Malaysia and South Africa case studies, are crucial in understanding the complexities and paradoxes of affirmative action and may also help us understand possible situations in other countries. Ethnic-based affirmative action has had its fair share of problems and there is a need to look again at its shortcomings for the purpose of moving towards more innovative alternatives.

References

Adam, H., F. van Zyl Slabbert and K. Moodley. 1997. *Comrades in Business: Post-Liberation Politics in South Africa*. Western Cape: Tafelberg.

Adams, C. and W. Cavendish. 1995. Background to Malaysian privatisation. In *Privatizing Malaysia: Rents, rhetoric and realities*, ed. K.S. Jomo (ed). Colorado: Westview Press: 45-58.

Adinkrah, M. 1995. *Crime deviance and delinquency in Fiji*. Suva: FCOS.

Agocs, C. 2009. *Measures to secure employment equity in the Canadian labour market*. Paper presented to Conference on Affirmative Action in the Labour Market: International Perspectives, British Academy, London, 2–3 November.

Ali, A. 1982. The politics of a plural society. In *Politics in Melanesia*, ed. R. Crocombe and A. Ali. Suva: Institute of Pacific Studies: 138-154.

Anand, S. 1981. *Inequality and poverty in Malaysia: Measurement and decomposition*. Oxford: Oxford University Press.

Australian Associated Press, 22 June 2002.

Baba, T. 1979. A challenge to the nation: The Fijian education problem. *Directions*, (2).

Bainimarama, F. 2011. Speech to UN General Assembly. 22 September. Ministry of Information *News Release*, 23 September: 1

Barr, K. 1990. *Poverty in Fiji*. Suva: Fiji Forum for Justice, Peace and Integrity of Creation.

Bavadra, T. 1986. Address by newly elected President of Fiji Labour. Suva: Fiji Labour Party.

Bayliss-Smith, T. and P. Haynes. 1988. Land development as a rural development strategy. In *Rural Fiji*, ed. J. Overton. Suva: Institute of Pacific Studies: 123-146.

Belshaw, C. 1964. *Under the ivi tree: Society and economic growth in rural Fiji*. London: Routledge and Keegan Paul.

Bernardino-Costa, J. 2010. *Affirmative action in Brazil*. Paper presented to Conference on Targeting Horizontal Inequalities: Affirmative Action, Identity and Conflict, University of Malaya, Kuala Lumpur.

Bobo, L. 1998. Race interests and beliefs about affirmative action. *American Behavioural Scientist*, *41*(April): 985–1,003.

Bowser, B. 2007. *The black middle class: Social mobility and vulnerability*. Boulder: Lynne Rienner.

Brookfield, H.C. 1979. Land reform, efficiency and rural income distribution: Contribution to an argument. *Pacific Viewpoint*, *20*(1): 10–25.

Brown, R.A. 1994. *Capital and entrepreneurship in South-East Asia*. London: St. Martins Press.

Bryant, J. 1993. *Poverty in Fiji*. Paper presented at School of Social and Economic Development, University of the South Pacific.

Burns, A. 1963. *Fiji: Report of the Commission of Enquiry into the natural resources and population trends*. London: HMSO.

Business Day, 9 May 1995.

———, 11 February 2008.

Business Report, 9 April 2010.

Business Times, February 1994.

Caliguire, D. 1996. Death of a dream. *Democracy in Action, 10*(15). 5-13

Cargill, J. 1996. Growing pains. *Democracy in Action, 10*(15): 5 –27.

Chand, S. 2007. 50-50 by 2020: Poverty and redistributive politics in post-independence Fiji. *Pacific Economic Bulletin,22*(2): 22–35.

Chaudhry, M. 1999. Address to the Great Council of Chiefs Meeting, *Fiji Times,* 14 June 1999: 22–23.

Chetty, K. and S. Prasad. 1993. *Fiji's emigration: An Examination of Contemporary Trends and Issues*. Suva: United Nations Population Fund.

Choo, H and M. Feree. 2010. Practicing intersectionality in sociological research: A critical analysis of inclusions, interactions, and institutions in the study of inequalities. *Sociological Theory*, June 28(2): 129–149.

Chowdhry, M. (ed). 1997. *Alternative perspectives in the third world development: The case of Malaysia*. London: Macmillan Press Ltd.

Chung, M. 1989. Ethnic politics and small business: The case of the Fiji poultry industry. *Pacific Viewpoint*, *30*(2). 15-29.

Citizens Constitutional Forum. 1995. *One nation, diverse peoples – Building a just and democratic Fiji: A Submission to the Constitutional Review Commission.* Suva: Conciliation Resources.

Cole, A. 1984. *Cole Report.* Suva: Fiji Government.

Collinicos, A. and J. Rogers. 1977. *South African Soweto.* London: Pluto.

Colonial Sugar Refinery. 1959. *Annual Report.* Lautoka: Colonial Sugar Refinery.

ConsWatch. 2008. 2(4), 4th Quarter, December: 1–3.

Daily Post, 17 June 1997.

————, 10 November 1998.

————, 13 March 1999.

————, April 10 1999.

Duncan, R. 2007. *Cultural and social norms and economic development in remote Aboriginal communities: Lessons from the Pacific.* Presentation to the Cape York Institute for Policy and Leadership Conference on Strong Foundations: Rebuilding Social Norms in Indigenous Communities, 25–26 June.

Emberson-Bain, A. 1994. *Labour and Gold in Fiji.* Cambridge: University of Cambridge Press.

Emsley, I. 1996.*The Malaysian experience of affirmative action: Lessons for South Africa.* Cape Town: Human Roussea Taelberg.

Enloe, C. 1980. *Ethnic soldiers: State security in a divided society.* Middlesex: Penguin.

Faundez, J. 1994. *Affirmative action: International perspective.* Geneva: International Labour Organization.

FEER, 13 April 1979.

Fiji Bureau of Statistics. 1983. *Statistical Data for Fiji.* Suva. Fiji Bureau of Statistics.

————. 1989. *Economic Statistics.* Suva: Fiji Bureau of Statistics.

————. 1991. *Statistical Data for Fiji.* Suva: Fiji Bureau of Statistics.

————. 1998. *Statistical Data for Fiji.* Suva: Fiji Bureau of Statistics.

————. 2011. *Poverty Figures.* Suva: Fiji Bureau of Statistics.

Fiji Central Planning Office. 1965. *Development Plan 5*. Suva: Fiji Central Planning Office.

———. 1970. *Development Plan 6*. Suva: Fiji Central Planning Office.

———. 1975. *Development Plan 7*. Suva: Fiji Central Planning Office.

———. 1980. *Development Plan 8*. Suva: Fiji Central Planning Office.

———. 1985. *Development Plan 9*. Suva: Fiji Central Planning Office.

Fiji Co-operative Department. 1948. *Annual Report*. Suva: Fiji Co-operative Department.

———. 1958. *Annual Report*. Suva: Fiji Co-operative Department.

Fiji Department of Road and Transport. 1994. *Annual Report*. Suva: Fiji Department of Road and Transport.

Fiji Development Bank. 1993. *Annual Report*. Suva: Fiji Development Bank.

———. 1994a. "Commercial Loans to Fijian Scheme-Review Board Paper No.7/362." Suva: Fiji Development Bank.

———. 1994b. "Review of Working Capital Loans for Retailing and Wholesaling Sectors of CLFC." Suva: Fiji Development Bank.

———. 1996a. "Annual Review of Commercial Loan to Fijians Scheme, Board Paper No. 11/396": Suva: Fiji Development Bank.

———. 1996b. "Commercial Loans to Fijians Scheme-Review." Suva: Fiji Development Bank.

———. 1996c. "Review of Real Estate Sector-Board Paper No. 11/391." Suva: Fiji Development Bank.

———. 1997a. "Board Paper No. 11/397: Annual Review for Commercial Loans to Fijians, Rotumans and General Electors (28 Feb)." Suva: Fiji.

———. 1997b. "Annual Review of Commercial Loans for Fijian Scheme, Board Paper No.11/398, 28 Feb." Suva: Fiji Development Bank.

Fiji Election Office. 1999. *Results for 1999 General Elections*. Suva: Fiji Election Office.

———. 2002. *Fiji Election Results*. Suva: Election Office.

Fiji Government. 1905. "Great Council of Chiefs Proceedings." Suva: Fiji Government.

————— 1938. *Annual Report*. Suva: Fiji Government.

—————. 1954. Annual Report, Secretary for Fijian Affairs, 1954-C.P.4/1947. Suva: Fiji Government.

—————. 1957. Economic Development Officers: Annual Report, 1957, C.P.38/1958. Suva. Fiji Government.

—————. 1966. *Employment Figures*. Suva: Fiji Government.

—————. 1970. *Constitution of the Republic Fiji*. Suva: Fiji Governments.

—————. 1974. *Current Economic Statistics*. Suva: Fiji Government.

—————. 1980. *Parliamentary Paper No.47*. Suva: Fiji Government.

—————. 1985. "The Wages Freeze: Summary of Government Position, Paper Presented to National Economic Summit." Suva: Fiji Government.

—————. 1990a. *Constitution of the Republic of Fiji*. Suva: Fiji Government.

—————. 1990b. *Fiji Republic Gazette*, 4 (83).

—————. 1993. *Opportunities for Growth: Policies and Strategies for Fiji in the Medium Term*. Suva: Fiji Government.

—————. 1997. *Constitution of the Republic of the Fiji Islands*. Suva: Fiji Government.

—————. 1999a. *Fiji National Budget*. Suva: Fiji Government.

—————. 1999b. *Public Service Act*. Suva: Fiji Government.

—————. 2000. 20 Year Plan (2001–2021) for the Enhancement of Participation of Indigenous Fijians and Rotumans for the Socio-economic Development of Fiji. Suva: Fiji Government.

—————. 2001. Blueprint for the Protection of Fijian and Rotuman Rights and Interests and the Advancement of their Development. Suva: Fiji Government.

—————. 2002. *Overview of Policy Government Policies*. Suva. Fiji Government.

—————. 2007. Fiji Independent Commission Against Corruption (FICAC) Decree. Suva: Fiji Government.

—————. 2009a. *National Budget for 2010*. Suva: Fiji Government.

—————. 2009b. *Public Emergency Decree, 2009*. Suva: Fiji Government.

————. 2009c. *Roadmap for Sustainable Economic Development (2009–2014)*. Suva: Fiji Government.

————. 2009d. *Strategic Plan*. Suva: Fiji Government.

Fiji Human Rights Commission. 2001. *Critique of affirmative action*. Suva: Fiji Human Rights Commission.

————. 2006. *Report on affirmative action in Fiji*. Suva: Fiji Human Rights Commission.

Fiji Inland Revenue Department. 1967. *National Accounts Report*. Suva: Fiji Inland Revenue Department.

Fiji Legislative Council. 1956. Paper No. 44 of 1956. Suva. Fiji Legislative Council.

————. 1960. Paper No. 1 of 1960. Suva: Fiji Legislative Council.

Fiji Ministry of Education. 1993. *Annual Report*. Suva: Ministry of Education.

————. 1996. *Annual Report*. Suva: Fiji Ministry of Education.

Fiji Ministry of Fijian Affairs. 1995. *Provincial Profile Project*. Suva: Ministry of Fijian Affairs.

Fiji Ministry of Information. 1994. *Fiji Focus*, May/June. Suva: Fiji Ministry of Information.

————. 2010. *News Release*, 16 April. Suva: Fiji Ministry of Information.

————. 2011. *News Release*, 20 December. Suva: Ministry of Information.

————. 2012. *News Release*, 9 March.Suva: Ministry of Information.

————. 2012. *News Release*, 14 March. Suva: Ministry of Information.

Fiji National Provident Fund. 1996. *Annual Report*. Suva: Fiji National Provident Fund.

Fiji Office of the Auditor General. 1994. *Annual Report*. Suva: Fiji Office of Auditor General.

————. 2002. *Annual Report*. Suva: Fiji Office of Auditor General.

————. 2005. *Annual Report*. Suva: Fiji Office of Auditor General.

Fiji Parliament. 1994. *Hansard Report*, 12 July. Suva: Fiji Parliament.

————. 2001a. *Hansard Report*, 21 November. Suva: Fiji Parliament.

———. 2001b. *Parliamentary Paper 28 of 2001*. Suva: Fiji Parliament.

Fiji Police Department. 1996. *Annual Report*. Suva: Fiji Police Department.

Fiji Public Service Commission. 1986. *Annual Report for 1985*. Suva: Public Service Commission.

———. 1988. *Annual Report for 1987*. Suva: Public Service Commission.

———. 1995. *Annual Report for 1994*. Suva: Public Service Commission.

Fiji Sugar Corporation. 1994. *Industrial Statistics*. Lautoka: Fiji Sugar Corporation.

Fiji Sun, 16 September 1977.

———, 17 April 1986.

———, 5 May 1975.

———, 8 March 2012.

Fiji Trade and Investment Board. 1997. "Record of Registered Fiji Companies." Suva: Fiji Trade and Investment Board.

Fijian Affairs Board. 1985. "Great Council of Chiefs Meeting Papers." Suva: Fijian Affairs Board.

———. 1990. *Annual Report*. Suva: Fijian Affairs Board.

Fijian Holdings Limited. 1984. *Annual Report*. Suva: Fijian Holdings Limited.

———. 1992. *Annual Report*. Suva: Fijian Holdings Limited.

———. 1993. *Annual Report*. Suva: Fijian Holdings Limited.

———. 1994. *Annual Report*. Suva: Fijian Holdings Limited.

———. 1995. *Annual Report*. Suva: Fijian Holdings Limited.

———. 1996. *Annual Report*. Suva: Fijian Holdings Limited.

———.2010. *Annual Report*. Suva: Fijian Holdings Limited.

——— .2011. *Annual Report*. Suva: Fijian Holdings Limited.

Fijian Initiative Group. 1992. *The Nine Points Plan*. Suva: Fijian Initiative Group.

Fijilive, 11 September 2008.

Financial Times, 21 November 1995.

Fine, B. and C. Stoneman. 1996. State and development: An introduction. *Journal ofSouthern African Studies, 21*(4): 5-26.

Fitzgerald, P., A. McLennan and B. Munslow, ed. 1997. *Managing Sustainable Development in South Africa*. Cape Town: Oxford University Press.

Fraenkel, J., S. Firth and B. Lal. (eds). 2009. *The 2006 military takeover in Fiji: A coup to end all coups*. Canberra: Australian National University E-Press.

GCC Review Committee. 2007. *Report of the GCC Review Committee*. Suva: Fijian Affairs Board.

Gelb, S. 1997. Kwazulu-Natal capacity to act independently limited. *Budget Watch, 3*(1A).

Gillion, K.L. 1962. *Fiji's Indian immigrants*. Melbourne: Oxford University Press.

Girardeau, S. 2000. *The laws of affirmative action: Twenty-five years of Supreme Court decisions on race and remedies*. New York: New York University Press.

Gomez, E. 2009. The rise and fall of capital: Corporate Malaysia in historical perspective. *Journal of Contemporary Asia,* 39 (3): 345–381.

——— 1994. *Political business: Corporate involvement of Malaysian political parties*. Townsville: James Cook University.

Gomez, E. and K. S. Jomo. 1999. *Malaysia's Political Economy: Power, Profits, Patronage*. Cambridge: Cambridge University Press.

Gopher://gopher.anc.or.za, 7 March, 1997.

Grattan, C.H. 1963. *The South West Pacific since 1900: A modern history*. Ann Arbour: University of Michigan Press.

Hailey, J. 1992. The politics of entrepreneurship: Affirmative action policies for indigenous entrepreneurs. *Small Enterprise Development2*(2): 4-14.

Harvey, C. 2010. *Affirmative action in United Kingdom and Ireland*. Presented to Conference on Targeting Horizontal Inequalities: Affirmative Action, Identity and Conflict, University of Malaya, Kuala Lumpur.

Horwitz, F. 2009. *Black empowerment and affirmative action in South African labour market*. Paper presented to Conference on Affirmative Action in the Labour Market: International Perspective, British Academy, London, November.

Howard, M. 1985. The evolution of industrial relations in Fiji and the reaction of public employees union to the current economic crisis. *South Pacific Forum* 2(2): 1-15.

———. 1989. State power and political change in Fiji. Paper presented to *Journal of Contemporary Asia,* conference, Manila, 10-12 November.

Hua, W. Y. 1983. *Class and communalism in Malaysia: Politics in a dependent capitalist state.* London: Zed Books.

Hyslop, J. 1998. *The African Renaissance meets the Asian Renaissance? The Malaysian impact on contemporary South Africa.* Paper presented at University of Sussex, February.

Iheduru, O. 1998. Black Entrepreneurs in Post-Apartheid South Africa. In *African Entrepreneurship: Theory and Reality,* ed. A. Spring and B. McDade. Gainsville: University of Florida Press: 30-49.

Iloilo, J. 2009. President's Speech to the Nation. Suva: President's Office.

Ishida, A. and A. Azizan. 1998. Poverty eradication and income distribution in Malaysia. *Journal of Contemporary Asia,* 28(3): 327-345.

Jain, H., P. Sloane and F. Horwitz. 2003. *Employment equity and affirmative action: An international comparison.* New York: M.E. Sharpe.

Jeffery, A. 2009. *People's war: New light on the struggle for South Africa.* Johannesburg and Cape Town: Jonathan Ball Publishers.

———. 2010. *Affirmative action in South Africa.* Paper presented to Conference on Horizontal Inequality and Identity, University of Malaya, 23–24 November.

Jenne, E. 2006. *Ethnic bargaining: The paradox of minority empowerment.* New York: Cornell University Press.

Jesudason, J. 1990. *Ethnicity and the economy: The state, Chinese business and multinationals in Malaysia.* London: Oxford University Press.

———. 1996. The syncretic state and the structuring of oppositional politics in Malaysia. In *Political oppositions in Industrialising Asia,* ed. G. Rogan. New York: Routledge: 128-160.

Jomo, K.S. 1986. *A question of class: Capital, the state, and uneven development in Malaysia.* Oxford: Oxford University Press.

——— (ed). 1993. *Industrialising Malaysia: Policy, performance, prospects.* London. Routledge.

———— (ed). 1994a. *Malaysia's economy in the Nineties.* Selangor Darul Ehsan: Pelanduk Publications.

———— (ed). 1994b. *Japan and Malaysia development: In the shadow of the rising sun.* London: Routledge.

———— (ed). 1995. *Privatising Malaysia: Rents, rhetoric, realities.* Colorado: Westview Press.

Jones, S. 1991. We are all cousins under the skin. *The Independent,* 12 December.

Kahn, J. 1992. Class, ethnicity and diversity: Some remarks on Malay culture in Malaysia. In *Fragmented Vision: Culture and Politics in Contemporary Malaysia,* ed. J. Khan and F. Wah (ed). North Sydney. Allen and Unwin: 158-178.

————. 1996. Growth, economic transformation, culture and the middle classes in Malaysia. In *The New Rich in Asia: Mobile Phones, McDonalds and the Middle Class Revolution,* ed. R. Robison and D. Goodman. London: Routledge. 69-89.

Kallaway, P. 1997. Reconstruction, reconciliation and rationalisation in South African politics of education. In *Education after apartheid. South African education in transition,* ed. P. Kallaway, G. Kruss, A. Fataar and G. Donn. Cape Town: University of Cape Town Press: 34-49.

Katznelson, I. 2005. *When affirmative action was white: An untold history of racial inequality in twentieth-century America.* New York: W.W. Norton.

Kellough, J. 2006. *Understanding affirmative action: Politics, discrimination, and the search for justice.* Washington DC: Georgetown University Press.

Kelly, J. 1990. Fiji Indians and commodification of labour. *American Anthologist,* 9(1): 11–25.

Kemp, N. 1992. Affirmative action: Legal obligation or prudent business? *Human Resource Management,* 8(6): 12-14.

Kingi, T. T. 2006. Communal land tenure and agricultural development in Fiji", *Development Bulletin, 70*: 80–83.

Knapman, B. 1987. Fiji's economic history, 1874–1939: Studies of capitalist colonial development. Pacific Research Monograph, No.15, ANU, Canberra.

Korovulavula, M. 1994. Speech to Fiji Senate on Fijian Holdings Limited, 12 July.

Kumar, B. 1980. *Fiji's Tripartite Forum*. Diploma in Industrial Relations Thesis, Victoria University, Wellington.

Lal, B. (ed). 1989. *Crossing the Kala Pani: A documentary history of Indian indenture in Fiji*. Canberra: Research School of Pacific and Asian Studies.

Lal, B. and M. Pretes. 2008. *Coup: Reflections on the political crisis in Fiji*. Canberra: ANU-E-Press.

Lamour, P. 2005. *Foreign flower: Institutional transfer and good governance in the Pacific Islands*. Honolulu: University of Hawaii Press.

Lau Provincial Council (nd), *Lau 21/45 Cane Cutting*, File in District Office, Lakeba.

Lee, A., E. Gometz and S. Yakob. 2010. *Affirmative action in Malaysia*. Paper presented to Conference on Affirmative Action, Inequality and Identity, Kuala Lumpur, 25 November.

Lee, H. G. 2005. Affirmative action in Malaysia. *South East Asian Affairs 2005:* 211–228.

Lee, R. 1990. The state, religious nationalism and ethnic rationalisation in Malaysia. *Ethnic and Racial Studies*, *13*(4): 482-502.

Lijphart, A. 1971. Comparative politics and the comparative method. *American Political Science Review 65*(3): 682–693.

Lim, T. G. 1971. *Peasant agriculture in colonial Malaya: Its development in Perak, Selangor, Negri Sembilan and Pahang, 1874–1941*. PhD Thesis, Australian National University.

Lin, T. Y. 1984. Inter-ethnic restructuring in Malaysia, 1970–80: The employment perspective. In *From independence to statehood*, ed. R. Goldman and A. Wilson. London: Frances Pinter. 92-130.

Lipson, H. 2006. *Talking affirmative action: Race, opportunity, and everyday ideology*. Lanham: Rowman & Littlefield.

Luiz, J.M. 1994. Constraints facing the socio-economic transformation in South Africa. *Africa Insight*, *24*(4): 230–235.

Lundahl, M. 1998. The post-apartheid economy, and after?. In *Post-Apartheid Southern Africa: Economic Challenges and Policies for the Future,* ed. L. Peterson. London Routledge. 34-50.

Maasdorp, G. 1992. Meeting expectations. In *Wealth or Poverty? Critical Choices for South Africa,* ed. R. Schnire. Cape Town: Oxford University Press. 14-26.

Madraiwiwi, J. 1997. Extracts from a letter to a friend. In *With Heart and Nerve and Sinew: Post-Coup Writing from Fiji,* ed. A. Griffen. Suva: USP. 10-15.

Malaysian Government. 1957. *Malaysian Merdeka Constitution*: Kuala Lumpur: Malaysian Government.

Malaysian Government. 1973. *Mid-term Review of Second Malaysian Plan.* Kuala Lumpur: Government Printing Department.

Malaysian Government. 1987. *FELDA Annual Financial Report.* Kuala Lumpur: Malaysia.

Manueli, I. 2001. $0.1m to woo island voters, Fiji Times 10 July.

Mara, K.K.T. 1999. Speech for Opening of Fiji Parliament. *Fiji Parliament Hansard Report*: Suva: Fiji Parliament.

Mbeki, T. 2006. State of the nation address to Parliament, February. *South African Parliament Hansard Report.* Capetown: Parliament of South Africa.

Means, G. 1991. *Malaysian politics: The second generation.* Singapore: Oxford University Press.

Michie, J. and L. Padayachee. (eds). 1997. *The political economy of South Africa's transition.* London: Dryden.

Muzaffar, C. 1989. *The NEP: Development and alternative consciousness.* Penang: Aliran.

Myburgh, J. 2006. *The African National Congress under the presidency of Thabo Mbeki* (1997–2002), DPhil Thesis, University of Oxford.

Naidu, V. 1986. The state, labour aristocracy and the Fiji Labour Party." Unpublished Paper.

———. 1989. *State and class in the South Pacific.* Unpublished DPhil Thesis. University of Sussex.

Narayan, J. 1984. *The political economy of Fiji.* Suva: South Pacific Review Press.

Narsey, W. 1979. monopoly capital, white racism and super profit in Fiji : A case study of CSR. *Journal of Pacific Studies, 5*:66–85.

———. 1985. The wage freeze and development plan: Contradictions in Fiji government policy. Paper Presented to the Fiji Trade Union Congress Labour Summit, Suva, 3–4 May.

National Council for Building a Better Fiji. 2008. *People's Charter for Change, Peace and Progress*. Suva: National Council for Building a Better Fiji.

National Federation Party—Fiji Labour Party Coalition. 1987. *Election Manifesto*. Suva: National Federation Party Labour Coalition.

National Federation Party—Fiji Labour Party Coalition. 1990. *A Fraud on the Nation*. Suva: National Federation Party—FLP Coalition.

Native Land Trust Board. 1975. *Annual Report*. Suva: Native Land Trust Board.

Native Land Trust Board. 1990. *Annual Report*. Suva: Native Land Trust Board.

Native Land Trust Board. 1995. *Annual Report*. Suva: Native Land Trust Board.

Native Land Trust Board. 1996. *Corporate Plan*. Suva: Native Land Trust Board.

Nawadra, T. 1995. *Ai Matai Malaya: 1st Battalion, Fiji Infantry Regiment, Far-East Land Forces, 1952–1956*. Suva: History & Archives Unit, Republic of Fiji Military Forces.

Nayacakalou, R.R. 1975. *Leadership in Fiji*. Melbourne: Oxford University Press.

Neblo, M. 2008. Three fifths a racist: A typology for analysing public opinion about race. *Political Behaviour*, *31*(1): 31–51.

———. 2009. Meaning and measurement: Reorienting the race politics debate. *Political Research Quarterly*, *62*(3):474–84.

Nkuhlu, W. 1993. Affirmative action for South Africa in transition: From theory to practice. In *Affirmative Action in a Democratic South Africa*, ed. C. Adams. Kenwyn: Juta.

Norton, R. 1994. *Race and politics in Fiji*. St Lucia: University of Queensland Press.

Office of Registrar of Companies. 1997. "List of Companies in Fiji." Suva: Office of Registrar of Companies.

Osman-Rani. 1990. Economic development and ethnic integration: The Malaysian experience. *Sojourn, 5*(1): 31-34.

Parikh, S., 2010. *Affirmative action in India*. Paper presented to Conference on Targeting Horizontal Inequalities: Affirmative Action, Identity and Conflict, University of Malaya, Kuala Lumpur.

P-E Corporate Services (SA) Pty Ltd. 2009. *P-E Human Resources Practitioners Handbook – South Africa*, September.

Pincus, F. 2003. *Reverse discrimination: Dismantling the myth*. Boulder: Lynne Reinner Publishers.

Plange, N. 1996. *The science of society: Exploring the links between science, ideology and theories of development*. Suva: Fiji Institute of Applied Science.

Prasad, K. 1978. *The Gujarat's of Fiji, 1900–1945: A study of an indian trader community*. PhD Dissertation, University of British Columbia.

Prasad, S. (ed). 1988. *Coups and crisis: Fiji – A year later*. North Carlton: Arena Publications.

Prothero, M. 1974. Foreign migrant labour for South Africa. *International Migration Review*, 8(3): 383–394.

Qalo, R. 1997. *Small business: A study of A Fijian family—The Mucunabitu Iron Works Contractor Cooperative Society Limited*. Suva: Mucunabitu Education Trust.

Qarase, L. 1994. *Ten-year Plan for Fijian Participation in Business*. Paper Prepared for Economic and Social Commission for Asia and the Pacific (ESCAP).

———. 2001. Speech to Parliament, 21 November. *Fiji Parliament Hansard Report*. Suva: Fiji Parliament.

———. 2004. *Report on the Affirmative Action Programme*. Presentation to Fiji Parliament, October 4.

Radio Australia, 13 March 2011.

Radio NZ, 13 October 2006.

Radio NZ, 2 November 2006.

Radio NZ, 18 January 2012.

Rasiah, R. 1998. Class, ethnicity and economic development in Malaysia. In *The political economy of South East Asia: An introduction*, ed. G. Rodan. Melbourne: Oxford University Press.

Ratuva, S. 1993. The rise and demise of Taukeism: Post-coup Fijian nationalism. *Review,13*(1): 58-64.

———. 2000. Addressing inequality? Post-coup affirmative action policies in Fiji. In *Confronting Fiji's Futures*, ed. H. Lodiar. Canberra: Asia-Pacific Press: 226-248.

————. 2010. Vakatorocaketaki ni Taukei: The politics of affirmative action in post-colonial Fiji. *Pacific Economic Bulletin*, (ANU) *25*(3): 168–192.

————. 2011. The Fiji military coups: Reactive and transformative tendencies. *Journal of Asian Political Science*, *19*(1): 96–120.

Ravuvu, A. 1991. *The Facade of Democracy*. Suva: Reader Publishing House.

Reddy, S. 1974. *Labour and trade unionism in Fiji*. Unpublished MA Thesis, University of Otago.

Reeves, P., T. Vakatora and B. Lal. 1996. *The Fiji Islands – Towards A United Future: Report of the Fiji Constitutional Review Commission*. Suva: Fiji Government Printers.

Republic of Fiji Military Forces. 2000. *Republic of Fiji Military Forces Board of Inquiry Report on 2000 Coup*. Suva: Republic of Fiji Military Forces.

Ro Temumu Kepa. 2012. Letter to Bainimarama, 11 April.

Robertson, R. 1982. Ratu Sir Lala Sukuna: Between Two Worlds. *Journal of Pacific Studies*. (12). 30-45.

Routledge, D. 1985. *Matanitu: The struggle for power in early Fiji*. Suva: Institute of Pacific Studies.

Sachs, A. 1993. Affirmative action and black advancement in business. In *Affirmative Action in a Democratic South Africa,* ed. C. Adams. Kenwyn: Juta.

Sadie, Y. 1995. Affirmative action in South Africa: A gender development approach. *Africa Insight,25*(3): 180–185.

Sanday, J. 1989. The coups of 1987: Personal analysis. *Viewpoint, 30*(2).

Santos-Paulino, A., M. McGillivray and W. Naude. 2010. *Understanding small-island developing states – Fragility and external shocks*. London: Routledge.

Scarr, D. 1980. *Ratu Sakuna: Soldier, statesman, man of two worlds*. London: Macmillan Educational Education ltd.

————. 1984. *Fiji – A short history*. Sydney: George Allen & Unwin.

Schultze, D. 1982. Credit unions of Fiji. *South Pacific Forum*, *2*(1): 5-13.

Scott, J. 1985. *Weapons of the weak: Everyday forms of peasant resistance*. New Haven: Yale University Press.

Sidiropoulos, E. 1994. The politics of black business. *Spotlight Paper*, No.3/94. South African Institute of race Relations, Johannesburg.

Skitka, L. and F. Crosby. 2005. Trends in the social psychology of justice. *Personality and Social Psychology Review*, 7(4): 282–285.

Sky TV Australia, 3 March 2012.

Sonn, F. 1993. Afrikaner nationalism and black empowerment as two sides of the same coin. In *Affirmative Action in a Democratic South Africa,* ed. C. Adams. Kenwyn: Juta. 1-14.

Soqosoqo Duavata ni Lewe ni Vanua Party. 2006. *Bill No.12 of 2006 (Qoliqoli Bill)*. Suva: Soqosoqo Duavata ni Lewe ni Vanua Party.

Soqosoqo ni Vakavulewa ni Taukei. 1991. *SVT Constitution*. Suva: Soqosoqo ni Vakavulewa ni Taukei.

South Africa Parliament. 1998a. *Parliamentary Bulletin*, 14 April.

South Africa Parliament. 1998b. *Parliamentary Bulletin*, 15 September.

South Africa Parliament. 1998c. *Parliamentary Bulletin*, 20 April.

SouthScan, 16 June 1995.

SouthScan, 18 September 1995.

Sowell, T. 2005. *Affirmative action around the world: An empirical study*. New Haven: Yale University Press.

Spate, O.H.K. 1959. *The Fijian people: Economic problems & prospects. A report for the Legislative Council of Fiji*. Council Paper No. 13 of 1959. Suva: Government Press.

Speight, G. 2000. Letter to Great Council of Chiefs, Thursday, 25 May. <http://www.scoop.co.nz/stories/WO0005/S00123.htm>

Stanley, R. 2009. *Attitudes of race, identity and politics in Brazil*. Stanford (Cal): Stanford University Press.

Star, 4 July 1995.

Sterba, J.P. 2009. *Affirmative action for the future*. Ithaca: Cornell University Press.

Stewart, F., G. Brown and A. Langer. 2007. Policies towards horizontal inequalities. CRISE Working paper No. 42, March 2007.

Sukuna, L.V. 1944. Memorandum to Administrative Officers conference. Suva: Fiji Government Archives.

Sunday Independent, 23 March 1997.

Sutherland, W. 1993. *An alternative history of Fiji to 1992.* Canberra: ANU Press.

————. 1998. Globalization, nationalism and the national agenda: The problematics of reform in Fiji and the Fijian question. Occasional paper with author.

Veitata, T. 1987. Radio Fiji Fijian Broadcast, 24 April.

Terreblanche, S. 1992. Equity and growth. In *Wealth or poverty? Critical choices for South Africa,* ed. R. Schrire. Cape Town: Oxford University Press.

The Fiji Times, 13 April 1987.

The Fiji Times, 11 January 1990.

The Fiji Times, 9 June 1991.

The Fiji Times, 18 November 1992.

The Fiji Times, 19 November 1992.

The Fiji Times, 28 November 1992

The Fiji Times, 15 December 1992.

The Fiji Times, 21 December 1992.

The Fiji Times, 23 December 1992.

The Fiji Times, 3 July 1997.

The Fiji Times, 10 July 2001.

The Fiji Times, 21 June 2005.

The Fiji Times, 2 July 2005.

The Fiji Times, 24 November 2005.

The Fiji Times, 16 November 2006.

The Fiji Times, 9 February 2008.

The Fiji Times, 24 February 2008

The Fiji Times, 14 January 2012.

The Review, July, 1995.

The Review, May, 1997.

The Review, June 1997.

Thomas, R. R. 1990. From affirmative action to affirming diversity. *Harvard Business Journal*. March–April: 107–117.

Thomas, W. 1995, Big bang shrinks to a whimper. *Democracy in Action*, 9(6): 10-20.

Tuatoko, A. 2004. Signed statement on the 2000 Coup. Copy with author.

Unit Trust of Fiji. 1996. *Annual Report*. Suva: Unit Trust of Fiji.

United Nations Committee on the Elimination of Racial Discrimination. 2003. *Report on Fiji*, 2 June.

Usiku, V., 2009. Affirmative action in Namibia. Paper presented to Conference on Affirmative Action in the Labour Market: International Perspective, British Academy, London, November.

Vusoniwailala, L. 1976. The free press in a developing multi-racial society: Fiji, a case study. *Journal of Pacific Studies*, 2(1): 10–16.

Walsh, C. 2009. *Political blogs on Fiji: Cybernet democracy or what?* Paper presented to Pacific Islands Political Studies Association Conference, University of Auckland, 4 December.

Ward, R.G. 1965. *Land use and population in Fiji: A geographical study*. London: HMSO.

Watters, R. F. 1969. *Koro: Economic development and social change in Fiji*. Oxford: Clarendon Press.

Whitehead, C. 1981. *Education in Fiji, 1939–1973*. ANU Research Monograph No. 6. Canberra: Australian National University.

Wilkinson, M. 1983. Fiji election: Australian strategy called 'Repugnant.'" *National Times*, 25 Nov.

Wise, T. J. 2005. *Affirmative action: Racial preference in black and white*. New York: Routledge.

World Bank. 1976. *Fiji: Appraisal of the sugar development project. Report No. 986a-FIJ*. Washington DC: World Bank.

————. 1989. *Fiji: Post Secondary Education and the Labour Market: Issues and Opinions. Report no. NV10522-EAP*. Washington DC: World Bank.

———. 1991. *Growth, poverty alleviation and improved income distribution in Malaysia: Country Report* 8667-MA.

———. 1993. *Pacific regional post-secondary school education study*. Vol 3. Fiji Country Dept 111 East Asia and Pacific Region. Washington DC: World Bank.

———. 1995. *Fiji: Restoring growth in a changing global environment. Report No. 13862-FIJ*. Washington DC: World Bank.

Young, J. 1984. The Lovoni land-purchase project: Case study in Fijian agricultural development. *South Pacific Forum. 2*: 14-20.

Young, J. and H. Gunasekera. 1982. Agricultural policy and projects in the Solomon Islands, Western Samoa and Fiji. *South Pacific Forum. 2*: 6-13.

Yudelman, D. 1984. *The emergence of modern South Africa*. Cape Town: David Philp Publishers.

Zhou, M.H. and A. Maxwell. 2009. *Affirmative action in China and the U.S: A dialogue on inequality and minority education*. New York: Palgrave Macmillan.

Zille, H. 2009. We will stop cadre deployment. *Democratic Alliance Newsletter*. Johannesburg: Democratic Alliance.

Index